INDIAN PHILOSOPHY OF RELIGION

STUDIES IN PHILOSOPHY AND RELIGION

Volume 13

For a list of titles in this series see final page of the volume.

INDIAN PHILOSOPHY OF RELIGION

edited by

ROY W. PERRETT
Massey University, Palmerston North, New Zealand

KLUWER ACADEMIC PUBLISHERS
DORDRECHT / BOSTON / LONDON

Library of Congress Cataloging in Publication Data

Indian philosophy of religion / edited by Roy W. Perrett.
p. cm. -- (Studies in philosophy and religion ; 13)
ISBN 0-7923-0437-3
1. Religion--Philosophy. 2. India--Religion. I. Series: Studies in philosophy and religion (Martinus Nijhoff Publishers) ; v. 13.
BL51.I595 1989
200'.1--dc20 89-37201

ISBN 0-7923-0437-3

Published by Kluwer Academic Publishers,
P.O. Box 17, 3300 AA Dordrecht, The Netherlands.

Kluwer Academic Publishers incorporates
the publishing programmes of
D. Reidel, Martinus Nijhoff, Dr W. Junk and MTP Press.

Sold and distributed in the U.S.A. and Canada
by Kluwer Academic Publishers,
101 Philip Drive, Norwell, MA 02061, U.S.A.

In all other countries, sold and distributed
by Kluwer Academic Publishers Group,
P.O. Box 322, 3300 AH Dordrecht, The Netherlands.

printed on acid free paper

Printed in The Netherlands

ACKNOWLEDGEMENTS

I am grateful to the contributors, without whom *this* book would never have existed; to the Dean of Humanities' Fund at Massey for assistance with production costs; and, most especially, to Sharon Cox who prepared the camera-ready manuscript.

CONTENTS

INTRODUCTION

With a few notable exceptions, analytical philosophy of religion in the West still continues to focus almost entirely on the Judaeo-Christian tradition. In particular, it is all too customary to ignore the rich fund of concepts and arguments supplied by the Indian religious tradition. This is a pity, for it gratuitously impoverishes the scope of much contemporary philosophy of religion and precludes the attainment of any insights into Indian religions comparable to those that the clarity and rigour of analytic philosophy has made possible for the Judaeo-Christian tradition.

This volume seeks to redress the imbalance. The original idea was to invite a number of Indian and Western philosophers to contribute essays treating of Indian religious concepts in the style of contemporary analytical philosophy of religion. No further restriction was placed upon the contributors and the resulting essays (all previously unpublished) exhibit a diversity of themes and approaches. Many arrangements of the material herein are doubtless defensible. The rationale for the one that has been adopted is perhaps best presented through some introductory remarks about the essays themselves.

Keith Yandell's opening piece on Indian theological dualism provides an obvious entry point into Indian philosophy of religion. Most recent analytic philosophy of religion has concentrated on (Western) Classical Monotheism. But there are also Indian varieties of Classical Monotheism, notably those developed by the Vedāntin philosophers Rāmānuja and Madhva. Yandell discusses a number of traditional issues raised by the theological dualism of Classical Monotheism, with particular reference to their treatment in the systems of Rāmānuja and Madhva. His approach recognizes not only important commonalities of structure and content of thought, but also the presence of significant differences between the Western and Indian monotheistic traditions.

Arindam Chakrabarti discusses a particular argument common in Classical Monotheism: the cosmological argument for the existence of God. However he is concerned with the Indian version presented by the Nyāya philosophers, particularly with their successive attempts at a better formulation of the argument within the terms of classical Indian logic. Once again, both the similarities and differences between the Indian and Western versions of the argument are very much in evidence.

But Classical Monotheism is by no means the only, or even the predominant, strand in the Indian religious tradition. This point is reflected in the chosen themes of the other essays in the volume. Thus Arthur Herman's essay concentrates on atheism in Hinduism and Buddhism. He addresses two questions: (i) in what sense can Hinduism and Buddhism be called "atheistic religions"; and (ii) what is the cause of that atheism? He attempts to display the various senses in which Hinduism and Buddhism are in fact atheistic religions and then argues for the thesis that historically it was the Indian confrontation with dysteleological suffering, leading to various failed attempts at theodicies, which was the principal cause of that atheism.

Shlomo Biderman is concerned with how philosophical scepticism in India accords with religion. He has in view here the Buddhist philosopher Nāgārjuna, who is

R. W. Perrett (ed.), Indian Philosophy of Religion, 1–3.

apparently committed to a kind of mystical scepticism. Biderman presents an interpretation of Nāgārjuna which seeks to resolve the apparent discrepancy between his scepticism and his mysticism, proceeding by way of a comparison with the areligious scepticism of Sextus Empiricus.

A well known trend in Indian religions is towards some kind of monism: most famously, perhaps, in the traditions of Mādhyamika Buddhism and Advaita Vedānta. Peter Forrest's essay explores the general question of what it means to be committed to monism. He presents a (partial) taxonomy of varieties of monism and sketches some of the logical relations between these varieties. Among other things, this taxonomy enables him to locate various forms of Mādhyamika and Advaita monism and their entailments: an essential part of the hermeneutical task of understanding what those mystics mean when they suggest that (in reality) all is one.

Of course Mādhyamika is only one school of Buddhist thought, notwithstanding its enormous influence. Thus it is entirely plausible to suggest that the themes of scepticism and monism are not at all paramount in early Buddhism, where the concepts of self and freedom are far more central. Drawing on the Pali canonical texts, David Kalupahana presents the early Buddhist doctrine of "no-self" (*anattā*) and the associated analysis of freedom (*nibbāna*) as these are traditionally supposed to have been expressed by Gotama Buddha himself.

The essays mentioned so far are mostly concerned with metaphysical issues. But Indian philosophy of religion is obviously not only metaphysics: there are, for instance, important epistemological and ethical dimensions, some of which are discussed by the other contributors to this volume. Thus Ninian Smart's essay focuses attention on the epistemological significance of the usual Indian inclusion of scripture and verbal testimony (*śabda*) as a source of knowledge. Smart espouses a soft non-relativism about worldviews and tries to connect appeals to the communitarian tradition of *śabda* with the communitarian enterprise of science. Appeal to tradition can then be regarded as affirming a hypothetico-deductive position with regard to a given worldview.

My own paper is concerned with the notion of omniscience. I begin with traditional Western treatments of God's omniscience and then go on to offer a general characterization of the concept. Utilizing this characterization, I discuss some traditional Indian debates about omniscience (*sarvajñatva*) and try to locate them in their religio-philosophical context (particularly with regard to the problem of justifying the authority of the religious scriptures).

Puruṣottama Bilimoria treats of the Mīmāṃsā notion of authorless revelation (*apauruṣeya*). Bilimoria attempts to explicate this theory by first sketching the problem situation that generates it and then outlining the complex theory of language Mīmāṃsā develops in order to make sense of the idea.

Julius Lipner is also interested in religious language: specifically Śaṃkara's account of metaphor with reference to his commentary on a passage from the *Bhagavadgītā*. He presents both the detailed theological context of Śaṃkara's view and his quite general insights into the nature of metaphor as contextual, cognitive, open-ended, differential.

The last two essays are both concerned with ethical themes and are both centred on the *Bhagavadgītā*. Shivesh Thakur is concerned with two questions: (i) is the pursuit of social justice compatible with the Hindu goal of salvation; and (ii) can the pursuit of social justice be said to be obligatory for the Hindu seeker of salvation? Basing his discussion on the *Gītā*, Thakur defends affirmative answers to both questions.

Bimal Matilal addresses the tension within Hinduism between the caste-hierarchy and the doctrine of karma. Matilal argues for the presence within the Hindu tradition of an internal critique of the prevalent heredity-based caste hierarchy and offers an interpretation of some passages of the *Gītā* to this effect.

There is, of course, much more in each of the essays than these brief remarks can indicate and the reader is therefore urged to turn to the original contributions themselves: as the Shaker proverb has it, God is in the details.

SOME VARIETIES OF INDIAN THEOLOGICAL DUALISM

Keith E. Yandell

University of Wisconsin, Madison

Introduction: A Three-fold Rationale

The doctrine of the creation of the world by God is an essential part of Classical Monotheism. It entails theological dualism - that there exist *at least* two sorts of entities: God, and God's creatures. God is viewed as having *independent* existence; there is nothing other than God whose non-existence would entail or cause His non-existence. God's creatures have *dependent* existence; God's non-existence would entail their non-existence. The notion of Classical Monotheism will receive further discussion below. My concern here is with the theological dualism of two Indian theologian-philosophers, Rāmānuja and Madhva.

Strictly, the discussion of a rich and complex theological-philosophical view requires no rationale other than the view being rich and complex, and Rāmānuja's and Madhva's certainly qualify. Here, however, there is an additional two-fold rationale.

One part of this rationale concerns the value of cross-cultural philosophical reflection that *exposes* shared structure and content of thought. Philosophical theology - the attempt to articulate the doctrines of a particular religious tradition in a philosophically informed manner, and to assess the results - is no longer a dead, or even a despicable, enterprise among philosophers who operate in an "analytic" tradition. (By "analytic" I have in mind philosophers who are not existentialists or phenomenologists, and who offer arguments and prize clarity; in this sense of the term, there have been plenty of Indian as well as Anglo-American "analytic" philosophers.) Philosophical theology can benefit from a wide variety of culturally diverse examples of religious traditions. Thus rationality regarding religious matters is served well by considering, among other things, varieties of Classical Monotheism that are Indian in origin as well as by considering varieties of Classical Monotheism that are non-Indian in origin.

The other part of this rationale concerns *exploiting* what has been exposed. Philosophy, theology, and *a fortiori* philosophical theology, are cross-cultural in several senses. Where a proposition *P* entails a proposition *Q* if and only if *P, but not*

R. W. Perrett (ed.), Indian Philosophy of Religion, 5–19.

Q is a contradiction, entailment is cross-cultural.[1] One comes to understand a belief, about mongeese or figs or Brahman or nirvana, by seeing what is true if it is - by learning what follows from it, and what does not. That is, one comes to understand a belief by coming to see what that belief entails. A belief entails what it does with necessity; Śaṃkara, Rāmānuja, and Madhva believe different things about Brahman. For a resident of Delhi, or of Detroit, to come to understand Śaṃkara's, Rāmānuja's, and Madhva's views of Brahman is, in each case, to come to understand the same set of entailments.

Similar traditions face similar issues in ways that are not cancelled by their occurring in different cultures. Divine foreknowledge and human freedom, salvation by works and salvation by grace, divine justice and divine mercy, knowledge through perception or inference and knowledge through revelation, the possibility of natural theology: these notions, and the issues that thinking them through raise, play important roles in Indian as well as in non-Indian Classical Monotheism. *At least* very similar dilemmas arise; *at least* very similar solutions are offered. Seeing these problems and solutions from different angles may serve both to emphasize the importance of the problems in question and suggest better ways of assessing solutions.

Some Varieties of Classical Monotheism

Recognizing the indicated commonality of structure and content of thought is perfectly compatible with recognizing the presence of significant differences. Judaeo-Christian-Islamic Classical Monotheism holds a doctrine of radical creation on which God brings the world into existence without there having been some "stuff" from which it came; creation is *ex nihilo* in the sense that the world is not viewed as having resulted from already-existing materials being brought into order. Radical creation is not a part of Vedāntic Indian Classical Monotheism. The doctrines of karma and rebirth are part of Vedāntic, but not of Judaeo-Christian-Islamic Classical Monotheism. The notion of God acting in history is importantly though subtly different in Judaeo-Christian-Islamic monotheism than it is in Vedāntic Indian monotheism; this is particularly so in the case of the Christian doctrines of the incarnation and resurrection of Christ. It is well worth exploring what differences such as these arise from, and what further differences they entail.

In addition, the imagery and metaphors as well as the rites and rituals and narratives differ as one crosses cultures and traditions, and these shifts are not unrelated to the core concepts of their respective traditions. Such differences yield complexity, not inherent incomprehensibility; religious traditions are typically cross-cultural.

Classical Monotheism holds that there exists an omnipotent, omniscient, morally perfect Person. It contains descriptions such as Rāmānuja's reference to "all the perfect attributes" that belong to Brahman - "those myriads of immeasurable, glorious, and innumerable perfections like omniscience, omnipotence, universal sovereignty, his being unequalled and unsurpassed."[2] Brahman is the "sole cause of creation" and "is opposed to all evil and is of wholly infinite perfection."[3] Brahman possesses "knowledge, strength, sovereignty, heroism, creative power, and splendour; qualities

---

[1]Staal (1988).

[2]*Vedārthasaṃgraha*, para.10; van Buitenen (1965).

[3]*Śrībhāṣya*, 2.1.14; Acharya (1948); cf. Thibaut (1904).

which are essential to him and of incomparable excellence."[4] Being unconditioned, Brahman is to be distinguished "from non-intelligent matter, which is subject to change, and from intelligent beings, which are linked with such matter in the created world...."[5]

Classical Monotheism contains similar descriptions such as these from Madhva: "God is the Independent Being possessed of all adequate and unrestricted powers in regard to the Cit (sentient beings) and the Acit (insentient beings) and who is all-knowing. He is the One who controls the Cit and Acit which are of a different nature from Him."[6]; "The Independent Being must, necessarily, be infinite in its attributes. Independent Being cannot possibly wish to be finite and limited in any sense."[7]

Such a view may contain a doctrine of creation *ex nihilo*, but it may not. Madhva, for example, states a position on which he and Rāmānuja are in agreement: " ... there is no birth of the Jīva as spirit. Passing *from one state of dependence to another* is itself a new birth [i.e., a new reincarnation] (in respect of eternal entities like the Jīvas)."[8] He also writes that; "Nowhere in experience has the insentient been known to be a product of the sentient, nor the sentient known to be a product of the insentient."[9] Aquinas held that, so far as philosophical reflection alone goes, it might be the case that the world stands in a relation of asymmetrical dependence on God; he held that revelation teaches creation *ex nihilo*. There seem to be two doctrines of creation that are consistent with other elements of Classical Monotheism. One holds that God created the world *ex nihilo*. The other holds that the world beginninglessly depends on God without God depending on anything for His existence. Nonetheless, Classical Monotheists hold that God is not only omnicompetent (omnipotent, omniscient, and morally perfect) but also Creator and Providence, Lord of nature and history.

The frequent suggestion that it is arbitrary to make God an exception to an otherwise universal dependence of one thing on another seems to me mistaken; an omnipotent, omniscient, and morally perfect being will also be an ontologically independent being.[10]

Some Further Alternatives Within Classical Monotheism

Critics of Classical Monotheism often too easily assume that if one way of spelling out the notion of omnicompetence is contradictory, then the concept of God itself is contradictory (whereas if one version of, say, materialism happens to be contradictory, then of course one replaces it by another). The practice of charity to one's own alone is not limited to politics and economics.

In fact, various notions of the essential divine attributes might do quite nicely for monotheistic purposes. To illustrate briefly, consider these rough characterizations of

---

4 *Vedārthasaṃgraha*, para.6.

5 *Śrībhāṣya*, 1.1.2.

6 Sharma (1961), p.96; *Tattvoddyota*, p.66. (References to the Sanskrit texts of Madhva's works are to the edition of Krishnacharya (1896).)

7 Sharma (1961), p.96; *Nyāya-vivaraṇa*, p.4.

8 Sharma (1961), p.111; *Brahmasūtrabhāṣya*, 2.3.9.

9 Sharma (1961), p.113; *Anuvyākhyāna*, 13b.

10 Yandell (1984), Ch.2.

divine omnipotence and divine omniscience:

> (D1) God is omnipotent if and only if, for every proposition *P*, if (a) *P* is not a contradiction, and (b) *God makes P true* is not a contradiction, then God can make *P* true.
>
> (D2) God is omniscient if and only if, for any proposition *P*, if *P* is true, and if *God knows that P* is not a contradiction, then God knows that *P*.

Consider (D1); clause (a) rules out God's making *The moon exists now and the moon does not exist now* true, and clause (b) rules out God's making *There is an uncreated universe* true. There is no possible state of affairs the obtaining of which would make it true that the moon both does and does not exist now. There is a possible state of affairs of there being an uncreated universe, but of course God could not create that state of affairs. Strictly, then, there is nothing that God, or any agent, might do that is ruled out by either (a) or (b). So far as I can see, assuming that (D1) expresses a consistent concept, God being omnipotent in the sense that (D1) characterizes is all that Classical Monotheism requires.

There are other analyses of divine omnipotence, and of course if one monotheist accepted (D1) and another accepted some other definition of omnipotence, they would disagree about what being omnipotent amounted to, and a critic might show that one of their definitions was inconsistent without being able to show this about the other. But note also that it is possible that two persons accept (D1) and yet have different views of the scope of divine omnipotence. Suppose Ray believes that *It is logically possible that a person's choices and actions be determined and that she nonetheless be morally responsible for them* is true and that Raji believes that it is false. Suppose also that both believe that God cannot act unjustly. Then Ray will suppose that God can both determine people's choices and hold people morally responsible for them and Raji will not believe this. They will both accept (D1) but will think differently regarding what God can do. Or suppose that Ray believes that while God will not act unjustly it is logically possible that He do so, and Raji believes that it is logically impossible that God act unjustly. Then a similar difference will arise about what God can do even though both hold that (D1) is the correct definition of omnipotence.

A similar difference will arise between them regarding the scope of divine knowledge if Raji believes that it is logically impossible that God know what the future free actions of agents will be and Ray thinks that this is not impossible; they may disagree about this even though they both accept (D2).

Alternatively, a Classical Monotheist might offer a different account of omnipotence or omniscience. Regarding any such account, three questions arise: (1) is it logically consistent; (2) in order to accept it, do I have to reject any philosophical (or other) claim that I have reason to think true; (3) in order to accept it, do I have to reject any claim that is constitutive of Classical Monotheism? (The third question, of course, may fall partially or entirely within the second.)

A Cultural Distinctive of Indian Classical Monotheism

Varieties of Classical Monotheism also differ in terms of the texts, if any, that they appeal to as doctrinally authoritative. For Indian Classical Monotheism, the Upaniṣads have authoritative status, as do various texts that serve as commentaries on them - e.g.

the *Brahmasūtra* of Bādarāyana,[11] comprised of some five hundred and fifty-five aphorisms said to provide a summary of Upaniṣadic thought. As one might expect, these aphorisms are themselves interpreted by each of the varieties of Indian Classical Monotheism. One feature of Indian thought (though not unique to India) that this text supports is the claim that the universe oscillates - that over periods of great length the physical universe goes from a state of chaos to a state of organization from which it returns to a state of chaos and so on forever.

The general view is that during periods of chaos, souls are disembodied and during periods of organization souls move from one embodiment to another according to their karma. The details of the various ways in which souls, matter, and oscillation are conceived are not our present concern. What is relevant is that both souls and matter are construed as being beginningless.

Another relevant feature is that the world is said to "proceed" from Brahman's "substance" - that, as it is often put, Brahman is viewed as the material cause of the world. Aphorism sixteen of Chapter Two tells us that: "the effect exists in the cause before it arises from it as effect". This Sāṃkhya view, B.K. Matilal notes, "means that the so-called effect pre-exists in its cause, causation being merely a change or transformation from one state to another, while the original thing... remains constant and unchanging. An effect means a change in only the attributes or characteristics of a thing, a new state of affairs means manifestation of what was *potentially* present... in the early state of affairs, that is, in its so-called cause."[12]

Madhva rejects this perspective, for according to him Brahman asserts: "Know me to be like the seed; for I am the cause of the manifestation of the world, as a seed is. But I am not the substantial cause which is subject to changes and manifests itself as a more gross effect. Indeed I am the Controller of such cause and effect."[13]

Along with there being different authorities appealed to, and different interpretations of the same authorities, the specific content of a variety of Classical Monotheism will depend on what claims (interpretive or noninterpretive of a text) are accepted concerning particular philosophical matters. For example, accepting one particular view of causality will give a version of Classical Monotheism a conceptual shape different from that of a version which accepts another.

Some Aphorisms of Bādarāyana

The second aphorism of Chapter One of Bādarāyana's work reads: "That from which the origin, substance, and dissolution of the world proceed is known as Brahman." Lying behind this second aphorism are such Upaniṣadic texts as these: "Being only was in the beginning without a second. It thought, 'May I be many; May I go forth.'" [*Chāndogya* 6:2]; "The Self was all this, one only in the beginning, and there was nothing else. He thought, 'Let me now create these worlds.'" [*Aitreya* 1:1:1]; "There are two forms of Brahman, the material and the immaterial, the mortal and the immortal..." [*Bṛhadāraṇyaka* 2; 3; 1]. Call such texts as these *one/many* texts.

The thirty-sixth aphorism of Chapter Three reads: "In the same way, because of the express denial of all other things, there is nothing but Brahman." Lying behind this aphorism are such Upaniṣadic texts as these "He [referring to Brahman] to whom there is nothing superior, from whom there is nothing different." [*Śvetāśvatara* 1:91]; "That

---

[11]Bahadur (1983).

[12]Matilal (1985), p.287.

[13]*Gītabhāṣya*, 7.10.

immortal Brahman is before, that Brahman is behind, that Brahman is right and left. It has gone forth below and above: Brahman alone is all this, it is the best." [*Muṇḍaka* 2:2:11]; "The Self is above, below, behind, in front, to the South and to the North. It is indeed all this world." [*Chāndogya* 7:25:2] Call such texts as these *all there is* texts.

Any variety of Indian Classical Monotheism will be expected to deal with the *one/many* and the *all there is* texts.

A Philosophical Red Herring

It is sometimes claimed that accepting the doctrine of the beginninglessness of the world solves (or precludes the raising of) an otherwise insoluble problem concerning the *timing* of the creation. (A similar virtue is sometimes claimed for the view that God is eternal.) If God creates the world at time *T*, the question arises as to why He created it at *T* rather than at some other time. Time slots, so to speak, are all equally receptive to creation's having occurred in them; whatever reason God had for creating at *T*, He would have for creating at any of an infinite number of times. So there could be no reason for His creating at *T* rather than at some other time. But God does not act arbitrarily, so if there is no reason for His creating at *T* than at some other time, He does not create at *T*. So if God creates at *T*, then God does not create at *T*; that is, the idea of God creating at a time - at one time rather than another - is contradictory. That the world is beginningless entails that God does not create at some time rather than another, and so does not entail the contradiction that this view entails.

The argument concerning timing can be countered as follows. The argument offered above for the claim that it is contradictory that God create the world in time requires the assumption that God never does anything without sufficient reason. Aphorism thirty-two of Chapter One says that: "Brahman's creative activity is mere sport, as is seen in [i.e., as is comparable to] ordinary life." The Vedāntic tradition takes divine play or sport - sheer creative effusiveness, as it were - to be the divine "rationale" for creation, though this "rationale" is compatible with, and supplemented by, more considerations. This seems to amount to this claim: that God creates freely, neither from some internal necessity nor from some rational or moral requirement that He do so. His nature as an agent makes it appropriate that He create if He wishes and the moral worth of what He creates is such as to make the creation a worthy divine activity. Further, that argument assumes that time is not *created with* the world (for were that so it could not go on to argue that if God created the world at some time *T*, then God would be arbitrary not to have created the world at some other time). Suppose that we grant the argument its assumptions.

Still, at any time, God exists independent of His creation and (unless He has promised not to do this) would not be blameworthy if He ceased to create. God has the same reason for creating at any one moment that He has at another; but since it is up to Him whether He ever creates, it is also up to Him whether He creates at any given time or not. If He does not create at a time *T*, this is not blameworthy or puzzling; His creating is not a duty or a necessary consequence of His nature. If He does create at a time *T*, His doing so is a matter of morally qualified creative effusiveness; this is so whether He creates at every time or only after some time. For the Vedāntic tradition, God creates at every time. For other sorts of Classical Monotheism, God creates only after some time. Precisely the same rationale can be offered for either alternative, and which alternative is correct is dependent on what God decided to do. If the only alternatives for what a question is are *conceptual* and *empirical*, where the answers to conceptual questions are always necessary truths, the question "Has God always created or did God create only after some time had elapsed?" is an empirical, not a conceptual, question. This is not affected by the fact, if it is one, that on the latter alternative an infinite amount of time will have elapsed before creation occurs; need the Ancient of Days be bothered by this matter of scheduling?

So far as I can see, then, the Vedāntic tradition itself, while in accord with other Indian traditions when it claims that the world is beginningless, equally well can accommodate the claim that the world was created by God at a particular time.

The view that *time is created along with persons and objects* is non-Vedāntic and we do not need to discuss it in order to show that the Vedāntic argument against creation-at-a-time fails. Nor need we enter into questions about any alleged divine atemporality or eternity.

Classical Criticisms of Classical Monotheism

Critics of Classical Monotheism often allege that it is contradictory. This criticism has various specific targets. A critic may claim that the concept of an omnipotent being, or of an omniscient being, or of a morally perfect being, is contradictory. Or a critic may claim that while the concepts of an omnipotent and of a morally perfect being are logically consistent, the concept of a being that is both omnipotent and morally perfect is inconsistent (or claim this about some other combination of concepts such that Classical Monotheism contends that the divine Person corresponds to or satisfies both of them). Or a critic may assert that the claim that there exists a morally perfect omnipotent and omniscient being is logically incompatible with some other claim that is essential to monotheism - say, that God created the world, or that there is evil. It is this last pair of criticisms - those centring on *creation* and *evil* - that interest us here.

Criticisms of Classical Monotheism based in one way or another on appeal to the fact of evil are common, and while I think that none of them succeed in showing Classical Monotheism to be false or unreasonable to accept, I will assume that the general rationale of such appeals needs no detailed explanation. But what, exactly, might appropriately arouse the critic's suspicion that the doctrine of creation is contradictory? That we cannot conceive of its *modus operandi*? An omnicompetent being needs none. That creation cannot be *ex nihilo*? It is not clear why not, and Indian Classical Monotheism does not include this doctrine.

The answer most relevant to Indian Classical Monotheism seems to centre on this contention: if *B* utterly depends for its existence on *A*, then *B* cannot be *entirely distinct* from *A*. But if *B* cannot be entirely distinct from *A*, then *B* cannot be *A*'s creation. Alternatively, if *B* is *part* of *A*, then *B* is *not ontologically distinct* from *A*, and necessarily a creature is ontologically distinct from its Creator. In these and other ways, the critic's worries concern the identity conditions of Creator versus creature. There are *epistemological* identity conditions; the epistemological identity conditions of *A* and *B* are what, if anything, allows us to distinguish one from the other. There are also *metaphysical* or *ontological* identity conditions; the metaphysical identity conditions of *A* and *B* are what, if anything, makes *A* and *B* non-identical. In any particular case of non-identical entities, the epistemological and the metaphysical identity conditions may, or may not, be the same. The critic's concern is with metaphysical identity conditions. The claim is that the sort of dependence involved in *B's being created by A* disallows there being any metaphysical identity conditions that differentiate *B* as one thing from *A* as another. Advaita Vedānta seems to be a system of thought in which this worry is transposed into a metaphysic.

Naturally Rāmānuja and Madhva are aware of such concerns. Not only are they also Vedāntins, albeit of non-Advaitic persuasion, but they know that making clear the Creator/creature relationship in such a way as to guarantee an absolute asymmetrical dependence of creature on Creator and specifying identity conditions in which the Creator is one thing and the creature another are essential tasks for Classical Monotheistic philosophers and theologians. The questions, then, are: (i) how do they attempt to do this; and (ii) do they succeed?

The General Classical Monotheistic Strategy

The general strategy for making a sharp Creator/creature distinction is straightforward and powerful. The general idea is that if *A* has a property that *B* lacks, then *A* cannot be identical to *B*. Then one chooses properties that are important ones for Classical Monotheism, and develops particular arguments that deal with these properties. Two examples are central. One is the *ontological independence* argument: If *A* can exist without *B* existing, then *A* is not identical to *B*, whether or not *B* can exist without *A* existing. The Creator can exist without the creation existing. So the Creator is not identical to the world - or, if you like, *there being a creation* is not essential to God's existing. The other is the *omnicompetent properties* argument: if *A* has one or more properties that *B* lacks, then *A* is not identical to *B*. God is omnipotent, omniscient, and morally perfect; the creation is not. So God is not identical to the creation.

The use of this perfectly appropriate strategy raises an interesting question about the relations between worshipping communities. According to orthodox Judaism, or Islam, God lacks the properties *being incarnate in Christ* and *being Trinitarian.* According to orthodox Christianity, He has these properties. Judaism, Christianity, and Islam hold that God has the property of having called the nation of Israel into being; the theistic varieties of Vedānta, of course, make no such claim. So do these religious communities worship the same God? I settle here for noting that appeal to the criterion and arguments just noted do not decide this issue. The reason for this is simple. Suppose that Kim is friend both to Surendranath and Samuel. Surendranath and Samuel both know that Kim is intelligent, honest, frugal, and reliable. But Surendranath believes Kim to be the author of a brilliant philosophical treatise and married whereas Samuel believes Kim to be an unmarried non-author. The difference in belief does not entail that the same Kim is not friend to both Suredranath and Samuel.

More generally, the issue has to do with connections between various epistemological and metaphysical identity conditions - a topic too broad to be tackled here. I mention it only to indicate that there is no necessary challenge to my use of the notion of Classical Monotheism in either the use of the *A*-and-*B*-are-identical-only-if-*A*-has-a-property-if-and only-if-*B*-has-it criterion or in the use of the ontological independence and the omnicompetent properties argument. In fact, these arguments appeal to *agreed-upon essential* properties of the God of Classical Monotheism.

I turn, then, to the objection concerning evil, and then to the objection concerning creation. I shall assume that it is well-enough known so as not to require documentation that Rāmānuja and Madhva accept a theistic version of the doctrines of reincarnation and karma.

Evil and Logical Consistency

The claim is often made that (1) *God is an omnipotent, omniscient, morally perfect Person* and (2) *There is evil in the world* are inconsistent propositions. A simple argument casts doubt on this claim. This argument invites attention to (1) and (2) above, but also to a third claim: (3) *God has a morally sufficient reason for allowing any evil that He allows.*

The argument can be constructed from these considerations: (i) no *single* member of the set (1-3) is contradictory; (ii) if a set of three propositions form a consistent trio, any pair of propositions from that trio are also consistent; (iii) the trio (1-3) is a consistent set. Of these claims, (ii) is a necessary truth. (i) is false if some single member of (1-3) is contradictory. If (2) is contradictory, there can be no evil. If (1) is contradictory, then perhaps the critic can show that (1) by itself is inconsistent. If so, then she need not bother worrying about the problem of evil. She need only show (by whatever argument she may have for this) that (1) is inconsistent, and we can examine her argument when it is presented. Showing that (3) is contradictory apparently would require showing that on the sense to be appropriately assigned to "morally sufficient reason", God cannot have a morally sufficient reason for allowing evil (or for allowing the evil that exists, or the like), and the critic will have to explain what the appropriate sense is that has these consequences. That, in turn, will either require deciding between competing moral theories, or else showing that theism itself entails a moral theory on which this claim about the appropriate sense to assign to "morally sufficient reason" is justified. That is a task the difficulty of which should not be underestimated, especially as it has never been done.

Suppose that (i) is true. Then, I suggest, a little reflection should be enough for one to see that (iii) is also true - that (1-3) is a consistent trio.

Suppose that (i-iii) are all true. Then the following argument has only true premises, and is obviously valid:

A. The set (1-3) is a consistent trio.
B. If (1-3) is a consistent trio, any set comprised of a pair taken from (1-3) will be a consistent set.
C. The set (1,2) is a set comprised of a pair taken from (1-3).
So:
D. The set (1,2) is a consistent pair.

That is, *God is an omnipotent, omniscient, morally perfect Person* and *There is evil in the world* are *not* logically incompatible propositions. At the *very* least, the attempt to show that they are is much harder than most critics have thought. This line of reasoning is as equally congenial to Indian Classical Monotheism as to non-Indian.

Evil, Karma, and Reincarnation

That *God exists* and *There is evil* are not logically incompatible does not fully answer all the objections that a critic might base on the existence of evil. For example, it is clear that people are born into different conditions. Some babies are healthy, some are not. Some have dispositions to crippling diseases, physical and mental, which others do not. Some have excellent parents, others parents who are tragically inadequate. Some are born into comfort, some into abject poverty. One person's "moral luck" differs from another - all of this in ways not correlated with personal merit or character. In sum, the world plainly seems not to be characterized by a just distribution of goods or of (what might be seen as) rewards and punishments. This is often said to show that the world is *unjust* in a way in which it would not be were it the creation of God.

It is also often suggested that the doctrines of reincarnation and karma solve this problem. If a soul is pre-existent to each of its embodied lifetimes, then its conditions of embodiment may reflect its character - its freely chosen merits and defects - in previous lives; so the apparently unjust distribution of goods, or rewards and punishments, in fact may be exquisitely matched to the real deserts of their recipients. The idea is that for any person - say, Sharma - born into particular circumstances, those circumstances are morally appropriate in the sense that they are the sort of circumstances in which a morally perfect being, fully informed and capable, would place a person with the karmic autobiography of Sharma. ("Sharma" should be taken here to refer to the *jīva* or soul or person who has been multiply incarnated and is now reincarnated under the conditions in question.) Inequities between conditions are not matters of moral luck, but of moral desert.

On such a pattern of thought, Sharma's life-conditions in lifetime *L* are a function of his moral conduct and character in lifetime *L*-minus-one (assuming for simplicity that a given life's karmic payoff comes in the very next life). The life-conditions of *L*-minus-one are to be explained by reference to *L*-minus-two; and so on. Call the life-conditions one is explaining the *currently considered* life-conditions. So one always has one set of life-conditions unexplained, namely that by which one is explaining the currently considered life-conditions.

This situation is isomorphic to that in which the existence of one dependent thing is explained by reference to another, and that to another, without ever coming to anything that exists independently. It is both true that for any dependent thing you like, its existence can be explained (by reference to another dependent being) but there is always one dependent being "left over" by virtue of one's most recent explanatory effort. For any dependent being you like, its existence can be explained; but there is no explanation of there being dependent things at all. In our case, there is an explanation of there being whatever set of unequally distributed life-conditions you please, but not of there being unequally distributed life conditions at all.

The objection is sometimes made there *is* nothing more to explaining that there are dependent beings other than explaining the existence of any dependent being you like by reference to some other, and of course it might be argued that there *is* nothing more to explaining there being unequally distributed life-conditions than explaining there being whatever such life-conditions you choose. This sort of reply seems to me inadequate; it is perfectly possible - it involves no contradiction - that there be no dependent things and no unequally distributed life conditions. Since that is possible, the question as to why there are any such things at all is a perfectly legitimate question, and the question *Why are there any X's at all*? is not answered by saying *Some X's cause others*.

Perhaps what lies behind the objection just noted - and in any case a consequence of it - is that there being dependent things, or there being unequally distributed life-conditions, is explanatorily primitive; it is the sort of thing by reference to which you explain other things but which itself is not explicable and/or requires no explanation. But then of course if one accepts this line of reasoning there being unequally distributed life-conditions is not explained after all. Further, there being unequally distributed life-conditions (and, it seems to me, there being contingent things) are not self-explanatory states of affairs. They have neither the property of *necessarily existing* nor the property of *necessarily being uncaused if they exist at all.*

I suggest, then, that the reincarnation-karma explanation of unequally distributed life-conditions (and of evil generally) fails. It does not, of course, follow that Vedāntic theological dualism cannot offer an explanation of there being (and also, differently, a justification for Brahman allowing) evil. It only follows that appeal to reincarnation and karma does not provide the sort of solution to the problem of unequally distributed life-conditions that it is often alleged to provide.

Rāmānuja and the Creator/Creation Distinction

In some ways, Rāmānuja's position seems positively to invite such criticism. Consider for example the use of a part/whole analogy in this passage: "That the world and Brahman stand to each other in the relation of part to whole, the former being like the light and the latter like the luminous body, or the former being like the power and the latter like that in which the power inheres... the soul; this *Parasara* and other Smṛti writers declare... the individual self is part of Brahman in so far as it is its body."[14] Still, even as he speaks of part and whole, he contrasts part with whole. Brahman is like light and power, the soul like what is illuminated and empowered. A few paragraphs later he adds: "Although the souls, as being part of Brahman, and so on, are essentially of the same character, they are actually separate, for each of them is of atomic size and resides in a separate body. For this reason there is no confusion or mixing up of the individual spheres of enjoyment and experience."[15] Each soul is distinct from both Brahman and every other soul.

His core analogy for the Brahman/world relationship is that of human soul to human body. He empathetically states the Sāṃkhya notion of a body: "The body of a being is that which has its nature, substance, and activity dependent on the will of that being."[16] His own fuller characterization runs: "Any entity that a sentient being is able completely to control and support for its own purposes, and the essential nature of which is entirely subservient to that self, is its body... In this sense then, all subject and non-sentient beings together constitute the body of the supreme Person."[17] In the *Vedārthasaṃgraha*, paragraph seventy-six, he is more specific still: "The relationship between the self and the body is: (1) that between the support and the thing supported, which is incapable of separate existence; (2) that between the controlled and what is controlled; and (3) that between the master and owner and what is subservient to him."[18] There is no suggestion here that Rāmānuja is unaware of, or could not use, the *asymmetrical dependence* argument.

Indeed, in the *Gītābhāṣya*, he does use it: "Know that they all originated from me. They abide in me; they are My body, but I am not in them, which is to say, *I do not depend on them.* In other cases, the self, though to be sure the one on whom its body depends, also derives some benefit from its body, but know that there is no benefit in

---

[14]*Śrībhāṣya*, 2.3.46.

[15]Ibid., 2.3.48.

[16]Ibid., 2.1.8.

[17]Ibid., 2.1.9.

[18]*Vedārthasaṃgraha*; van Buitenen (1965), p.76.

them for me. My purpose is only and entirely sport."[19] Again, "I pervade the universe as its Inner Controller, in order to support it, and by virtue of being its Owner... I am the supporter of finite beings, but *I derive no benefit from them.*[20]

So Brahman does not depend on the world, and does not (among other possible benefits He does not receive from it) receive the benefit of existence or continuing to exist. To drive the point fully home, Rāmānuja becomes even more explicit: "My existence is not under their control, which means that *they are not helping in any way in My existence...* I am the supporter of all beings; they are no help at all to me at any time. What I will in My mind itself causes the existence of all beings and also supports and controls them."[21]

Many monotheists, of course, have rejected the soul/body analogy as a proper way to think of the Creator/creation relationship. This is not hard to understand. Ordinary experience, let along neurophysiology, makes plain that mental capacities are intimately connected with the state of our physical organism - something that mind/body dualists have been as aware of as materialists and that is perfectly compatible with either position. Thus it is easy to suppose that if the world is God's body, it follows that (at least in principle) a really talented but perverse society of nuclear physicists could do nasty things to God's capacity for thought, and from a monotheistic perspective this is absurd. Further, from a Hebrew (and so to a considerable degree from a Christian or Islamic) perspective, *being human* (or, perhaps, *being fully human*) entails *being embodied* whereas *being divine* entails neither *being embodied* nor *creating a world.* So everyday experience and theological considerations often combine to exclude soul/body from the relationships on which God/world relationships may be modelled.

While the topic is too complex to enter into here (involving differences between various Graeco-European and Indian conceptions of what a mind is and of the identity conditions of disembodied as well as embodied minds, and the like), on a perspective in which reincarnation occurs and for which a soul's karma in past lives affects the manner of one's current embodiment, one's relationship to a particular body (or any resurrected successor) seems "loosened". Further, Rāmānuja's use of "body" is technical, intended to capture the use of the term as it appears in the texts he regards as scriptural. This, of course, places constraints on the Brahman/world analogy (as there are on all analogies), one of them being that in the Brahman/world case Brahman's karma plays no role (there being none) and another being that in the Brahman/world case souls comprise parts of the relevant body whereas in the human soul/human body case they do not. "The Supreme Brahman (has) the whole aggregate of non-sentient and sentient beings for its body."[22]

Madhva on the Creator/Creation Distinction

Madhva too seems to so put his position as to invite the critic's comments. He describes Brahman as the "essence" and "seed" of the world. Taken in their usual senses, the critic may say, if *A* is *B*'s essence then *A* is a set of properties that constitutes *B*'s nature and if *A* is *B*'s seed then *A is B* at an early stage of *B*'s development or *A* is *B*'s nature-bearing product. But Madhva uses these terms in a

---

[19]*Gītabhāṣya*, 7.12; my italics. Cf. Sampatkumaran (1969).

[20]Ibid., 9.4; my italics.

[21]Ibid., 9.4-5; my italics.

[22]*Śrībhāṣya*, 1.4.23.

technical sense. He tells us that "To say that the [Brahman] is the 'essence' in the waters and other elements means that he himself is the determining Cause of the distinctive nature, inner potency and the very quintessence of a thing's essential nature and principal character. It is not to be thought that these... are determined by the intrinsic natures of the substances themselves."[23] In a passage already cited, Brahman is described as "seed" of the world in the sense of being its cause and Controller; not Himself a part of the contingent sequences of causes and effects, but the sustaining providential cause of the whole series of dependently existing things.[24]

He expands on this theme as follows. "Since the essence, i.e., the very nature of the soul, consists only of wisdom, bliss, and other qualities similar (in some degree) to those of Brahman, there proceeds the statement that the soul is one with (like) Brahman; just as in the text, 'All indeed is Brahman' (Chand. Up. 3.14.1), Brahman is spoken of as identical with all (the world) on account of there being qualities in Brahman which are predicated of the whole world. The following is in the *Bhavushyat Purāṇa*: 'The souls are separate, the perfect Lord is separate, still owing to the similarity of intelligent nature they are spoken of as Brahman in the various Scriptural disquisitions.'"[25] Consider these Madhvian comments: Brahman "enters into Prakṛti and energizes it to transform in various ways and assumes many forms to control such modifications."[26]; "The Supreme Being, possessed of infinite powers, enters into various stages of evolution of matter and brings about each and every such stage of such manifestations of things, Himself."[27] Madhva, then, makes explicit use of the *omnicompetent properties* argument.

Rāmānuja, Madhva, and the Ontological Independence and Omnicompetent Properties Arguments

It seems to me plain that, given the materials cited and discussed, both Rāmānuja and Madhva are in the position of being able to offer both the ontological independence and omnicompetent properties arguments. The ontological independence argument is explicit in our Rāmānujan texts and the omnicompetent properties argument explicit in our Madhvian texts. But in each case the other sort of argument is implicit in, and easily constructed from, the views expressed. Similarly, I shall take it as fairly obvious how Rāmānuja and Madhva read the *one/many* and the *all there is* texts.

The Argument Concerning Autonomy

There is at least one other argument that the critic might use with the hope that it may succeed where the arguments that we have considered fail. This argument concerns autonomy. It can either maintain that if an all-powerful, all-knowing being exists then no human being can have autonomy, or else claim that a *deterministic* monotheism is incompatible with human autonomy and that Rāmānuja and Madhva

---

[23] *Gītabhāṣya*, 7.8.

[24] Ibid., 7.10.

[25] *Brahmasūtrabhāṣya*, 3.3.29.

[26] Sharma (1961), p.110; *Brahmasūtrabhāṣya*, 1.4.27.

[27] Sharma (1961), p.110; *Brahmasūtrabhāṣya*, 2.3.11.

are determinists.

Treat making a choice as itself a kind of action. Then a person's having autonomy regarding some choice or action can be defined as follows: Manindra has autonomy regarding action *A* at time *T* if and only if it is actually within Manindra's power at *T* to perform *A* and it is actually within Manindra's power at *T* to refrain from performing *A* - whether Manindra performs *A* or not is up to Maninindra, not *if* something were to obtain that does not obtain, but under the actually prevailing conditions.

I do not know of any argument that is sound and valid that begins with *There is an omnipotent, omniscient being* and ends with *No human being has autonomy*. Attempts at such arguments sometimes confuse *Necessarily, if God knows that Jane will choose onion soup for lunch, then Jane will choose onion soup for lunch*, which is true and irrelevant, with *If God knows that Jane will choose onion soup for lunch, then necessarily Jane will choose onion soup for lunch*, which is relevant but false; God's knowing a logically contingent proposition does not change the modal status of that proposition from *contingent* to *necessary*. Sometimes such attempts forget that what makes a proposition true is the obtaining of the state of affairs that the proposition says obtains; what makes *John chooses to lie at T* true is John's choosing to lie at *T*. If *John chooses to lie at T* is true, say, a thousand years before time *T*, that does not change the fact that what makes it true is John's choice; it is the choice that determines the truth value of the proposition, and not conversely, and this is so whether or not John's choice is free (and hence the proposition being true a thousand years before the choice is made is perfectly irrelevant to - save as being determined by - whether John chooses autonomously). Sometimes such arguments assume that if God knows in advance what choice Paul will make, then God must cause Paul to make that choice, which is plainly false. Sometimes such arguments assume that if God knows what choice Pauline will make, He must *infer* that knowledge from some other information, and that whatever makes that information reliable must be something that predetermines how Pauline shall choose; but there is no reason why any of an omniscient being's knowledge should be inferred knowledge. So far as I can see, Augustine is correct when he notes that what God may know regarding my choices is how I shall freely make them.

Perhaps at the base of the critic's intuitions about divine creation is some such view as this. Consider the highly plausible claim that necessarily for any item *A*, time *T*, and property *P*, either *A* has *P* at *T* or else *A* lacks *P* at *T*; in that sense, whatever exists is *fully determinate*. Now for God to create something is for God to create *that* thing rather than any other. Since whatever exists is fully determinate, for God to create is for God to create a fully determinate thing. And since for God to create is for Him to create one thing rather than another, for God to create anything is for him to determine the precise manner in which that thing is fully determinate. This line could be put in a slogan: *Necessarily, to create is to determine the manner in which the created becomes fully determinate.* Or the slogan might be: *Necessarily, creating is a deterministic activity, so the creation is deterministic.* (Madhva's notion that God determines the particular nature of karma-bearers so that they come to have the karma they do at least in part due to their natures may reflect thinking somewhat along these lines, but that is a complex matter.)

This is certainly not the only way to think of the act of divine creation or of its resultant creation. One might instead distinguish between *baptismal* and *non-baptismal* properties. A baptismal property is a property that God can fiat that a creature shall have. *Being male*, *being female*, and *belonging to a particular caste* are baptismal properties. *Autonomously telling the truth, freely becoming virtuous*, and *freely electing to embrace Thugee* are non-baptismal properties. For God to create a being *A* at time *T* indeed will involve God's determining what baptismal properties *A* shall have at *T*. It will also be to decide whether *A* shall have any non-baptismal properties or not; after all, *being an autonomous moral agent* is a baptismal property, and in creating *A* God must decide whether *A* shall have that baptismal property or not. But if *A* is given that baptismal property, then what non-baptismal properties *A* comes to have will be up to *A* (and since what non-baptismal properties *A* comes to have may influence what baptismal properties *A* comes to have, some of *A*'s baptismal properties - properties that God *could* have fiated that *A* have or lack - may be properties that *A*'s autonomous choices and actions play a role in determining). So while *A* will be fully determinate with respect to all properties, baptismal or non-baptismal, at all times, the manner in which *A* is fully determinate need not be determined by God. The slogans are false.

The other line the critic may take concerning autonomy is more promising. Its basic idea is this. Suppose that *A* and *B* are related in the following manner: every thought, feeling, choice, action, or other state, event, or property of *B* is a forseen effect of something that *A* autonomously does. Then *B* at most is *A*'s agent, and indeed seems but an extension of *A* - a mode or state or emanation of *A*. But modes or states or emanations of *A* in fact are parts of *A*; they are some aspect of *A*'s being or some modality of *A*'s existence, or the like. But for a deterministic monotheism, the creation is related to God as *B* is to *A*. So a deterministic monotheism has no room at all for *creation*, or for a *Creator/creation distinction*. This may be correct; note that, if it is, the way of "conceiving of creation" that the slogans summarize turns out *not* to be a way of thinking of creation after all. If it is correct, then the crucial question regarding Rāmānuja and Madhva is whether they are deterministic monotheists. That important exegetical question I leave for another occasion.

REFERENCES

Acharya, N.R. (1948). Editor. *The Brahma-Sūtra-Bhāsya*, 3rd ed. Bombay.
Bahadur, K.H. (1983). *The Wisdom of Vedānta*. Delhi: Sterling Publishers.
Krishnacharya, R.T. (1896). Editor. *Collected Works of Madhvācarya*. Bombay: Nirnayagasar Press.
Matilal, B.K. (1985). *Logic, Language, and Reality*. Delhi: Motilal Banarsidass.
Sampatkumaran, M.R. (1969). *The Gītā-Bhāsya of Rāmānuja*. Madras.
Sharma, B.N.K. (1961). *Madhva's Teachings in His Own Words*. Bombay: Vidya Bhavan.
Staal, Frits (1988). *Universals*. Chicago: University of Chicago.
Thibaut, George (1904). Translator. *The Vedānta-Sūtras with the Commentary by Rāmānuja*. Delhi: Motilal Banarsidass, 1966.
van Buitenen, J.A.B. (1965). Editor and translator. *Rāmānuja's Vedārtha-Saṃgraha*. Pune: Deccan College Postgraduate and Research Institute.
Yandell, Keith E. (1984). *Christianity and Philosophy*. Grand Rapids: Wm. B. Erdmanns.

FROM THE FABRIC TO THE WEAVER?

Arindam Chakrabarti

University College London

... *suchelakebhya iva tatkuśalah kuvindah* - Jayantabhaṭṭa

... *everything that begins to exist is put forth by a will directed power* - Martineau

I. Is It a Cosmological Argument?

Whether God exists, clearly, is not a controversy concerning God. It is an issue about the world. This can be said without having to pronounce that existence is not a genuine property of individuals.[1] In the classical Indian inference-schema:

> *A* has *f*,
> Because it has *g*,
> Like *B*.

the subject of the conclusion (*A*) must be agreed by both parties to be real on pain of the fallacy of "unestablished place".[2] Accordingly, the changeful universe or the cosmos is the undisputed *place* with respect to which the putative property of *having a creator* is to be inferred on the basis of some mark (reason, or ground - '*g*' in the schema) which will be demonstrably present in the place - the cosmos - and established to be invariably co-located with (or *pervaded* by) the property of having a creator.

Before a philosophical examination of the argument can take off, we have to determine, therefore, at least three things. What is precisely the *place* (or subject) of this inference? What is the *property to be inferred* (or probandum)? What is the proposed *mark* (or probans, or ground, or reason)? The present paper is a modest attempt at recording, connecting and criticising most of the answers given in the

---

[1] Gaṅgeśa not only uses "The cow exists" as a paradigm example of an informative subject- predicate sentence, but explicitly argues for the position that universal properties like existence and knowability are genuine properties even if nothing lacks them.

[2] I have throughout translated "*pakṣa*" as "place", "*hetu*" as "mark" and "*sādhya*" as "inferable property".

R. W. Perrett (ed.), Indian Philosophy of Religion, 21–34.

history of Indian thought to these three questions. It at most tries to clear the ground for actually assessing some of the theistic proofs.

The history of theistic arguments and their refutations in India - which runs parallel to the history of Indian logic from Gautama to Gadādhara - is basically the story of successively suggested changes and reformulations of the subject, inferable, and mark of this essentially causal argument.[3]

It is amazing that, contrary to the wide-spread prejudice that classical Indian philosophy has been predominantly *religious* and *faith-bound*, belief in anything like a Creator God found almost[4] its sole defender in the Nyāya-Vaiśeṣika philosophers - who had constantly to fight against the atheism not only of heterodox schools like the Cārvāka, Jaina and Buddhist, but also of the godless but mainstream orthodox schools like Sāṃkhya and Mīmāṃsā. Even Gautama - the father of the Nyāya tradition - talks about God only non-commitally as one theory among many of the origin of the universe. In his brief report of the ancient controversy, however, he starts by identifying Īśvara (= God) as the *cause* of the world-order (not necessarily in his own view, though) because human effort is often seen to fail.[5] An objection follows in the natural rhythm of his style. After all, God cannot be the sole or whole cause because without human actions no fruits can be brought about. Then the objection is answered. Even human efforts are brought about ultimately by God and cannot succeed without God's agency. Although we vaguely see the outline of a *causal* argument of some sort here, we are not sure whether this is quite the *cosmological* argument as we know it in Western thought. The moral order (where good acts bring about happiness and bad acts suffering) is looked upon as an extension of the natural order. The need for a just overseer is felt urgently by some - though not all - philosophers who look upon "merit" and "demerit" not only as "unseen", but also in a profound sense *unseeing*, blind or inert. Thus the inference assumes more and more the form of a *moral* argument. Some later formulations make the special arrangement of parts in natural objects a *mark* for inferring an intelligent architect. Thus a *teleological* dimension is also added to it. So it is a causal argument with *cosmological*, *moral* and *teleological* variants. Yet, in so far as the core of the argument remains a passage from the phenomenal world as an effect to its sentient efficient cause we are more or less justified in calling it the Nyāya version of the cosmological argument for the existence of God. The argument does not quite proceed from the *existence* of a complex physical universe to the existence of God (as Swinburne recently requires), but it surely proceeds from the *complexity* of the physical universe to the existence of some one intelligent cause.

It would be exciting in this context to compare Udayana's "Five Bouquets" with Aquinas' "Five Ways".[6] Although it is only in the bunch of positive "reasons" offered in the fifth and final bouquet that Udayana gets down to the crucial causal argument, this work has been regarded as the classic compendium of all the reasoned replies to

---

[3]See Vattanky (1984), pp.3-150 for an authentic survey of the field.

[4]Some Kashmir Śaiva thinkers like Sadyojyotih and Viśiṣṭādvaitins like Yāmunācārya endorse a similar position but they use the essentially Nyāya argument from effecthood to a conscious agent.

[5]*Nyāyasūtras* 4.1.19-21.

[6]The striking *dissimilarity* between these two sets of basically cosmological arguments is that Aquinas uses the fundamental contrast between necessary and contingent beings (note that even necessary beings can be created and destroyed), which is a distinction unavailable to Udayana; whereas Udayana's God creates according to the blueprint of individual souls' moral "savings" and out of preexistent material atoms, which is an idea quite foreign to Aquinas.

atheism, as well as of all the possible proofs of a Creator God. In Patañjali's *Yogasūtras*[7] we get the independent argument from degrees of knowledge which anticipates the insight behind Aquinas' fourth way (except that the latter talks about graduation of "goodness, nobleness and truth"). Resisting, on this occasion, the temptation to plunge into a comparative account of such arguments in the two traditions (historically mostly insulated from each other) I wish to go back to the heart of the issue: which, if any, is the flawless formulation of the age old argument that mountains, places and animal bodies must have an original maker, because they are composite non-eternal effects, like a jar or a piece of fine fabric. We must remember that the very two competing and collaborating traditions which gave sophisticated shape to Indian logic - viz. the Nyāya and the Buddhist philosophers - were precisely the propounders and the attackers of this argument. So, along with the metaphysical and logical development of these two schools of thought, the limbs of the argument - the place (subject), the mark (the reason) and the inferable (property to be established in the place) - were given sharper, and more and more careful formulations.

II. What Sort of God?

The burden of the proof was heavy indeed. It intended to prove the existence of a God who:

(1) Is a super-soul with eternal knowledge of everything.[8]

(2) Has natural control or lordship over the material universe and other souls[9] whose bodies he creates according to their beginninglessly earned merits and demerits.

(3) Joins the equally eternal atoms in the beginning of each cosmic cycle (giving rise to the twoness of a dyad by his primordial act of counting).

(4) Makes the otherwise unconscious law of moral retribution work.

(5) Acts directly through his eternal will and agency without the mediation of a body.[10]

(6) Composes the Vedas which tell humans how to live a good life, through

---

[7]*Yogasutras* I, 1.25

[8]Potter calls God truly and shockingly "an unliberated soul" because, unlike a liberated soul, God always has knowledge, desire (to create, sustain, destroy), agency and perhaps even happiness of a sort - properties which the Nyāya-style liberation deprives you of.

[9]In interpreting the invocation verse of *Ātmatattvaviveka* all the commentators, including Raghunātha, take "*jagat*" (which ordinarily means the material world) to mean "all the embodied persons", of which God is said to be the natural father.

[10]Since God does not have a body, there is no question of God's being a man or a woman. Yet I have, alas, had to keep faithful to the general practice of calling God "he" - although the concept of *God the mother* is very common among Hindu religious thinkers. The "Mother" cult seems to be more inclined to pantheism and monism. Goddess Durga remarks, "I alone exist in this Universe; where is a second other than me?"

"do-s" and "don't-s".

(7) Establishes the conventional connection between primitive words and their meant items.

(8) After creating the world also sustains and destroys it (according to the ripeness of the accumulated "unseen" seeds of the actions of creatures).

(9) Showers grace on humans and other creatures so that each soul can ultimately become liberated.

(10) Remains constantly and uniformly happy or contented through all these actions which do not touch his changeless, blissful essence.

Naturally, *almost* each of those alleged attributes of the Creator came under severe attack for centuries from Buddhists, Jains, Mīmāṃsakas and Sāṃkhyas. Questions like the following became standardised in the polemical literature on this subject before Udayana's time (the eleventh century):

(a) How can an eternal changeless object be a cause, mover or initiator of change at all?

(b) Why do we *need* a creator at all if the universe is beginningless and the so called "cycles" begin and end according to the accumulation or expiry of the fructifying seeds of the actions of individual conscious agents?

(c) How can a bodiless substance even *try* to join physical atoms?

(d) What would motivate a perfect being to start creating the world?

(e) Why doesn't the putative "maker" start making the world at any point of time earlier than when he actually does it? In so far as his knowledge of the constitutents and his will to create are eternal and uncaused, why does not he create everything at a time rather than waiting for a successive or gradual unfoldment?

(f) What explains the discrimination and cruelty so apparent in the scheme of creation if the Agent behind it is infinitely kind and neutral and just?

(g) Even if there is a maker behind each non-eternal effect which constitutes the cosmos, why must there be only one and the same maker for all of them? What stops us from imagining a plurality of makers?

(h) Knowledge - or at least direct perceptual knowledge - is generated in a soul by the sense-object contact. How can God have any knowledge, having no sense organs? Isn't the concept of *ungenerated* knowledge inconsistent anyway?

(i) Either evil acts are committed completely independently by mortal individuals, in which case God's mastery over them is mutilated; or these acts are prompted by God himself, in which case God is either unwise or deliberately mischievous. Why should an omniscient and all-good propeller of all human action prompt us to do wrong things? The answer that it is his game or spontaneous sport paints god as a wanton and mean figure rather than a graceful one.[11]

(j) If the whole of the cosmos requires a *maker* because it undergoes change, even God undergoes change in so far as he sometimes creates, sometimes destroys, sometimes just sustains this or that cycle of the universe. Should not he, by the same token, require a further maker?[12]

We shall not have either the space or the occasion to enter into each of these interesting complaints against the Nyāya-Vaiśeṣika concept of God. Neither shall we be able to demonstrate how each of the above mentioned tenfold attributes of God was felt to be necessary by the theist logicians, who were of course all too happy to raise these atheistic complaints and fortify their notion of a Deity by what they considered to be well-argued replies to these objections.

We shall confine ourselves to a systematic study of the different formulations of this broadly causal argument for the existence of God.

III. The Subject (or Place) of the Inference

We began by noting that the place (*pakṣa*) of the argument must be the *world.* But there are three sorts of elements in this world as we find it.[13] Certain things are taken even by the theist to be as eternal and uncreated as God himself (unlike in most Christian theology of antiquity where time itself is supposed to have come into existence due to God's will). Individual souls; space; time; the indivisible infinitesimal atomic elements of earth, fire, water and air; the universals; the relation of inherence are all such parts of the world. To include them in the "subject" of an inference which establishes the predicate "is created by an intelligent maker" will be to incur the fallacy of contradicting established facts.

There are other things which are obviously known or seen to be "made" - built or constructed out of materials by conscious agents. Palaces, gates, pots and carriages are made by human agents. (Or in the case of nests, by birds etc.). To prove about them that they are preceded by intelligent makers will be to incur the fallacy of "proving the obvious". The freshness condition is as important for knowledgehood generally in Indian epistemology as the coherence, truth and justification conditions. So these two sorts of things - even if parts of the world - could not be included within the subject of the inference in question.

The third category consists of things about which there is disagreement or doubt as to whether they are made by a conscious agent or not. Bodies of animals, trees, mountains and rivers are such changeful composite objects which are not known to be

---

[11]See Prajñākara on *Pramāṇavārttika* 2/10, verse 261: "One gets a moment's fun, lots of others lose their lives."

[12]See Guṇaratna's commentary on Haribhadra's *Ṣaḍdarśanasamuccaya*, verse 46, par.22: "... if being an effect means being susceptible to change even the Supreme Lord should be an effect ... how can he be active without undergoing change?"

[13]This distinction is first clearly drawn by Vācaspati in his elegant Sanskrit in the *Tātparyaṭīkā*.

either definitely beginningless or definitely constructed by embodied conscious agents with limited abilities. So it was proposed that we should formulate the "place" of the inference as:

(P_1) That about which there is doubt whether it has a maker or not.

But whose doubt are we talking about? The theist has no doubt that products of earth (like animal bodies), trees, rivers, etc. do have a maker. The atheist is equally certain that they do not have any maker. The neutral judge in the middle, if any, has a doubt *only* after the theist and atheist have produced their respective inferences proving opposite properties in the same *place*. The identification of that place cannot *depend* upon the doubt of the neutral judge, which is epistemically subsequent to the formulation of the inferences and hence of the place itself, without an obvious circularity. So, even if we get at the right sort of items through this mode of presentation, the property of *being the topic of doubt about having a maker* cannot serve technically as the limitor of placehood (the epistemically prior means of characterising the subject of the inference).

So we can try taking simply the *earth* as the subject. Of course, we have to avoid the atoms of earth and jars etc. made by human potters for we don't want either to prove the patently false or the patently true. But shall we then just go on enumerating things like mountains, plants, bodies individually as all or each forming the place of the inference? And then of course we cannot stop with only middle-sized *earthly* objects; we have to include everything *produced*, all non-atomic water, air, fire etc.; also, they do not have anything in common except that they are all *produced*. So try:

(P_2) Things produced (but not by embodied beings).

But then what are we eventually inferring in this place? It is also the *property of being produced* (but not by an embodied being). So upon this formulation again we shall have a tautology as the conclusion of the inference, which hardly needs any ground or reason to get established. Hence we have to try taking the immediate effects of atomic particles - the first dyads which are made at the very beginning of creation. Surely, we cannot introduce them as *place* or subject of inference, *as* "the dyads at the first moment of creation". For such a beginning of creation itself is questioned by the atheist who has to grant the *place* as uncontroversial. But dyads themselves can be quite non-controversial, at least for philosophers (even materialists or realist Buddhists) who see how compelling the atomistic hypothesis is as an explanation of emergence of visible and tactile objects (an archaic view had "whatever is accessible to two different sense-organs" as the *place*). So we can try as the subject of the inference:

(P_3) Dyads.

Some modern commentators take the usual expression "earth-sprouts" to mean earth-*dyads*[14]. For like the first-found effect of a seed which later brings out the huge fullgrown tree, the dyads are the first evolute of the atoms which are seeds of the "tree of the cosmos". Now there can be two reasons why, even upon the general Nyāya-Vaiśeṣika story of cosmic evolution, one can balk at arranging the theistic inference as simply: "Dyads have a maker because they are effects". For one thing, this suggests

---

[14]See Kṛṣṇavallabhācārya's elucidation of *Mūktāvalī* (Chowkhamba, 1972, p.16).

that the rest of the building up of the material universe - like the formation of the planets, the solar system, the constallations of stars, the intricate putting together of delicate and elaborate machines like human bodies - all this is supposed to happen quite independently of divine agency. Obviously if God is to be required as a cause, he is not required *only* to put together couples of atoms.

Secondly, all theists and definitely all atheists will not accept this particular account of the origin of the world as a step-by-step process where dyads necessarily figure as the first step. Even if they do, there are technical problems in recognizing "dyad-hood" as a genuine universal (the "impediment" of *intermixture* seems to be operative against it) which limits the placeness of the place - to allow myself a bit of Navya-Nyāya jargon!

Gaṅgeśa has proposed several other formulations of the subject of the inference. Finally he proposes:

(P4) Everything which is produced but not through the unseen (merits or demerits) and not through an agency which is itself produced, and which is such that it *inheres* in something.

This is his own (characteristically complicated) favoured subject of the inference. All that is produced by human agency is thereby excluded, because human agency to an action is itself produced by a desire to act (which is caused by the knowledge of the appropriate kind). Only God's agency is said to be uncaused.

In this connection we can briefly address the troubled question of God's motivation for and agency towards creation. It might seem that, in order to have the will to initiate this endless series of changes in the cosmos, God will have to be full of movements and changes, whereas God is known to be unmoved and unchanging. The classic answer to this - both in the East and in the West - has been that *willing a change is not changing a will.*[15] God could eternally have willed all these temporally ordered changes - like a certain housewife's fixed plan made first thing in the morning to act according to a certain busy schedule of various successive activities during the whole day. She does not have to will before each act separately. The theory of divine action, like the theory of divine knowledge and divine desire, of course has to run somewhat differently than the theories of human action, desire and knowledge. In the case of God the causal sequence

cognition → desire → agency

is not operative at all. Neither is his cognition supposed to be *caused* (and not causally because more of his cognitions can be *generated*); his eternal desire and eternal volition also relate directly to their intended series of objects, rather than via the causality of knowledge. These are, expectedly, deeply controversial metaphysical issues. Each difficulty in this area assumes the form of an atheist objection. As to the motivation for creation, three sorts of views have been put forward. Sometimes it has been said that he creates out of kindness towards the creatures. Now, even if we don't interpret kindness as suffering at another's suffering (which is the usual form of pity) because God cannot suffer,[16] we are not allowed to see in God a permanent or beginningless wish to relieve the pain of other souls without making the *sufferings* of

---

[15]See Sorabji (1983), pp.240-241.

[16]See Śaṃkaramiśra's gloss on the word "*kṛpā*" (mercy) in the invocation of the *Ātmatattvaviveka*.

these souls to be as beginningless as his kindness on account of it. This, of course, would not daunt the Indian theists who do not believe in a "Fall" which human or divine aid could have helped. The chain of suffering is indeed believed to be without a beginning. But this explanation is rejected because if just kindness were the reason for creation, God would have only created happy creatures, or at least made them do actions which can earn happiness for them.

Since creation is not at all free of first and second order evil, the kindness motivation is rejected. Sometimes it is proposed that God creates to show off his power. This is easily refuted, for it suggests that he feels unfulfilled until he has displayed his power to his subordinate creatures - which after all is the mark of a very insecure boss.

Finally, the favoured hypothesis is that God creates because it is his essence or nature to create. He creates not to have fun or a game (that is not quite the meaning of "*līlā*"!) - because he always is having enough fun. Rather, like a happy artist's, his creativity emanates spontaneously out of an excess of happiness in him.

But this creates a different problem for the Nyāya metaphysicians. Is God even happy? Happiness is said to be caused by virtuous acts, or merit due to such acts. If God enjoys unmerited happiness there will be a serious breach in the inexorable law that "No one enjoys what one has not earned". Some theists have gone to the length of ascribing *merit* to God due to his primordial good acts (interpreting the Upaniṣadic reference to God's *tapas* - austerities practised in order to create the world - as his making the *resolution* to generate a multifarious universe). But later Nyāya philosophers have mostly opposed this view and have supposed that God is not "happy" in the usual sense. He is just free from any touch of pain. Like the question of whether there is positive joy in the state of final liberation for an individual soul, the question of God's blissfulness has remained an open question for the theists.

Minus this account in terms of overflowing happiness (which might have seeped into Nyāya from the Kashmir Śaiva Schools) the mere answer that God automatically or mechanically or motivelessly creates is not going to satisfy the atheist. A Jaina would say, "Why then cannot we ascribe to inert matter the same automatic instinctive tendency to build up a world?"

IV. What Is To Be Inferred

Let us now look at the issues concerning the property to be inferred (the *sādhya*). The straightforward property which a cosmological argument usually ascribes to the cosmos is "having a first cause". They want right away to prove the existence of a conscious, or even an omniscient, maker from the meagre mark of something being an effect. This will ultimately commit them to the now obsolete theory of all causation being ultimately governed by some conscious agency or will. To use the words of Martineau: "neither phenomena, nor thing, nor force but *will* will have to be taken as the first cause of every movement or effectuation."[17] So

(S1) Having a maker

is the property to be inferred in the place: viz, things which are produced but not by a produced volition etc. But what is it to have a maker? A maker is a conscious agent who has (a) direct knowledge about the material causes; (b) a desire to make

---

[17]See *Study of Religion*, Vol.1, Book II, Sections IA and IB.

something out of those causes; and (c) volition to combine the same material causes into the form of the product. The weaver has such knowledge, for example, of the threads, and wishes and acts to make a piece of cloth out of them. So

> (S_2) Being *immediately* caused by a being who has direct knowledge, desire, and volition about the material causes of those very products

is the refined probandum. Such a probandum precludes the proposal of substituting human agents as ultimately responsible for the creation of the world (through their accumulated unseen again, which necessitates a world to be enjoyed or suffered, to bear fruits) the human agents do not have direct (perceptual) knowledge of atoms which are ultimately the material causes of the corporeal world. It also excludes human agents as the inferred cause of the world because their causal role is mediated by their merits and demerits and is not *immediate* like God's.

In this connection we can look back at the crucial Buddhist objection: why cannot we just stop with inferring many such intelligent architects who collaborate to give this world its present shape? After all, a complex building or machine could be the handiwork of many jointly working artisans. Two arguments can be collected from the monotheistic literature in Indian philosophy against a plurality of creators. First is the favourite Nyāya consideration of ontological economy: if one omniscient and omnipotent God is adequate to explain the bringing about of this universe, why infer more?[18] The other argument is sketched in the commentary on *Yogasūtra* I.25. If more than one such intelligent architects are presupposed *(each equally independent or free)*, the logical possibility will remain that one of them wills x to be f while the other freely wills it at the same time *not* to be f. Since only one of these wishes is going to be carried out, only one will come out as the Supreme Lord. Call that "God".

This, obviously, does not settle the issue. But the theist does hope somehow to include the unity of the maker into the property to be inferred, or at least deduce it as a consequence of that property.

V. What Is the Mark or Reason?

We have to prove the conclusion that dyads and other products are caused directly by some one being who knows the atoms directly. But what will be the mark or reason (*hetu*) which can bear such a load of proof? The proposals are amazingly simple. Dyads (or mountains, oceans, animal bodies etc.) must have such an intelligent maker because

> (H_1) they are effects;
>
> (H_2) they have unconscious material causes;
>
> (H_3) they have an origin;
>
> (H_4) they are inherent in something else while they have a pre-orginatory absence;

---

[18]See Hayes (1988) for Buddhist arguments against the *unity* of conscious causes of the cosmos and Bhattacharya (1961) pp.151-159 for replies.

(H_5) they have parts;

(H_6) they have medium-size (they are non-atomic and non-ubiquitous in dimension;

(H_7) they move by fits and starts, not constantly or mechanically.[19]

Without going into detailed reasons for preferring any one of these alternative formulations to any other, let us directly plunge into the possible and standard objections against this as a ground for inferring an intelligent maker for all those disputed cases of produced but not humanly produced material objects.

A valid and sound mark is expected to have the following characteristics:

(i) It must exist in the place or subject of inference (otherwise the mark is "essentially unestablished").

(ii) It must *not* (only) exist in those places only where the probandum or inferable property is known to be absent (otherwise the mark would be "contrary").

(iii) It must exist in those places (other than the place of inference) where the inferable is known to be present (otherwise the mark is "unexampled").

(iv) It must not have a rival mark which establishes the opposite conclusion, i.e. a mark which supports an inference of the absence of the inferable property in the same place (otherwise the mark will be "counterarguable").

(v) It must not support a conclusion which is patently false or against agreed philosophical theories or empirical facts (otherwise the mark will be "flouted by fact").

(vi) The mark should be established to be pervaded by, i.e. invariably co-located with the inferable property, in an unconditional manner. (If *g* is the mark for infering *f* in *A*, that wherever there is *g* there is *f* must be ascertained independently of any suspected further factor *h* which ensures the presence of *f*, given the presence of *g*. Otherwise the mark will be "deficient in pervasion".)

Now the theistic inference has been faulted on almost *all* those counts. The mark of "being an effect" (or any one of its variants) has been found to be essentially unestablished, contrary, lacking in a proper example, counterarguable, flouted by fact, as well as very much deficient in pervasion.

If "being an effect"[20] is interpreted as "being an effect of conscious volition", such a mark is clearly going to be found by the atheist "unestablished" in places like

---

[19]This last mark ("*sthitvā sthitvā pravṛttih*") could tantalize some philosophers of science who find unpredictable quirks in the behaviour of matter to be signs of a free agency behind it. But we won't discuss it here.

[20]The most trenchant and incisive attack on this mark is to be found in Guṇaratna's commentary on *Ṣaḍdarśanasamuccaya*, verse 46, pars.18-22.

mountains and rivers. It is as controversial as the property to be inferred. If it is interpreted as "being an absentee to a pre-originating absence" (in other words, as having come into being at a point of time) this surely cannot be ascribed to the *whole world*, which in some form or other could be said to have been always there.

Finally, the mark can fail to exist in the place because the *place* is a nonentity - giving rise to the *fallacy of unreal subject*. Śāntarakṣita has insisted that since Buddhists don't admit *wholes* like mountains, rivers, or bodies to be unitary substances distinct from their component parts, the marks cannot be present in the proposed places of inference because there simply are no such places. The above charges of unestablished mark are all somewhat contrived or based on partisan views in metaphysics. If the attempted inference tries to establish the stronger conclusion that some *omniscient bodiless* maker must be responsible for producing the disputed effects like dyads, the mark could be charged of *contrariety*. All the known cases of effects are produced by a non-omniscient embodied maker, if any. So also we get the notorious *counterargument*:

> Earth, trees, bodies, etc.
> Are not produced by any agent
> Because they are not-due-to-the
> action-of-any-*body*
> Like, the sky or the atoms.

The idea is that whatever can be produced by an agent can be produced only through the activity of the agent's body. The blacksmith has to use his hands. A supposed bodiless entity can never bring any effect into being.

The conclusion of this counterargument has been sometimes put as a well-established fact against which the theistic inference absurdly militates. It is not rare nowadays to appeal to established scientific theories (although cosmologists are not so sure that anything is established in this area) to the effect that the universe, if it began at all, began without any conscious agency. Such an appeal will be considered, in the classical logical language of India, to be bringing the charge of fact-floutedness against the mark.

As to whether a bodiless will can bring about a change, the issue is an ancient one and it is transculturally shared.[21] Not *every* feature of the established examples is supposed to carry over to the disputed cases where the mark is applied. We have to abstract certain features of the mark (in this case *being an effect*) and certain features of the inferable property (*having a component-conscious agent*) and then carry on the inference. Otherwise no inference will be possible. There will always be *some* feature of the inferable *as found in the examples* which will be hopefully *inessential* to the abstracted mark and not expected in the place of inference. We do not expect to find kitchen-fire in the hill because we have inferred fire from smoke as a mark, having established the mark as a mark of fire from the case of a *kitchen*-smoke.

However an atheist can here raise a serious difficulty. The passage from kitchen-fire to hill-fire is not quite parallel to the pasage from human agency to divine agency. At least kitchens, fires and hills are separately equally uncontroversial. But in the case under consideration we know agency in humans to be *caused* (by knowledge etc.), to be co-present with a *body*, to be acting through a body etc., whereas none of these would apply to the putative probandum of a divine agency of an omniscient being. Do

---

[21] See Sorabji (1983), p.246.

we have any *pervasion* at all here; any form of agency which is universal enough to span across the radically different modes of operation? The Naiyāyika thinks we do have a generic notion which can serve as the inferable which the mark claims to be unconditionally colocated with. The atheist differs. Dharmakīrti scoffed at this mark of "being an effect" or "having a special arrangement of component parts" by giving the example of ant-hills. Even ant-hills are *produced* and have very clever designs sometimes. Are they therefore produced necessarily by agents who had awareness of the elements or a fully formed intention to build that particular structure? Even if we suppose that they do, is there *one* intelligent agent behind it?

Of course, the Nyāya philosopher would bring all such apparently purposeless or undesigned structures of nature under the general rubric of "things produced but not by human agency" - and then shove them into the *place* of our inference.[22]

VI. Concluding Considerations

To conclude, I must mention some other aspects of the causal argument and the kind of God it hopes to establish in Indian philosophy (especially in Nyāya).

First, God is supposed to be only the efficient cause and not the material cause of the universe. To use Professor Matilal's language, it is the "potter-model" where the ingredients are distinct from and uncreated by the maker.[23] The objects made are still *created* by the maker, because the metaphysics of causation is - literally - "beginning-ist": one which considers the emergent whole to be *absent* prior to the proper putting together of the parts. It is definitely *not* the "spider-model" where God's own essence *becomes* the world; *nor* the "magician-model" where creation is but an illusion created by the Sole Reality, namely God or the Absolute (all effects being ultimately "appearance".)

Secondly, God does not have the freedom to create arbitrarily ignoring or superseding the results of the actions of individual souls in their previous births. As Vācaspati remarks: "Although he is compassionate, although his power or greatness excels that of any other soul, he cannot possibly reverse the essential potentialities (causal powers) of inanimate things."[24] The same unseen laws, which require the almighty to govern them or put life into them, seem to limit the power of the governor by their inexorable nature. Even God cannot upset the metaphysics of morality which lies at the back of the Nyāya cosmology.

Thirdly, God's omniscience has been proved on the basis of the eternity of his knowledge. If he had only a limited number of things to be known his knowledge would be limited in time too. I don't know how good this argument is, because even given an infinite expanse of topics he could be said to know any one of them relentlessly, unlike us who know one thing after another. The objection that in order to really share all *our* pieces of cognition he will have to share our errors also I think can be taken care of by Gaṅgeśa's insightful remark that "someone who knows a mistake (is aware of what mistake has been made) is not necessarily mistaken".[25]

---

[22] Vācaspati, *Tātparyaṭīkā*: "It is not proper to complain that the universal-rule is confuted by the counterexample of trees in a forest growing without any conscious effort, because all such examples are included within the subject of the inference and are hence objects of dispute" (p.601).

[23] Matilal (1982), p.31.

[24] *Tātparyaṭīkā*, 4.4.21, (p.596).

[25] See *Śabdaprāmanyavāda* of *Tattvacintāmaṇi*.

Fourthly, not only creating but sustaining and destroying are also said to be the job of the same benevolent Father of the Universe. Udayana also argues that the world must have a destroyer because it is destructable. It is considered to be merciful of God not to let a tattered and dirty fabric of the universe go on. And this is not all that absurd. Witness the remark made by a contemporary physicist:

> ... if the universe continues to expand, it may never reach precise thermodynamic equilibrium ... *Only a supernatural God could truly wind it up again.*[26]

We must remember that the divine destroyer's dance has a rhythm. There is method in the madness of a Maheśvara! The forms of Brahma, Viṣṇu and Rudra are not three distinct gods, but roles taken up by the same Controller of the Cosmos who makes or unmakes always according to the total maturity of the merits and demerits earned by individual conscious beings. Let us not commit the mistake which Kant made in *interpreting* the cosmology of the Hindu theist when he remarked,

> ... that a Fall into evil (moral evil ...) presently hurried mankind from bad to worse with accelerated descent ... In some parts of India the Judge and Destroyer of the world, Rudra (sometimes called Siwa or Siva), already is worshipped as the reigning god - Vishnu, the Sustainer of the World, having some centuries ago grown weary and renounced the supreme authority which he inherited from Brahma, the Creator.[27]

Fifthly, it is not only the material universe which is taken as an effect of the divine will. Even language is taken as an *artifact* which can be ultimately traced back to God's will (unlike in Mīmāṃsā where the word-meaning relation is supposed to be eternal and originless). The usage which is handed down to us as determining the semantic relationships is made also a place, where the property of "being established by a supreme teacher of all teachers" is inferred by the single mark that it is a usage at all, like the man-made usage of a proper name to denote a new object.[28] This raises interesting issues about how God can be made responsible for even newly invented words meaning or referring to what they do. The strategy (shown by Gadādhara) is to ascribe to God a generally formulated *will* which empowers subsequent humans to establish further semantic conventions or name-object relations.

Finally, the question of God's body remains an open one even within the theistic camp. Not everyone recognizes God to be necessarily bodiless. According to Rāmānuja and his followers the individual souls and the material world constitute the body of the Supreme Self (God). Udayana suggests that God can assume corporeal bodies for special purposes on occasions (which is a very precarious position given God's immutable nature). There is also in place a suggestion that since God's will acts

---

[26] Davies (1983), pp.212-213.

[27] *Religion Within the Limits of Reason Alone*, Bk.1; Kant (1960), p.15.

[28] See Chemparathy (1972) pp.95-96.

directly upon the atoms, the atoms themselves constitute the body of God.[29] We must remember however that such an account will come closer to the "spider-model" than to the "potter-model"!

REFERENCES

Bhattacharya, Gopikamohan (1961). *Studies in Nyāya-Vaiśeṣika Theism.* Calcutta: Sanskrit College.

Chemparathy, George (1972). *An Indian Rational Theology.* Vienna: De Nobili Research Library.

Davies, Paul (1983). *God and the New Physics.* Harmondsworth: Penguin.

Hayes, Richard P. (1988). "Principled Atheism in the Buddhist Scholastic Tradition" *Journal of Indian Philosophy* 16: 5-28.

Kant, Immanuel (1960). *Religion Within the Limits of Reason Alone*, trans. T.M. Greene & H.H. Hudson. New York: Harper & Row.

Martineau, James (1888). *A Study of Religion*, Vol.1. Oxford: Oxford University Press.

Matilal, Bimal Krishna (1982). *Logical and Ethical Issues of Religious Belief.* Calcutta: University of Calcutta.

Potter, Karl H. (1977). Editor. *Indian Metaphysics and Epistemology.* Princeton: Princeton University Press.

Sorabji, Richard (1983). *Time, Creation and the Continuum.* London: Duckworth.

Vattanky, John (1984). *Gaṅgeśa's Philosophy of God.* Madras: Adyar Research Centre.

---

[29] Madhusūdana, while reporting the Nyāya view and defending it against Sāṃkhya atheism, conjectures that: "Whatever is the recipient of direct volition of a person is his body. It is the atoms which directly receive the volition of the Supreme Lord and get activated. So God should be correctly argued to have atoms as his body." He ascribes this view to Udayana on the basis of a suggestion of the latter in the context of explaining the idea "the Universe is God's body" in Vācaspati's *Ṭīkā* invocation verse. See my translation of Madhusūdana's "Towards an Unfoldment of Our Knowledge of God" (*Īśvarapratipattiprakāśa*), forthcoming in the *Journal of Indian Philosophy*.

RELIGIONS AS FAILED THEODICIES: ATHEISM IN HINDUISM AND BUDDHISM

A.L. Herman

University of Wisconsin, Stevens Point

INTRODUCTION

This essay intends to pursue two questions: First, in what sense might Hinduism and Buddhism be called "atheistic religions"; and, second, what is the cause of that atheism?

I shall attempt to display the various senses in which Hinduism and Buddhism are, indeed, atheistic religions; and demonstrate that it was the Indian confrontation with unjustifiable, dysteleological suffering leading to various failed theodicies that was the chief cause of that atheism. I shall try to demonstrate that these various failed attempts at theodicies provided the impetus and the energy for the religious evolution and philosophic change seen throughout the early history of both Hinduism and Buddhism. It was, in other words, the repeated failure at theodicy that led time and again to new theodical schemes, schemes involving sacrificial compulsion and ritual magic, the celebration of a new mythology, together with the introduction of a whole host of new concepts, such as *tapas, ṛta, pāpa, Brahman, Ātman, māyā, saṃsāra,* and the law of karma.

Let me say something, to begin with, about "theodicy" in precisely the sense I shall employ thoughout this essay:

> By theodicies one means defences of the highest wisdom of the creator against the complaints which reason makes by pointing to the existence of things in the world which contradict the wise purpose. One calls such defence a "plea for God's cause".[1]

It is human suffering, of course, that "contradicts the wise purpose" of God and it is "the plea for God's cause" that will provide the fuel for the changes in Hinduism on which I shall be focusing. The contradictions to the wise purpose shall take many forms, ranging from the apparently dysteleological evil mentioned above to more

---

[1] Immanuel Kant, "On the Failure of All Attempted Philosophical Theodicies (1791)", translated by Michel Despland in Despland (1973), p.283.

R. W. Perrett (ed.), Indian Philosophy of Religion, 35–60.

simple evils, such as failed health, unanswered prayers, and disappointed expectations.

"Atheism" in the Indian texts is usually translated from Sanskrit words like "*anīśvaram*", "without a God" or "*anindrāh*",[2] "persons who do not believe in Indra as Lord" or, more in line with the God that Kant's theodicies are attempting to defend, "*nāstika*", "unorthodox" or "heterodox" which means, *inter alia*, "the denial of the existence of a Creator".[3] However, for the purposes of this chapter, by "atheism" I will mean the view that denies "theism", which is the view that there is a God, whether Creator or not, who is all-powerful, all-just, and all-knowing. This is the God that the theodicies both East and West have been and are seeking to justify and explain, and this is the God whose existence can be found and defended in the Vedas, as we shall see below in our examination of Vedic theism.[4]

The Theological Problem of Evil

With these definitions of "theodicy" and "atheism" in mind, let me say a final word about the theological problem of evil. The theological problem of evil will arise wherever both theism and suffering exist. No religion can or has escaped this ubiquitous puzzle; and nowhere is the problem better illustrated than in the early history of both Hinduism and Buddhism where the God-threatening nature of the problem is all too clearly displayed. The theological problem of evil can be stated as follows:

1. If God is all-powerful, all-good, and all-knowing then why is there evil (horrendous suffering) in the world? For God could prevent it (God is all-powerful), God would want to stop it (God is all-good) and God would know when it occurred (God is all-knowing).
2. But there is evil (horrendous suffering) in the world.
3. So why doesn't God prevent evil?

Theodicies, Failure and Atheism

The theological problem of evil leads to theodicies, i.e., attempts to justify the ways of God to man, or in Kant's memorable words, they attempt to find "defences of the highest wisdom of the Creator against complaints". When these theodicies fail, as fail they all do or must, they lead inevitably to atheism. The formal argument supporting this atheism looks like this:

---

[2] *Bhagavad Gītā* 16.8.

[3] See Smart (1964), p.23: "Atheism involves disbelief in a Creator...."

[4] This definition of "theism" and "God" builds on Arthur Keith's reference to the "high gods" of the *Ṛg Veda* by explicating his concept of "supernatural power" in such a way as to include a theistic Buddhism which accepts "gods," as Keith defines them, but which does not accept "God":

> ...in the main the high gods of the Rigveda should be essentially conceived as human, as men of supernatural power, and free from death, but still as subject to birth and akin in their family relation to men. Keith (1925), Vol.1, p.58.

Our examination of Varuṇa in the *Ṛg Veda* will clarify below precisely what I intend by "God" and by "theism" and, thereby, through them, of "atheism", as well.

1. If theism is true (if God exists) then there should be no evil (horrendous suffering).
2. But there is evil (look around!).
3. Therefore, theism is false (God does not exist).

Failed or failing theodicies are a real and constant threat to theistic religions. This is especially clear when we remember that evil can take very varied forms ranging from unfulfilled ritual requests, and unanswered prayers, to the tragic loss of loved ones and friends, to pain, anxiety, and death for oneself and others.[5]

In what follows I want to examine briefly the development of Indian atheism in three historic periods, viz., the Vedic period, the Upaniṣadic period, and the early Buddhist period. I will conclude this chapter with a fourth and final section on the problems and speculations which this study of Indian atheism may have engendered.

My thesis, which will answer both of the questions that we are pursuing, will be that Hinduism and Buddhism (and all religions) are ultimately theodicies, that all theodicies must inevitably fail, and that those failures account for the evolution of Hinduism and Buddhism (and all religions), an evolution towards, and finally into, atheism.[6]

I. RELIGIOUS ATHEISM IN THE VEDIC PERIOD

The Vedic period (1200-800 B.C.E.) is witness to the evolution of religious theism into ritual atheism. This evolution ranges from the earliest Vedas, such as the *Ṛg Veda* (ca. 1200 B.C.E.), through the *Atharva Veda* (ca. 800 B.C.E.) and the Brāhmaṇas (ca. 900 B.C.E.). It is a period that exhibits gradual loss of faith in the Gods[7] and in their ability to carry out the purposes for which the religion of the Āryans seems to have been originally designed, viz., to solve the problem of suffering in both this world and the next. The Vedic period is a time, from a theodical point of view, of religious challenge and response to what can only have been repeated failures in those responses. The challenges, i.e., the contradictions to God's or the Gods' wise purpose,

---

[5]Not to mention the suffering of sentient creatures other than man. On sub-human (animals) and super-human (demons and devils) suffering as added dimensions of the theological problem of (human) evil, see Herman (1976), pp.90-92.

[6]My thesis is really an exploratory extension of Max Weber's assertion:

> All Hindu religion was influenced by [the problem of theodicy].... even a meaningful world order that is impersonal and supertheistic must face the problem of the world's imperfections. In one form or another, this problem belongs everywhere among the factors determining religious evolution and the need for salvation. Weber (1964) p.139.

See O'Flaherty (1976) for a grand discussion of the problem of evil in the classical texts and mythological epics of Hinduism. See especially pp.1-16 and her conclusion: "But there are problems of the theodicy type in many texts of the Vedas and Brāhmaṇas .... the patterns of theodicy were established before the [Upaniṣadic] doctrine of karma and continued to develop alongside it." (p.16)

[7]I see no reason to drop honorific initial capital letters in mentioning these Vedic deities. I suspect that it was originally merely a Judaeo-Christian monotheistic conceit that relegated pagan "Gods" to "gods", and, since there are no upper case letters in Sanskrit to separate *"deva"* from *"Deva"*, who could gainsay the practice? Throughout this chapter, "Gods" are Beings with Power, while "gods" lack that Power.

appear as ordinary and extraordinary suffering.

Extraordinary suffering includes the pains caused by cataclysmic natural events, such as famine, earthquake and flood, horrendous and continuous pain over days, months and years, as well as anxiety over health, wealth, long life and progeny, pains for which the general machinery of religion may have no ordinary answers and to which it must then make extraordinary responses. Should the sufferings persist, then the theological problem of evil becomes a religion-threatening and ultimately a God-threatening problem: The religion becomes a theodicy. Should the theodicy fail to meet the extraordinary responses to suffering, the result could be a denial of the Gods and their power, i.e., the Gods become gods. The consequence is that the religion has evolved from a theism into one or more of the different varieties of atheism.

Religious Theism in the Vedic Period

In order to understand what Vedic atheism was all about, it might be helpful to see what Vedic theism was all about. I take this theism to be a norm from which later atheism will deviate.

I begin with several assumptions about religions: That religions are societal systems designed to meet human needs; that the greatest human need is to be protected from suffering but especially extraordinary suffering; that the principal purpose of religion is to solve the problem of human suffering; and that nowhere is that purpose pursued with greater expectation of success than in religious theism. For religious theism holds that the central problem of human existence, suffering, can be solved by the supernatural intervention of God or Gods who have the Power to relieve that suffering.

Religious theism received its clearest expression in the early Vedic period where those who suffer, or are about to suffer, approach the Gods in order to stop or assuage the real or the threatening evil.[8] Man gives something to the Gods and the Gods return the favour. Vedic religious theism can be summarized under the following four headings:

1. There are Gods with Power.

The early Āryan brahmins who chanted the hymns of the Vedas seldom doubted the existence of the Gods or the supernatural Power of the Gods whom they worshipped. This hymn to Indra is typical:

> Indra is sovereign lord of earth and heaven;
> Indra is lord of waters and mountains.
> Indra is master of those who prosper and of the wise.
> Indra must be invoked at work and at rest.
>
> Greater than days and nights, the Giver of all,
> He is greater than the earth's and the oceans' waters,
> Greater than the limits of earth and the wind's expanse.

---

[8] Let me say at the outset that I don't believe that anyone can really enlighten us on what the Vedas are really all about except the Vedic *ṛṣis* themselves and they are all dead. This hard fact makes Vedic studies or comparative studies using the Vedas both heady stuff, almost anything works, and at the same time risky stuff, almost nothing works. The reader is forewarned.

> Greater than all rivers and all our lands, greater than all of these is Lord Indra.[9]

2. Man Wants and Needs that Power.

It goes without saying that extraordinary suffering can only be met by extraordinary responses. The Gods' Power could secure wealth, keep anxiety at bay, forgive sins and relieve sickness, and save one from death and death's destructive aftermath. This hymn to Varuṇa, a Vedic Saviour, is typical:

> May we be in your keeping, Oh Saviour, wide-ruling Varuṇa, the lord of many heroes.... Save us, admit us to your friendship.
>
> Release me from sin as from a bond that binds me; may we strengthen the foundation of your order. Let not my thread be cut while I weave my prayer, nor may life-work be crushed before my life has ended.
>
> Remove far from me what ever sins I have committed; let me not suffer, Oh God, for the sins of others. Many full morns have yet to dawn upon us; while we live in those morns, Oh Varuṇa, we pray you to give us guidance.[10]

3. There is a Way to that Power.

The Gods have the Power, man needs the Power, so the way to that Power becomes all-important. The way, of course, lies in either the public or the household sacrifices and rituals conducted by the priests or the householder. The *soma* sacrifice is typical of the ways to the Power of the Gods as the sacrificer calls upon God to deliver the favour requested in exchange for the shared inebriating offering of *soma*. This hymn to Indra is, again, typical:

> Drink, Indra; the juice is shed to make thee joyful....
> Drink this soma... for power and rapture.
> The men, the pressing-stones, the cows, the waters have made this soma ready for your drinking.
> Let this sacrifice increase your strength.[11]

And the glorious results that follow are typical as well:

> We have drunk the soma, we have become immortal, we have reached the light, we have found the Gods.[12]

The Gods are fed and they feed man in return as this religious theism culminates in a *quid pro quo* relationship between the Gods and man. J. Gonda has put the matter in

---

[9] *Ṛg Veda* X. 89. 10-11. Griffith (1889), p.601. I have used Griffith's translations throughout this chapter and made minor changes where appropriate.

[10] *Ṛg Veda* II. 28.3,5,9. After Griffith (1889), pp.148,149.

[11] *Ṛg Veda* VI. 40.1,2,4. After Griffith, p.307.

[12] *Ṛg Veda* 8. 48. 3. After Griffith, p.435.

this fashion:

> [M]an adds to the god's power, that he [the god] may have power to reciprocate and that life processes may not stagnate because of any lack of potency.[13]

Dependency on man and the sacrifice does not detract from the Gods' Power. It merely gives man the opportunity for both increasing and directing that Power.

4. The Vedas Describe that Way

The hymns of the Vedas give descriptions of what must be done and sung in order to mitigate suffering. In doing so they lay the foundations for the solution to the problem of suffering pursued by Vedic men and women.

Varuṇa as Vedic Saviour

The theism of the *Ṛg Veda* is probably best and most clearly represented in the personality of Lord Varuṇa. Varuṇa, among his other roles in the Vedas, is a Saviour who has the power to forgive sins and save his worshippers from the consequences of their suffering-producing indiscretions. From the hymns that have appeared above, it is clear that Varuṇa must be both omniscient and omnipotent. He is omniscient for he must have the power to know when those who pray to him are truly contrite; and he must be omnipotent for he must have the power to ward off any and all untoward consequences from occurring to his truly contrite devotees. In addition, Lord Varuṇa is not only all-knowing and all-powerful but he is, in addition, all-just. Varuṇa is bound by his nature, it was believed, to punish the unrepentantly wicked and reward the repentantly good. These properties of Varuṇa are all nicely reflected in the following hymn as the all-just, the all-wise, and the all-powerful Lord is lovingly described:

> Oh God, Oh Varuṇa, when we as men violate your law day after day,
>
> Then give us not as prey to death, to be destroyed by you in your wrath or in your fierce anger when displeased.
>
> To gain your mercy, Varuṇa, we bind your heart with hymns, even as the charioteer binds his tethered horse....
>
> Varuṇa knows the path of birds that fly through heaven, and, master of the sea, he knows all the ships thereon.
>
> True to his holy law, he knows the twelve moons with all their progeny as the months with all their days....
>
> He knows the pathway of the wind, the spreading, high and mighty wind; he knows the Gods who dwell above.

---

[13]Gonda (1965), pp.214-215.

> Varuṇa, true to holy law, sits down among his people; he, the most wise one, sits there to govern all.
>
> From there he perceives all wondrous things, both what has been, and what hereafter will be done.[14]

Conclusion

From what has been said above the theism of the Vedas, from one period of their development and evolution, seems obvious. There were Gods, powerful, knowing and just Gods, who were willing to share their Power. What these Gods received from their worshippers in exchange for their favours was varied, food for Indra, moral behaviour and loyalty for Varuṇa, but essential to their continued survival and to the survival of their Power. But challenges to that theism also existed, sceptical challenges at first, and then, as I shall hypothesize, a growing challenge leading to atheism. This latter challenge was brought about by a growing disappointment with both the promise of theism to relieve suffering and the theistic institution that supported that promise. That disappointment is translatable into the theological problem of evil and atheism. We turn next to the scepticism and atheism of the Vedic period.

Vedic Scepticism

The appearance in the later Vedic period of sceptical comments with respect to the Power of the Gods or the Gods' ability to manipulate that Power may be the first indication that we have of problems, unsolvable problems, developing in the religious theism of the earlier period. The following sceptical comments and questions are typical:

> No one knows from whence this creation has come - maybe it made itself, maybe it did not - maybe the God who looks down on it from the highest heaven knows, and then again maybe he doesn't know.[15]

And about Indra:

> Men have stopped pressing the *soma*; they do not count Indra as a God.[16]
>
> One and another say that Indra does not exist. For who has seen him? Who then shall we praise?[17]

But there is more than scepticism about the Gods and their Power arising in this later period of religious theism. The Gods themselves came to be sacrificers, for their Power and their status depend on the sacrifice. The *quid pro quo* relationship that had existed between the Gods and man is now revealed as a terrible existential dependency

---

[14]*Ṛg Veda* I. 25.1-3,7-11. After Griffith, p.15.

[15]*Ṛg Veda* X. 127.7.

[16]*Ṛg Veda* X. 86.

[17]*Ṛg Veda* VIII. 89. See also *Rg Veda* II. 12.

which the Gods had upon the sacrifice. The human sacrificer, the patron, and the priests who do the sacrificing discover that what was wanted all along was the Power that the Gods possessed and not the Gods themselves. The Gods' limited nature is now made all-too-plain:

> Who really knows? Who will proclaim it? Whence was it produced? Whence is this creation? The gods came afterwards, with the creation of this universe? Who then knows whence it has arisen?[18]

The "Gods" have become "gods".

Nowhere is the transition from religious theism to religious atheism made more plain than in two later compositions from the Vedic period, viz., the *Atharva Veda*, the last and latest of the Vedas from about 800 B.C.E., and the Brāhmaṇas, late commentaries on the Vedic sacrifice from about the same period. Let's look briefly at the development of two atheisms, magical atheism and ritual atheism, from these two compositions.

Magical Atheism in the *Atharva Veda*

The *Atharva Veda*, as Louis Renou reminds us, was a collection of hymns intended for domestic, as opposed to public, use and sacrifice; and for the performance of special magical rites. The *Atharva Veda* "...either minimizes the importance of the gods or leaves them altogether out of account." Instead, what we find in the *Atharva Veda* as a solution to the problem of suffering is an appeal to black and white magic, and to demonic forces:

> The divinities have become merely decorative in function; the activities they preside over are ill-defined; the part they play is sometimes ludicrous. Indra is a shadowy figure of magic; Varuṇa loses his virility.[19]

This is atheism pure and simple: The Gods have become gods. Their power is now seen as negligible and ineffectual while the Power over which they previously had control is now seen as separable from them and independently accessible. The magical ritual supplants the ritual sacrifice, where the Gods had a place of importance, and the newly discovered Power becomes controllable by that magic. For all practical purposes the Gods have ceased to exist. If atheism is the view that there are no Gods, then this is precisely the view being expressed by the *Atharva Veda*.

Franklin Edgerton speaking to the *Atharva Veda's* disinterest in the Gods and its new interest in the Power to which the Gods had previously had access comments:

> It is a commonplace of Atharvan psychology that *knowledge* of the end to be gained is a prime means of gaining it. "We know your name, O assembly!" says AV. 7. 12. 2, in a charm to get control of the public assembly. "I have grasped the names of all of them," says a medical charm, AV. 6. 83. 2, of the scrofulous sores it intends to cure. No more

---

[18] *Ṛg Veda* 10. 129. 6, from the beautiful translation of O'Flaherty (1981), p.25.

[19] Renou (1968), p.23.

> fundamental idea can be found in the whole range of Atharvan magic.[20]

It is that knowledge that the new priestly seers are striving for and, in particular, it is the knowing of the name of the entity striven for that is tantamount to controlling the entity: "who knows thus" (*ya evam veda*) the name of the Power ("*brahman*") has that Power:

> Verily, who knows that citadel of *Brahman*, covered over with immortality, to him *Brahman* and the powers of *Brahman* grant sight, life-breath, offspring.[21]

The Gods, as well as the gods, have now become supernumeraries as the priests realized that it was the Gods' (gods') Power that was wanted all along. The way of sacrificial ritual had ceased to secure, we must suppose, the "sight, life-breath and offspring" that had formerly been of easy access to the brahmins through the Gods.

Finally, we might conjecture that the discovery that theism is false follows from the realization that the Gods (gods) are powerless to provide "sight, life-breath and offspring". This realization, in turn, signals, surely, the recognition that the Gods (gods) are no longer either all-powerful, or all-just, or all-knowing. In other words, the inability of the Vedic *ṛṣis* to solve the theological problem of evil has led to the magical atheism we find in the *Atharva Veda*.

Ritual Atheism in the Brāhmaṇas

A similar state-of-affairs has developed in the Brāhmaṇas of the late Vedic period. Consequently, similar conclusions about the impotency of the Gods (gods) in securing "sight, life-breath and offspring" can also be drawn. In particular, as in the *Atharva Veda*, the power of knowledge gave the sacrificer power over that which was known. It was even considered unnecessary to perform the ritual sacrifice: "If you know it, you have as good as performed it."[22] Moreover, the meaning of *brahman*, "holy word", now came finally to signify the impersonal Power inherent within the holy word.[23] Further, the Brāhmaṇas underscore this atheism when they say, "There is nothing more ancient or higher than this Brahman."[24]

A final step is taken in the Brāhmaṇas. Expanding on a view that may have originated in the *Atharva Veda* that identifies the Self, *Ātman*, with that which is "desireless, wise, immortal, self-existent, filled with enjoyment, and not deficient in any respect", i.e., all-knowing, all-powerful and all-good,[25] the Brahman and this ever-present Ātman are identified. It is knowledge of this Self, ultimately, that frees one

---

[20]Edgerton (1965), p.22.

[21]*Atharva Veda* 10. 2. 29; Ibid., p.90. See also a fine discussion of these matters in Hopkins (1971) pp.31-35.

[22]Edgerton (1965), p.23.

[23]Ibid., p.24.

[24]*Śatapatha Brāhmaṇa* 10. 3. 5. 10; Ibid., p.24 n.2.

[25]*Atharva Veda* 10. 8. 44; Edgerton's translation ibid., p.103.

from pollution by works: The Self (self) has become God.[26]

The Vedic atheism that we have been tracing receives even further expression in the Brahmanas as the gods, "exhausted by their functions... their strength spent"[27] are supplanted by the Brahman-knowing priests: The priests ("Priests"?) become Gods. The *Śatapatha Brāhmaṇa* puts the matter this way:

> Verily, there are two kinds of gods; for, indeed, the gods are the gods, and the brahmins who have studied and teach sacred lore are the human gods.[28]

Troy Wilson Organ comments on this priestly theism:

> The "human gods" who controlled the sacrifices were the real agents of control. The sun did not rise because of Ushas; the sun rose because the sacrifice made it rise, and the priest controlled the sacrifice.[29]

Summary

Vedic theism, the view which states, "There are Gods", has evolved into transcendent atheism, "There are no Gods", which has now evolved into an early form of Ātman theism, "The Self is God" or priestly theism, "The priests are Gods".

But how do we account for the necessity for this change by the time of the end of the Vedic period (ca. 800 B.C.E.) from Gods to gods, from Godly Power to godly power, to godly impotence; from the priests as servants of the Gods to the priests as rivals of the Gods and then as replacements for the Gods; from views about the Gods (theology) to new views about Brahman (Brahmanology) and Ātman; from theism to atheism? What was it that forced these changes and speculations?

My own view, once again, is that the evolution was brought about by the failure of Vedism to deal adequately with the problems of human suffering, either for this world or the next. This repeated failure led in turn to doubts about Vedic theism and finally to its eventual dissolution and replacement. The forms that that replacement took were many and varied, ranging from magical atheism, ritual atheism, scepticism, and finally the internalization of that Power that the priests were eager to protect. The one common thread running through all of these views, Ātman-theism and priestly-theism to the contrary notwithstanding, is atheism.

We turn next to the Upaniṣadic period as the atheism begun in the Vedic period continues.

II. METAPHYSICAL ATHEISM IN THE UPANIṢADIC PERIOD

The Upaniṣadic period (800-200 B.C.E.) is witness to the evolution of the religious theism and the magical and ritual atheisms of the Vedic period into a "metaphysical

---

[26] See Keith (1925), Vol.2, p.450 where Keith discusses this view, from the *Taittirīya Brāhmaṇa* III.12.9 and *Śatapatha Brāhmana* X.6.3, as transitional to the more clearly expressed Upaniṣadic theme of the identity of Brahman and Ātman.

[27] Renou (1968), p.24.

[28] *Śatapatha Brāhmaṇa* 10.5.2.9 in Organ (1974), p.91.

[29] Ibid., p.91.

atheism" of this new age. It would be a mistake to believe, of course, that either religious theism or magical atheism or ritual atheism became moribund; they remain alive and active within Hinduism to this day. Metaphysical atheism is expressed through a network of interlocking concepts, e.g., Brahman, Ātman, *saṃsāra,* the law of karma, *jñāna yoga,* and *mokṣa,* that collectively tend to reinforce the atheism of evolving Hinduism.

The *Bṛhadāraṇyaka Upaniṣad* as a Metaphysical Atheism

This oldest of the Upanisads (ca. 750 B.C.E.) expresses a number of atheist themes that come rumbling out of the previous centuries. The magical theism of the *Atharva Veda,* as well as the ritual atheism of the Brāhmaṇas, receive early recognition in the *Bṛhadāraṇyaka.* Oddly enough it is an impersonal entity called "breath", *prāṇa,* that is given the place of honour early in this Upaniṣad. *Prāṇa* appears as part of an argument for solving the problem of suffering. The argument contains several familiar features:

1. Breath is identical with everything.
2. To know breath is to control breath.
3. Therefore, to know breath is to control everything.[30]

A similar argument is then brought out with respect to Ātman:

1. Ātman is identical with everything.
2. To know Ātman is to control Ātman.
3. Therefore, to know Ātman is to control everything.[31]

But how do these *prāṇa* and Ātman arguments, each an echo of the magical and ritual atheisms of the Vedic period, fit into the metaphysical atheism of the Upaniṣadic period?

A Vedic-Upaniṣadic Overview

We can put both of these arguments into the language of suffering and atheism by suggesting that the move in the *Bṛhadāraṇyaka* as well as in the other older Upaniṣads is to covertly support the atheism that has been long in the making. The theodicy developed in the earlier Vedas to explain why, for example, Varuṇa doesn't answer one's prayers, involved the development of two new concepts, *tapas* and *pāpa.* Imagine this probable scenario. The blame for suffering cannot fall on God, the Vedic *ṛṣis* had to say, therefore it must fall, somehow on the sacrificer, or the patron, i.e., on man. Who else was to blame for the lack of success in controlling the suffering? Perhaps the sacrificer chanted wrongly, or moved or poured incorrectly during the ritual. Good enough; another priest was added, the brahmin, to observe the other priests in order to make sure that no ritual mistakes were made. But still the failures occur, the disappointments remain: Suffering is apparently uncontrollable. But now we can't blame God and we can't blame the external performance of the ritual. So the

---

[30]See *Bṛhadāraṇyaka Upaniṣad,* I. 3. 1-28. *Prāṇa* talk goes back to the Vedas (RV 10. 90. 13 and AV 11. 4) and is not original to the Upaniṣads, though this *prāṇa* argument seems unique to the *Bṛhadāraṇyaka.* But see AV 11. 4. 18.

[31]Ibid., I. 4. 1-17.

blame must lie within, inside the hearts and minds of the men who carry out the ritual performance. Perhaps they are not empassioned enough, i.e., they lack the fire and faith and fervour that was called *tapas*;[32] or perhaps they are not morally pure, i.e., they are filled with *pāpa*, sin. In both cases it is the performing subject that must change and on whom the blame for the suffering must securely fall. The objective elements of the Vedic system, God and God's ritual sacrifice, are saved. Thus Vedic theodicy tends to place the blame for suffering on man and not on the Gods.

But this probable move to save the Gods won't work either. The theodicy must fail. For the suffering wasn't controlled else nothing would have changed.

At this point the *Atharva Veda* and the Brāhmaṇas enter to recast the entire theodicy. The failure of Vedic theodicy is emphasized, as we have seen, as magical atheism and ritual atheism tend to remove religious theism from the Vedic scene. The Gods become gods and the Power is transferred to the knowing priests.

Brahmadicy, Yoga, and Metaphysical Atheism

In keeping with our central argument that all religions are theodicies and, ultimately, failed or failing theodicies, we won't have to seek far to see the Upaniṣads attempting a theodicy of their own as they continue the theodical tradition begun in the Vedic period. With the Gods now become gods, and with impersonal Brahman now become the holy Power of the universe, and with that holy Power reflected as the very Self of man, a new problem of suffering arises. Call this new problem, paralleling the Vedic problem of evil, "the Brahmanological problem of evil." It will look like this:

1. If Brahman is all-Powerful then Brahman could protect the world from suffering, i.e., there should be no suffering.
2. But there is suffering.
3. Therefore, Brahman is not all-Powerful.

At this point, the Upaniṣads introduce their own versions of Vedic *tapas* and *pāpa* in order to protect Brahman in the same way that Varuṇa and the other Gods had been protected in the Vedic period. The plea for God's cause now becomes the plea for Brahman's cause. This new theodicy ("Brahmadicy"?) calls forth two new ways or yogas, *dhyāna*, "meditation", and *jñāna*, "knowledge", both paralleling Vedic *tapas*; and it introduces *saṃsāra*, "rebirth", together with the law of karma, parelleling Vedic *pāpa*, in order to solve the new problem of sin within a highly original solution to the old Vedic theological problem of evil. In each instance the suffering that is experienced in this life is due not to the holy Power of the universe nor is it due to the true Self within.

Nor can that Power help man in any direct way to overcome his or her sufferings. Brahman remains all-powerful. Suffering is entirely man's fault, either because he or she hasn't tried hard enough in this life to overcome the present suffering (the new yogas can eliminate all present suffering), or because of bad karmic effects inherited from a previous life (*saṃsāra* and the law of karma can explain and justify all of those effects). The atheism, the metaphysical atheism, is complete.

This new way out of the problem of evil is presented in the *Bṛhadāraṇyaka* and the

---

[32] *Tapas* is "heat", "ritual austerity" or "ascetic penance". It is the precursor of *yoga*, "internal mental discipline", and was practiced in order to bring about some great event. See *Ṛg Veda* X. 154; X. 129; and X. 190: "From *tapas* kindled to its utmost were Ṛta and truth born...."

other early Upaniṣads. The way out comes from one's own effort, yoga, as one comes to realize, *jñāna*, that the Self within is identical to the holy Power of the universe. Only then will present suffering cease and only then will liberation from future sufferings be possible. The prescription for liberation lies in going from suffering to yoga to knowledge to liberation; it is mechanical and metaphysically certain that if one applies the yogas to the causes of the problem, then one will surely reach the solution to the problem. Once again, the atheism is complete.

Saṃsāra, the Law of Karma, and Metaphysical Atheism

This metaphysical atheism is made clear in the *Bṛhadāraṇyaka*. Amidst the debris of references to Vedic magic and ritual, it introduces all of the basic concepts necessary for the metaphysically mechanical operation of liberation. At one point, it asks the intriguing question.

> Do you know why heaven is not filled up with the many who go there again and again?[33]

And it answers that heaven doesn't fill up because the many are born back into this world.[34] The law of karma, as it will be called, guarantees *saṃsāra*, "rebirth", for all those in whom the urge or desire to be reborn has not been eliminated; for it is the desire for *saṃsāra* that makes *saṃsāra* possible:

> To whatever his mind is attached the self becomes that in the next life. Achieving that end he returns again and again to this world. This happens to the man who desires.[35]

And this rebirth happens because of the stricly automatic operation of the law of karma:

> Truly, one becomes good by good action, bad by bad action.[36]

Or more fully stated:

> According to the way one acts, according to the way one behaves, just so does one become. The doer of good becomes good and the doer of evil becomes evil. One becomes good by good action and evil by evil action. As is his desire such is his will; and as is his will, such is the action that he performs; and whatever he does, that he gets back. For a person is not made of acts but of desires.[37]

Saṃsāra is caused by desire and this principle of moral causation says that everyone gets what's coming to them, if not in this life then in the next.

---

[33] *Bṛhadāraṇyaka Upaniṣad* VI. 2. 2.

[34] Ibid., VI. 2. 15-16.

[35] Ibid., IV. 4. 6.

[36] Ibid., III. 2. 13.

[37] Ibid., IV. 4. 5.

The way out of *saṃsāra* lies in eliminating desire by knowing that the Self is Brahman:

> Consider the man who does not desire. He who is without desire, who is liberated from desire, whose desire is Ātman: His breaths do not go on. Being Brahman, he goes to Brahman.[38]

And the *Bṛhadāraṇyaka* concludes:

> When all desires are finally liberated from one's heart, then the mortal becomes immortal. Then he becomes Brahman.[39]

Liberation from rebirth is achieved through knowledge of the Self. Again, it is a purely mechanical process. The problem of evil, the questions concerning the origin or cause of one's sufferings, are located in one's desires either from this life or inherited from a previous life. The Gods are unnecessary either as Saviours or aids in the liberation process. A metaphysical principle (the law of karma), a metaphysical process (*saṃsāra*), a metaphysical agent (*kāma* or desire), a metaphysical Being (Brahman-Ātman), and a metaphysical practice (*jñāna yoga*), are all that are necessary to explain suffering and the release from suffering. The atheism is complete.

Some Atheistic Second Thoughts

But the atheism sat uneasily upon the heads of many Upaniṣadic *ṛṣis*. Whether it was the prospect of an impersonal and coldly indifferent Reality dominating the universe, or of having to assume total responsibility for one's actions, past and present (and it is terribly nice to be able to blame the Gods for one's predicament now and again), or the awful realization that the end of *saṃsāra* meant the end of personality, consciousness, and memories for the liberated, is not clear. But that all of these factors, in one way or another, entailed futures too terrible to contemplate became obvious to many. Besides, as it now turned out, with the theological problem of evil apparently solved, there was no longer any need for an impersonal Brahman and Its attendant metaphysical atheism. The Upaniṣadic theodicy, after all, had cleared the Gods of any possible blame in the world's sufferings. The way had been cleared for a return of the Gods.

It was obvious that metaphysical atheism and its implications had alarmed many of the Upaniṣadic seers. Nowhere is this alarm more clearly portrayed than in the following story from the *Chāndogya Upaniṣad* of about 650 B.C.E.:

Second Thoughts: Indra's Panic in the *Chāndogya Upaniṣad*

Indra had gone to the Lord of Creation, Prajāpati, for instruction in the new Brahmadicy, the views that we have been discussing above. The atheism of the early Upaniṣads is nowhere more clearly expressed than in the roles that the new *ṛṣis* assign to these formerly prestigious Vedic Gods: Prajāpati is a *guru* and Indra is his *chela*. The Gods have become gods. Indra has come to hear all about the new Brahman in order that he, too, presumably, might be liberated from *saṃsāra*.

---

[38] Ibid., IV. 4. 6.

[39] Ibid., IV. 4. 7.

First, Prajāpati, after thirty-two years, teaches Indra that Brahman is to be identified with the waking state of the body. But Indra, after leaving his teacher, realizes that were this identification between the waked body and Brahman true then when the body perishes, Brahman would also perish. He returns to Prajāpati with his objection and asks for further instruction.

He remains with Prajāpati for another thirty-two years. This time Indra learns that Brahman is the dream state or a dream. Once more Indra sets forth. But on considering what he has been taught he realizes that Brahman cannot be identified with the dream state. For it It were, then on waking Brahman would cease to exist.

Returning to Prajāpati, Indra remains for another thirty-two years and is instructed this time that Brahman is the dreamless state, the state of void and nothingness. Now this is what the Upaniṣads have indeed been saying about Brahman all along and this teaching constitutes orthodox Upaniṣadic metaphysics: The holy Power of the universe is *neti neti*,[40] "not this, not that", beyond description and predication, for It has no properties, no personality. Further, reaching Brahman, being liberated into Brahman, is to reach the state of nothingness where no desire, no personality, consciousness, or memory survives. Indra suddenly sees the Upaniṣadic point and being the heaven-wise Vedic being that he is, he recoils in horror. In his panic he cries out:

> I would become like a man who has gone to absolute annihilation. I see nothing enjoyable in this.[41]

Metaphysical atheism has failed to appeal to one of the deepest longings of the human spirit, the desire for continued personal survival. The myth is at this point an affront to that ultimate desire for continued conscious existence. So Indra in his panic hastens back to Prajāpati with his objection and asks for further instruction.

Prajāpati instructs Indra to remain with him for another five years. What he learns now is that Brahman is the Self, Ātman, and that the Self is qualified by enjoyment, *ānanda*. Hence on reaching Brahman one will reach enjoyment. The consequence of this metaphysical retreat is the promise, in effect, that one will enjoy eternal happiness in Brahman. Indra's panic is assuaged. But the way is open for other changes in the manner in which impersonal, qualitiless Brahman is to be conceived. The slide from metaphysical atheism back to religious theism is about to begin. The slide starts with the attempt to personalize Brahman, an attempt aptly illustrated in the following story from the *Kaṭha Upaniṣad* of about 500 B.C.E.

More Second Thoughts: Personal Brahman in the *Kaṭha Upaniṣad*

The *Kaṭha Upaniṣad* relegates another Vedic God, Yama, the Lord of the dead, to the role of a *guru*. Yama instructs a brahmin boy, Naciketas, in the new metaphysical atheism much as Prajāpati had previously instructed Indra in the *Chāndogya*.

---

[40]Ibid., IV. 4. 22.

[41]*Chāndogya Upaniṣad* VIII. 11. 1.

Naciketas has been sent by his father to Yama.[42] The boy waits three days for the tardy Yama to return to his underworld dwelling. On his arrival Yama is upset that because of his absence the laws of hospitality to this young brahmin have been violated. So to make amends he offers three wishes to Naciketas. The boy chooses, first, to be allowed to return to his father and to the earth; second, he wishes to be taught a fire sacrifice that will get him to heaven; and, third, like Indra he wants instruction in the new Brahmanology, i.e., "What happens to a man when he dies?"

There follows, not unexpectedly, a lecture by Yama on Brahman-Ātman metaphysics and the path that one must follow in order to teach the knowledge of the Self. But it is a very personal Ātman that is being presented:

> The Self is not born, He does not die. He has not come from anywhere, He has not become anyone. Unborn, constant, eternal, the first and the last. He dies not when the body dies.
>
> Smaller than the smallest, greater than the greatest, the Self is set in the heart of all creatures. The man freed from desire beholds Him, and becomes forever freed from suffering.[43]

Immediately following these passages about the personal Self, we have this very theistic assertion by Yama:

> This true Self, this Ātman, is not to be obtained by instruction, nor by learning. He is to be obtained only by those whom He chooses. To such a one the Self reveals his own nature.[44]

If there is a slide back into theism, it begins in these early and middle Upaniṣads with Indra's panic and Yama's lecture on the personal Self that makes choices.

Still More Second Thoughts: God in the *Śvetāśvatara Upaniṣad*

The slide culminates in the *Śvetāśvatara Upaniṣad* from about 400 B.C.E. In it the personal God, Rudra, is identified with Brahman, and Īśvara, the omniscient and omnipotent Lord, is seen as an emanation from Brahman and worthy of worship and devotion. And through it all Ātman is both personalized and given a specific bodily residence:

> A Person the size of the thumb is the inner Ātman that dwells in the hearts of all men. He is the lord of knowledge and framed by the heart and the mind. Whoever knows this will never die.[45]

---

[42] What looks like a theodical myth turns out in the end to be a Brahmadical myth. The descent theme, the initiation into the nature of Brahman, the justification of the necessity of suffering in order to realize the Self, the condemnation of the Vedic sacrifices, rituals and gods, and the return of the hero to the world of the living with the hard won transforming knowledge intact, are all elements of the myth of mystical liberation.

[43] *Kaṭha Upaniṣad* I. 2. 18, 20.

[44] Ibid., I. 2. 23.

[45] *Śvetāśvatara Upaniṣad* III. 13.

Even Indra would have been happy with this discovery. The *Kaṭha* theme of God choosing those whom he favours continues:

> Smaller than the smallest, greater than the greatest is the Self that lives in the heart of all creatures here. One beholds Him as being without desire and becomes freed from suffering, when through the grace of the Creator he sees God and his greatness.[46]

The way is now open, of course, for the bhaktism of the *Bhagavad Gītā*, the Purāṇas, and later Hinduism. Perhaps the way was never closed. Theism returns. Perhaps it never left. Theism returns with a theodicy which it did not previously possess. But it seems to have taken a flirtation with three atheisms, magical, ritual, and metaphysical, to make the world safe for that theism.[47]

Another atheism appears during this same period. It is more derisively and more baldly stated than any atheism met thus far. It will serve as a conclusion to the atheism of the Upaniṣadic period as well as being a good introduction to the atheism of early Buddhism.

Philosophic Atheism Among the Lokāyatas

Lokāyata (or Cārvāka) philosophic atheism with its attendant scepticism, empiricism and materialism is worth recalling and for three reasons: First, Lokāyata is the earliest and clearest expression that we have, though existing only in fragments which their enemies and time have spared, of an atheism that is undoubtedly pre-Buddhist and which probably dates from the time of the Brāhmaṇas; second, Lokāyata was very likely the first expression of the views of rebellious priestly-seers who had the courage of their philosophic convictions and used reasoned arguments, as well as wit and ridicule, to make those convictions clear; third, and finally, Lokāyata provides us with a clue to the real reason for resorting to atheism in the Vedic and Upaniṣadic periods in the first place, viz., the inability of theism to solve the problem of human suffering, i.e., the inability to find a satisfactory solution to the theological problem of evil, and it explains thereby the move to metaphysical atheism during the Upaniṣadic period.

Consider now the unalloyed atheism of these lines from a tradition that goes back to the *Bṛhaspati Sutra* of about 600 B.C.:

> ...the only God is the earthly monarch whose existence is proved by all the world's eyesight; and the only liberation is the dissolution of the body.[48]

The overt atheism of the Lokāyata contradicts and ridicules the Vedas, the priests, the

---

[46]Ibid., III.20.

[47]See Hopkins (1971), p.69 who has a good discussion of this "new theism" of the Upaniṣads in contrast to the earlier "old atheism" that "undercut the entire Vedic pantheon". But, Hopkins argues, even this personalized Brahman was not a *deva* in the older Vedic sense: "The personal Brahman was always secondary, and never had the characteristics of a clearly defined god" (p.69).

[48]Mādhavācārya, *Sarvadarśanasaṃgraha* in Radhakrishnan and Moore (1957), p.230.

sacrifice, and the orthodox Vedic traditions, in general:

> There is no heaven, no final liberation, nor any soul in another world,
> Nor do the actions of the four castes, orders, etc., produce any *real effect*.[49]

The Lokāyata philosophic or formal argument for atheism looks like this:

1. If theism is true (i.e., if God, heaven, final liberation and immortal souls exist) then there should be no evil, i.e., there should be *real effects* now.
2. But there is evil (i.e., dysteleological evil), i.e., there are no *real effects* now.
3. Therefore, theism is false.

The emphasis here is on the inefficacy of the theistic tradition and that tradition's ritual activities. In other words, pragmatically speaking, they just didn't work. The Gods failed; the ritual failed; and the tradition failed. Failed to do what? Failed to solve the problem that I am assuming from the start is the business of religions to solve, viz., the problem of human suffering. In other words, the concern with the theological problem of evil seems to be at the heart of Lokāyata atheism. The ridicule continues:

> The *Agnihotra* [the daily fire sacrifice], the three Vedas [but not the fourth, the *Atharva Veda*!], the ascetics' three staves, and smearing oneself with ashes, were made by Nature as the livelihood for those destitute of knowledge and manliness.[50]

But it is the attack on the ritual sacrifice, the very centre of Vedic theism, that is of chief interest here:

> If a beast slain in the Jyotiṣṭoma rite [a *soma* sacrifice] will itself go to heaven,
> Why then does not the sacrificer forthwith offer his own father?
> If the Śrāddha [offerings to the dead] produces gratification to beings who are dead.... [and]
> If beings in heaven are gratified by our offering the Śrāddha here,
> Then why not give the food down below to those who are standing on the housetop? [i.e., those more eager to receive it and for whom it would do more good.][51]

The ridicule is aimed at one of the most sacred rituals of Hinduism, the Śrāddha ritual to the dead, by urging that the offerings to the dead be reserved for those more able to use and enjoy them in this world. The entire attack ends as the Lokāyata author enjoins his listener:

> While life remains let a man live joyously, let him feed on ghee [the

---

[49]Ibid., p.233. Emphasis added.

[50]Ibid.

[51]Ibid.

> clarified butter reserved for the very rich and for the Gods in the Vedic sacrifice] even though he runs into debt.[52]

Another group of Indians, echoing the atheism of the Lokāyatas together with their irony and ridicule, was also buying none of the second thoughts of Upaniṣadic neo-theism. The theological problem of evil, the problem that will not go away, will return with this new atheist philosophy to challenge anew the rising, or continuing, theism of Hinduism. Once again it is the ubiquitous problem of suffering that will prove to be the puzzle that will spell destruction for Upaniṣadic neo-theism. This resurgent theism comes up hard against the theological problem of evil clearly, rationally, and boldly with the Buddhists. We turn very briefly to early Buddhism and to its view of philosophic atheism.

III. PHILOSOPHIC ATHEISM IN EARLY BUDDHISM

Buddhologists are as divided on the nature of the atheism of Buddhism as Hindologists have been on the possibility of atheism in Hinduism. As usual, the squabble is over the meaning of a word.

Nancy Wilson Ross in her popular book on Buddhism writes:

> Actually, Buddhism is no more atheistic than it is theistic or pantheistic. The charge of atheism can hardly be laid at the door of a Teacher who could declare of the universe or cosmos in its wholeness (or *thusness*): "There is an unborn, an unoriginated, an unmade, an uncompounded."[53]

Walpola Rahula in an equally popular book sounds a more negative note declaring, "According to Buddhism, our ideas of God and Soul are false and empty."[54]

Helmuth Von Glasenapp admits gods but not Gods into the Buddhist cosmology:

> Buddhism believes in the existence of a great number of impermanent gods (*devas*) and of men who became gods (*buddhas*). It believes in a moral world order (*dharma*), but emphatically denies the existence of an eternal creator and ruler of the world.[55]

Von Glasenapp admits, however, after carefully placing some quotation marks:

> That Buddhism was an "a-theist" religion from the beginning is supported by the evidence of other non-theist religions.[56]

Charles Prebish, working without benefit of quotation marks, prefers the concept "nontheistic" to that of "atheistic":

---

[52] Ibid., p.234.

[53] Ross (1981), p.30.

[54] Rahula (1974), p.52.

[55] Glasenapp (1966), p.15.

[56] Ibid., p.43. Von Glasenapp has in mind Jainism, "an atheistic pluralism", as well as the two *darśanas* of Mīmāṃsā and Sāṃkhya.

> Needless to say, Buddhism's position on the absolute is clear and explicit. Buddhism employs no god concept and must necessarily be regarded as nontheistic.[57]

David Kalupahana, on the other hand, admits to gods in Buddhism and insightfully points to their function in that religion:

> Realizing that man's fundamental nature is to hanker after happiness and detest pain, the Buddha seems to have utilized the beliefs in gods and spirits as *regulative* concepts.[58]

The overwhelming modern and scholarly opinion regarding the theism-atheism-nontheism controversy for Buddhism leans, therefore, decidedly towards either atheism or nontheism. The solution to this verbal dispute must be decided, however, on manipulating some definitions and making some distinctions.

Buddhist Atheism and Nontheism: *Anitya* and the Silence of the Buddha

From one point of view, early Buddhism, that is, the view held by the Buddha, himself, is "atheistic". Following his *nirvāṇa*, "awakening", the Buddha realized and announced his intuitive discovery of the principles of *anitya*, "universal restlessness", and *pratītyasamutpāda*, "causal dependency". Together these great truths rule out the existence of any and all unchanging or permanent absolutes whether they be Gods, or Brahman or Ātman, Creators, Saviours or metaphysically real entities of any sort. The Buddha states:

> ...it remains a fact and the fixed and necessary constitution of being, that all its constituents are transitory [*anitya*].[59]

From which it follows that there can be no Brahman, Ātman, or God. From this point of view, early Buddhism is atheistic, i.e., it denies the existence of unchanging, Brahman-like, Ātman-like Reals.

From another point of view, early Buddhism is "non-theistic". This follows from the famous "silence of the Buddha" on all matters that neither lead to, nor are conducive to, *nirvāṇa*. According to the *Majjhima-Nikāya*, the Buddha refused to take a stand, to give any answer at all, to a number of questions the speculations on, and the answers to, which are inconsequential, if not downright detrimental, to the search for awakening. The Buddha criticizes all those who seek answers to unanswerable and meaningless questions including, presumably, questions about the existence of God, and the reality of Brahman and Ātman. Such questions would be among those which lead neither to edification nor enlightenment:

> These theories the Buddha has left unelucidated, has set aside and rejected, - that the world [or God, or the Gods] is eternal, that the world is not eternal, that the world is finite, that the world is infinite, that the

---

[57]Prebish (1979), p.183.

[58]Kalupahana (1976), p.65.

[59]*Aṅguttara-Nikāya* III. 134 in Warren (1963), p.viii with minor changes.

> self and the body are identical, that the self is one thing and the body another, that those who are enlightened exist after death, etc., etc. [These views] are a jungle of theorising, a wilderness of theorising, the bondage and the shackles of theorising, attended by anxiety, distress, perturbation and fever; it leads not to detachment... to knowledge, wisdom of nirvāṇa. This is the danger I perceive in these theories which makes me discard them all.[60]

The questions about the existence of God or the Gods, or about God's or the Gods' nature, are questions which lead not to enlightenment. About them the Buddha had no opinion. From this point of view, early Buddhism is nontheistic, i.e., neither affirming nor denying theism.

Buddhist Atheism: Two Philosophic Arguments

But early Buddhism, despite its leanings towards nontheism, does record two arguments for atheism that tend to mark it plainly as an atheistic religion. The two arguments can be gleaned from three devastating observations made by the Buddha and recorded in the *Jātaka*, "the previous lives of the Buddha", that leave little doubt as to how early Buddhism felt about Hindu theism and why. Referring directly to "Brahmā", the post-Vedic and early Buddhist name for God,[61] the Buddha begins by stating the theological problem of evil, clearly and succinctly:

> If Brahmā is Lord of the whole world and Creator of the multitude of beings, then why has he ordained misfortune in the world without making the whole world happy; or for what purpose has he made the world full of injustice, deceit, falsehood and conceit; or the lord of beings is evil in that he ordained injustice when there could have been justice.[62]

The arguments contained in this passage are from a text that dates at least from the first or second century B.C.E.[63] It offers two *modus tollendo tollens* arguments, each expressing the theological problem of evil and each leading to an atheistical conclusion. Here are those two arguments from this brief but compact passage; call the first "the good God argument" and the second "the hidden purpose argument":

The Good God Argument

1. If God exists (as an all-good and all-powerful Lord) then there should be happiness and justice (i.e., there should be no suffering because if

---

[60]*Majjhima-Nikāya*, Suttas 63,72. Ibid., pp.117, 122, 124 with some minor changes.

[61]Hiriyanna (1932), p.95. See also Thomas (1933), p.87: "...for the Buddhist Brahma is a personal god who is also recognized by the Brahmins. But he, like the other Vedic gods, is only a manifestation of the ultimate reality Brahman. This neuter Brahman is never mentioned by the Buddhists...."

[62]*Jātaka* VI. 208 in Jayatilleke (1963), p.411. See also O'Flaherty (1976), p.5.

[63]The *Khuddaka-Nikāya* contains verses belonging to some 547 *Jātaka* stories; the *Khuddaka* was compiled in Pali in Sri Lanka probably in the first or second centuries B.C.E. See Thomas (1931), pp.272, 274.

God is all-good, He would want to stop it; and if He's all-powerful, He could stop it).
2. But there is unhappiness and injustice (i.e., dysteleological suffering).
3. Therefore, God does not exist.

The Hidden Purpose Argument

1. If God exists (as an all-good and all-powerful Lord) then God would have revealed His purpose for allowing suffering (i.e., there should be no concealing of purpose because if God is all-good, He would want to reveal his purpose, and if He's all - powerful, He could reveal His purpose).
2. But God has not revealed His purpose for allowing suffering.
3. Therefore, God does not exist.

The two Buddhist arguments are valid and either one, if sound, would be sufficient to sink the theocentric proclivities of theistic Hinduism. What is at issue here, however, is not merely the existence of Brahmā. The early Buddhists do not appear to have denied his existence. What they did contest was that he was Ruler or Creator of the universe, or Real or Absolute. Brahmā is merely a god, hence as much subject to bondage in the chain of birth and death as any other creature.[64]

Of the two arguments, the good God argument is the more familiar statement of the theological problem of evil and, consequently, the less interesting of the two. However, despite its rather tiresome familiarity, it is the kind of argument that forces theists to scurry about looking for a theodicy. It also forces Vedic and Upaniṣadic *ṛṣis*, as we have seen, into taking seriously concepts like *tapas* and *pāpa*, *saṃṣāra* and the law of karma: Harried theists who cannot blame God for the suffering in the world, turn their attentions to man. The good God argument compels the God-defending theist to say things like, "Man didn't perform the sacrifice correctly." If that fails then one says, "Man didn't know that which was necessary for the correct functioning of the sacrifice, i.e., man didn't know *Om* or Brahman's name, or Brahman or Ātman". We've seen all of this work previously in our discussion of the Vedas, Brahmanas and Upanisads. In all of these instances the aim appeared to be to solve the problem of suffering either theoretically, by thinking about a solution to the theological problem of evil, or practically, by doing the ritual or chanting the formula or knowing the Reality, in new and more compelling ways. By blaming the sacrificer, by saying that the patron or priest lacked faith, or fervour, or devotion, or the right actions, or the right knowledge, God could emerge unscathed. Man was to blame for the continued suffering. Theism is safe.

But the hidden purpose argument threatens to centre the blame for suffering back onto God. As with the good God argument, the blame will ultimately be attached to man. For the hidden purpose argument can be answered by simply saying, "God *has* revealed his purpose. Man was simply too ignorant to see that purpose." And with that theism is safe, once again.

Philosophic atheism in early Buddhism probably depends, then, on these two arguments and on Hinduism's or the theists inability to find solutions to them.

---

[64]David Kalupahana (1976) puts the matter extremely well: "But compared with the Buddha and the arahants, the gods are inferior beings, for, while occupying a position in which they become engrossed with sense pleasures, they are unable to attain freedom from suffering" (p.65).

From what we have seen already in our discussion of Hinduism, above, the theists have no answer to the theological problem of evil save a retreat into atheism. But the coming centuries will see the resurgence of theism in Hinduism, with the rise of interest in the theology of the *Bhagavad Gītā* (ca. 200 B.C.E.), and in Buddhism, with a similar rise of interest in Mahayana Buddhism and its *Prajñāpāramitā* literature (beginning ca. 100 B.C.E.). The rise of theistic devotionalism in Hinduism, with Lord Kṛṣna, and in Buddhism, with the Boddhisattva-ideal, atheistic arguments to the contrary notwithstanding, will provide Gods and Saviours in abundance in both religions. The religious life without Saviours, Avatārs, Bodhisattvas, God and Gods would seem to be impossible, unpreventable and, perhaps unbearable.[65] But so also it seems is it equally impossible and unpreventable to have the religious life without suffering and without theodicies. The theistic stage will be set, once again, for a renewed battle as dysteleological suffering and the theological problem of evil come once more to the fore and theists turn, even again, to the hunt for a theodicy.

Summary of Buddhist Philosophic Atheism

Buddhism emerges as a theodicy, but a failed theodicy, to be sure. The Buddha recognized the central truth of human existence to be suffering. He also recognized that there can be no theoretical solution to such a problem, for suffering is still with us despite all the theories. He knew that a practical, existential problem demanded a practical, existential solution. Like the other atheists contemporary with him, the Lokāyatas and the Sāṃkhyas, the Buddha was able to marshal philosophic arguments for his atheism, and those arguments may well be the arguments that we have mentioned, above.

IV. SOME ASSUMPTIONS AND CONCLUSIONS AND PROBLEMS

Let me make plain the assumptions and the conclusions that have motivated this study of the nature and cause of atheism in early Hinduism and Buddhism. My central argument, that all religions are failed theodicies, rests upon three assumptions and several conclusions that can be drawn from those assumptions:

First, I have assumed that all religions are social systems whose principal purpose is to solve the problem of human suffering.

Second, I have assumed that suffering is ubiquitous and destabilizing.

Third, I have assumed that if any social system works well (whatever its purpose), then either that system will not change or that it will change in insignificant ways.

From these three assumptions several conclusions follow, all of which are hypotheses that I have been at some pains to try to demonstrate in this essay by focusing on early Hinduism and Buddhism:

First, all religions have been overtly or covertly concerned with attempting to solve the theological problem of evil. The statement of that problem is the attempt to

---

[65] I am reminded of something that Gilbert Murray once wisely wrote about Western Saviours:

> But in the later development of Greek thought, as is well known, Saviour religions developed with immense vigour, and the reason of their success was just that, without some Saviour, the government of the world seemed evil and the lot of mankind intolerable. Hence the widespread worship of Asclepios, the divine Healer; of Mithras, the Redeemer; of Serapis, the Saviour; of the many "Deliverers" of Hermetism and Gnosticism. Murray (1924), p.85.

conjoin certain properties of God with the simultaneous existence of apparently dysteleological suffering. The theological problem of evil is religion's statement of its concern regarding the first assumption.

Second, the failure to solve the theological problem of evil leads to atheism, i.e., a religious system changes from a theism to an atheism. The argument, which we have mentioned before, looks like this:

1. If theism is true then there should be no evil (dysteleological suffering).
2. But there is evil.
3. Therefore, theism is false, i.e., atheism is true.

This follows from the second assumption regarding the adamantine nature of evil and from the first conclusion, above.

Third, the theological problem of evil may well be unsolvable. That is to say, the problem seems to be empirically impossible of solution, for no solution has yet been found; and it may be logically impossible of solution, in which case no solution will ever be found. The empirical part of this conclusion follows from the second and third assumptions above and from the previous conclusion.

Problems and Questions

The two questions with which our lengthy study began have now, however unsatisfactorily, been answered. Early Hinduism and Buddhism are either atheistic religions or they are in the process of becoming atheistic religions. The chief cause of this atheism lies in the destabilizing effect of evil and in the inability of either religion to solve the problem of evil. The consequence is that each religion has evolved as either a failing or a failed theodicy.

The critic might now respond to the above conclusions and arguments in some such fashion as this:

Your central and most important argument, if I can cut through all of the assumptions and conclusions that you have thrown into our eyes, seems to be this:

1. All religions are theodicies.
2. All theodicies are failures, i.e., either failed or failing theodicies.
3. Therefore, all religions are either failed or failing theodicies.

To begin with, the critic might continue, the first premise of this argument is patently false. You are guilty of the fallacy of hasty generalization in going from an examination of a few religions to a conclusion about all religions. Religions serve many functions and they don't exist just to solve human problems. Further, the so-called "theodical religions" that you have described, also serve other ends or purposes than that of being merely problem-solving human institutions. And, finally, many problems which religions attempt to solve have nothing to do with human suffering. From all of this I conclude that religions exist for other purposes than meeting theodical needs. For example, the Vedic sacrifice that fed the Gods, or the prayers to Varuṇa that attempted to assuage sin, or the *jñāna yoga* that sought union with Brahman, or the *anitya* that defined human existence, might all have been proposed or practiced for reasons that had nothing to do with theodicy or the attempt to solve human problems. They might all have existed solely to express some aesthetic need, or some emotional urge, or some basic intuitive or empirical discovery about the way the world really is or ought to be. And while I'm at it, let me say that religions evolve and change for reasons that may have nothing to do with the failure to solve the problems of human suffering. Your first premise is not only false but it is outrageously false.

My own response to the critic's several comments would be to reiterate the assumption and conclusions on which that first premise was based. The examples mentioned by the critic were each of them classical instances of theodical responses to the destabilizing activity of suffering as it is stated in the theological problem of evil. I believe the evidence from early Hinduism and Buddhism substantiates this conclusion and that the evidence from other religions would probably do the same. I will admit that the generalization in the first premise is a generalization from limited cases, i.e., from five or six phases of Hinduism (counting early Buddhism as a logical extension of early Hinduism). But that's what empirical generalizations in fact do. I see nothing sinister or unfair in that logical move here.

Second, the disgruntled critic might continue, the second premise of this argument, that all theodicies are failures, is also patently false. Millions of people have found emotional solace and philosophical satisfaction in any number of the proffered solutions to the theological problem of evil. Theodicies haven't failed, but you have!

My own response to the critic's comment is two-fold: The theological problem of evil may be empirically impossible to solve, i.e., all attempted solutions have so far failed, each one having been found wanting in some respect, those millions of solaced and satisfied people to the contrary notwithstanding. Secondly, the theological problem of evil may, indeed, be logically impossible to solve, i.e., the empirical impossibility may be underlain by a logical difficulty such that the properties of God, notably goodness and justice, may be inconsistent with the world's evil and suffering.[66] If the latter is the case, then the theological problem of evil would be ultimately insoluble, and the inevitability of atheism in the world's religions would be all the more obvious. In other words, all pleas for God's cause would be doomed.

REFERENCES

Despland, Michel (1973). *Kant on History and Religion.* Montreal: McGill-Queen's University Press.

Edgerton, Franklin (1965). *The Beginnings of Indian Philosophy.* Cambridge, Mass.: Harvard University Press.

Glasenapp, Helmuth von (1966). *Buddhism - A Non-theistic Religion*, trans. Irmgard Schloegel. New York: George Braziller.

Gonda, J. (1965). *Change and Continuity in Indian Religion.* The Hague: Mouton.

Griffith, Ralph T.H. (1889). *The Hymns of the Ṛgveda.* Delhi: Motilal Barnarsidass, 1976.

Herman, Arthur L. (1976). *The Problem of Evil and Indian Thought.* Delhi: Motilal Banarsidass.

Herman, Arthur L. (1986). "The Problem of Suffering in the *Bhagavad Gita*". In

---

[66]For a discussion of the empirical and the logical impossibilities of a solution to the theological problem of evil see Herman (1976), pp.112-139 and pp.99-104, respectively. While the theological problem of evil may be insoluble, two variants of this puzzle, the Krisnalogical problem of evil and the Karmalogical problem of evil, may both be capable of solution. For a discussion of the former see Herman (1986), especially pp.83-85. For a discussion of the latter see Herman (1987).

Kapil N. Tiwari (ed.), *Suffering: Indian Perspectives*. Delhi: Motilal Banarsidass.
Herman, Arthur L. (1987). "Karmadicy: Karma and Evil in Indian Thought". In S.S. Rama Rao Pappu (ed.), *Dimensions of Karma*. Delhi: Chanakya Publications.
Hiriyanna, M. (1932). *Outlines of Indian Philosophy*. London: Allen & Unwin.
Hopkins, Thomas J. (1971). *The Hindu Tradition*. Encino: Dickenson.
Jayatilleke, K.N. (1963). *Early Buddhist Theory of Knowledge*. London: Allen & Unwin.
Kalupahana, David J. (1976). *Buddhist Philosophy: A Historical Analysis*. Honolulu: University of Hawaii Press.
Keith, Arthur Berriedale (1925). *The Religion and Philosophy of the Veda and Upanishads*. Delhi: Motilal Banarsidass, 1970.
Murray, Gilbert (1924). *Aeschylus*. Oxford: Oxford University Press.
O'Flaherty, Wendy Doniger (1976). *The Origins of Evil in Indian Mythology*. Berkeley: University of California Press.
O'Flaherty, Wendy Doniger (1981). *The Rig Veda: An Anthology*. Harmondsworth: Penguin.
Organ, Troy Wilson (1974). *Hinduism: Its Historical Development*. Woodbury, N.Y.: Barrons Educational Series.
Prebish, Charles S. (1979). *American Buddhism*. North Scituate, Mass.: Duxbury Press.
Radhakrishnan, Sarvepalli & Moore, Charles A. (1957). Editors. *A Sourcebook in Indian Philosophy*. Princeton: Princeton University Press.
Rahula, Walpola (1974). *What the Buddha Taught*. New York: Grove Press.
Renou, Louis (1986). *Religions of Ancient India*. New York: Schocken.
Ross, Nancy Wilson (1981). *Buddhism: A Way of Life and Thought*. New York: Vintage.
Smart, Ninian (1964). *Doctrine and Argument in Indian Philosophy*. London: Allen & Unwin.
Thomas, Edward J. (1931). *The Life of Buddha as Legend and History*. London: Routledge & Kegan Paul.
Thomas, Edward J. (1933). *History of Buddhist Thought*. London: Routledge & Kegan Paul.
Warren, Henry Clarke (1963). *Buddhism in Translations*. New York: Atheneum.
Weber, Max (1964). *The Sociology of Religion*. Boston: Beacon Press.

SCEPTICISM AND RELIGION: ON THE INTERPRETATION OF NĀGĀRJUNA

Shlomo Biderman

Tel Aviv University

In one of the best-known passages of the *Treatise of Human Nature*, Hume makes a strikingly pessimistic statement. He does not flinch at all when he describes the difficult situation in which a philosopher like himself may be caught. He sees this situation as the inevitable consequence of the submission of all knowledge-statements to a genuinely philosophical scrutiny. The result, as he describes it, is a state of total despair. Hume testifies that when he is in such a state he resolves to perish on the barren rock on which he finds himself rather than to venture upon the boundless ocean of philosophical uncertainty.[1] Hume then gives a vivid description of the difficult frame of mind in which, as a sceptic, he finds himself:

> I have exposed myself to the enmity of all metaphysicians, logicians, mathematicians, and even theologians; and can I wonder at the insults I must suffer? I have declared my disapprobation of their systems; and can I be surprised if they should express a hatred of mine and my person? When I look abroad, I foresee on every side dispute, contradiction, anger, calumny, and detraction. When I turn my eye inward, I find nothing but doubt and ignorance.[2]

It would appear natural for such a difficult state of mind to be expressed in a vocabulary that lacks the consoling expressions, such as serenity, tranquility, bliss, and the like, that used to mark the language of religious philosophers. To judge from Hume, the verdict of "No peace of mind for the sceptic" is made with the same assurance as the prophet's promise of "No peace for the wicked". A man who sees all claims as equal, who refuses to pass judgment, who maintains that truth, though desirable, is impossible to find, who appears eager to deconstruct all philosophical arguments, to destroy the very foundations of philosophical theories, and to pour scorn and contempt on all philosophical efforts to reach truth, must be regarded as "wicked" in the eyes of anyone whose doctrine offers either a peaceful, harmonious life or

---

[1] Hume (1962), Book One, Part IV, Section vii, p.313.

[2] Ibid., p.314.

R. W. Perrett (ed.), Indian Philosophy of Religion, 61–74.

eternal salvation. Enemies of the sceptic include, therefore, not only philosophers and scientists, but, as Hume accurately remarked, theologians as well. Scepticism is likely to view religion as an extreme case of unfounded dogmatism, while religion is likely to view scepticism as anathema. The language of religion and the language of scepticism seem to be diametrically opposed to each other.

If we go back to scepticism in its most radical manifestation, that is to say, to the Pyrrhonistic kind of sceptic, the gap between religion and scepticism seems unbridgeable. A Pyrrhonist is a daring thinker who is unwilling to take anything for granted, who sees all conflicting arguments as equally balanced, and who consequently rejects all knowledge claims not only as equally uncertain but also as equally improbable. How can a sceptic adhere to any form of religious belief or doctrine without giving up his scepticism? It would appear, therefore, that if we happen to discover a sceptic who, despite his scepticism, accepts a religious view or acts in accord with a certain religious form of life, this "inconsistency" would justify Hume's claim that "to whatever length any one may push his scepticism, he must act,... and live, and converse, like any other man."[3] More generally, a "religious" sceptic would demonstrate Russell's verdict according to which, "Scepticism, while logically impeccable, is psychologically impossible, and there is an element of frivolous insincerity in any philosophy which pretends to accept it."[4] It is only by maintaining some faith that the sceptic can act like a normal human being, who, after all, leaves a room through the door and not the window[5], and so shows that scepticism is psychologically untenable.

The philosophical scene in India yields perhaps the most appropriate illustrations for the, at least apparent, conflict between radical scepticism and religion. In the present context, I take the term *religion* to apply to the belief in release that is common to all the major Indian philosophical viewpoints. The posssibility of release (*mokṣa*, *nirvāṇa*) is no doubt a cornerstone of the structure of Indian thought. One can even see it as the primary presupposition of Indian thought, the core around which all other arguments and beliefs evolve. Of course, *nirvāṇa* is often presented as something that is beyond perception and beyond comprehension; sometimes it is even declared to be totally ineffable. One may indeed refer to *nirvāṇa* in different and contrasted ways: it can be characterized positively as Being, or hinted at negatively as Nothingness, or even presented paradoxically as that which is neither Being nor Non-being. All the same, the basic noetic quality of *nirvāṇa* remains intact. It remains a self-evident possibility, a real alternative to the cycle of birth and death (*saṃsāra*) and suffering; whatever it is considered, whether a value, a regulative Idea, a mystical experience, or anything else, it cannot be denied.

In India, the sceptic may therefore seem to find himself in an intolerable situation of conflict. On the one hand, any attempt to cast doubt on the possibility of release undermines perhaps the most basic constitutive rule of Indian thought. On the other hand, to accept the possibility of release is to admit that total and radical scepticism is indeed impossible. At this point, one might assume that the theoretical alternatives are: either to be sceptical or to be nirvanic, to be philosophical or to be religious in a utopian sense. For this reason, one might easily be surprised to find a radical sceptic in India who accepts the possibility of *nirvāṇa*. And should the odd phenomenon of a

---

[3]Hume (1948), Part I, p.9.

[4]Russell (1948), p.9.

[5]See Hume (1948), p.7.

religious sceptic be discovered, it would seem just to declare him to be absurd or insincere.

It would seem impossible for an Indian philosopher to undertake to be the necessarily disbelieving sceptic and yet to declare that his motives and purpose were strictly religious. However, this is precisely what happened in the second century A.D., when the Buddhist thinker Nāgārjuna launched his sceptical war against dogmatic Indian philosophers of every kind. Nāgārjuna's powerfully sceptical arguments need not concern us here. Nor is it necessary for us to decide whether or not Nāgārjuna succeeded in his radical scepticism. For our purpose, only one point need be stressed: by destroying the authority of all knowledge claims, Nāgārjuna did not wish to leave us to fall prey to a nihilistic state of mind. On the contrary, his express objective is to console rather than to terrify. As Matilal nicely puts it, "The sceptic's argumentation... is supposed to lead one to an *insight* into the nature of what is ultimately real (*prajñā*). This transition from radical scepticism to some sort of mysticism (where the truth is supposed to dawn upon the person if he can rid himself of all false or unwarranted beliefs) is very pronounced in the Indian tradition."[6] Matilal thus acknowledges the link that exists between Nāgārjuna's scepticism and his mysticism. Moreover, according to Matilal this link is not as paradoxical as it may look at first sight. Mysticism need not always be interpreted as a derogatory term.[7] Mystical experience can be seen to stem directly from the sceptic's suspension of judgments, that is to say, from the realization that in fact we do not possess any certain knowledge either of the world or of ourselves. This awareness of ignorance has a liberating impact: "As we realize more and more the limits of language in our analytical struggle, the idea of something inexpressible may well dawn in our mind although it would be difficult to make a logical appraisal of this 'inexpressible'."[8] The transition from radical scepticism to some sort of mysticism is similar to the celebrated ladder of Sextus Empiricus: the sceptical procedure is nothing but a means, a ladder on which to climb up and then throw away.[9]

Although we may grant that Nāgārjuna in some way holds to a mystical faith, it would be unfair to see his standpoint as a religious doctrine charged with arbitrary dogmas concerning release or salvation. Nāgārjuna implicitly accepts mysticism; but his standpoint can be characterized as "minimal mysticism", by which I mean mysticism without ontological suppositions, mysticism independent of any metaphysical world-view. But although his mysticism may be minimal in nature, we cannot avoid asking the crucial question on the coherence of a mystico-sceptical standpoint. Is even such a minimal mysticism possible for a radical sceptic?

How can the radically sceptical and yet believing mysticism of Nāgārjuna be defended? In his works Nāgārjuna is often anxious to emphasize that his consistency remains unimpaired because he himself does not have any thesis (*pratijñā*) to propose. If he has no argument to be proved, he repeats, how can he be at fault?[10] In this emphasis on having no standpoint to defend, Nāgārjuna is strikingly similar to Sextus Empiricus, who proclaimed that "the sceptic determines nothing, not even the very

---

[6]Matilal (1986), p.67. See also p.22, where Nāgārjuna's philosophy is named "mystical scepticism".

[7]See Matilal (1971), p.147.

[8]Ibid., p.147.

[9]See Sextus (1936), *Adv.log.* II. 481, p.489.

[10]See Nāgārjuna (1978), Verse 29.

proposition 'I determine nothing'."[11] (A similar exposition can be found in India about a thousand years later in the writings of the Advaitin mystic Śrīharṣa.) The total absence of any positive statement is what makes such scepticism, as even its bitter opponents are bound to admit, logically impeccable. But this logical impeccability is demolished when *nirvāṇa* gets into the sceptic's picture. As I have pointed out, speaking of *nirvāṇa* involves accepting the possibility of release, that is, accepting something, while the success of the sceptic's endeavour is wholly dependent on the absence of any assent whatever. Would it not, then, be reasonable to conclude that the Indian sceptic of Nāgārjuna's kind is not really a radical sceptic but rather a "methodical" one, since his sceptical procedure is only a means to establish what may be considered a minimal absolutistic position?[12]

In what follows I will attempt to suggest a solution to the apparent inconsistency between scepticism and religion. More precisely, I will offer what appears to me as a feasible way of reading Nāgārjuna's claims concerning the possibility of *nirvāṇa*. The reading I propose will present these claims as compatible with Nāgārjuna's scepticism or even as stemming directly from it. It is my conviction that Nāgārjuna himself was aware of the apparent discrepancy between his scepticism and his "minimal" mysticism and that he offered an original solution to it which can be discovered by a careful reading of his works. A proper understanding of Nāgārjuna's views will shed light not only on his position but also on the mutual relationship between philosophy and religion in India.

In order to clarify the novelty of Nāgārjuna's sceptical view, I should like to begin with the affinity between his doctrine and that of Sextus Empiricus as a methodical starting point. I propose to distinguish between the sceptical claims that can be found in the writings of both Sextus and Nāgārjuna and the sceptical claims that are unique to Nāgārjuna. I shall use the word *traditional* to characterize Nāgārjuna's claims that bear a close similarity to those of Sextus, and the word *original* to characterize Nāgārjuna's claims that cannot be found, to the best of my knowledge, in Sextus. It is self-evident that I do not wish to imply that Nāgārjuna was in any direct or indirect way influenced by Sextus, or vice versa. Nor do I wish to make an elaborate comparison between those two fascinating sceptical thinkers. My references to Sextus will serve a single purpose: to shed a light on Nāgārjuna's sceptical position and to help distinguish Nāgārjuna's scepticism from the scepticism of other philosophers. It seems to me that by using Sextus as a yardstick of scepticism, we can point out more clearly the distinctive aspects of Nāgārjuna's thought. When we have made out what is distinctive in Nāgārjuna's thought, we may be better able to understand how Nāgārjuna can accept the possibility of release at the same time as he continues to insist on his scepticism. When we understand Nāgārjuna's position, we may be better able to understand how Indian thinkers coped in general with the problem of release in their philosophy, which was, after all, the context of Nāgārjuna's thought.

There are a number of features that are common to the scepticism of both Sextus Empiricus and Nāgārjuna. First and foremost is the extensive use of a form of argument that is commonly called *reductio ad absurdum*. By the use of this form of argument, each of the two thinkers puts philosophical doctrines to an implacable test, the result of which is, to quote Naess, that the sceptic "finds no better grounds for

---

[11] Sextus (1933), I.197, p. 115.

[12] As Matilal claims, the Mādhyamika is in favour of some Absolutism in philosophy. See Matilal (1971), p. 147.

accepting the arguments in favor of the doctrine than for accepting those against it."[13] In the present essay, however, my interest lies not in the sceptical procedure itself but in its outcome. In this respect, Sextus and Nāgārjuna seem to share a "traditional" feature: both sceptics are eager to present the sceptical course of action as a novel means of mental therapy. Both regard philosophical dogmatism as a kind of mental disease that scepticism is able to cure, not by offering still another version of a philosophical doctrine, but rather by showing that all doctrines are equally exposed to doubt and uncertainty. Doubt and contradiction can cause feelings of frustration and become an obstacle to understanding.[14] But if, as the sceptic's argue, doubt leads to total suspension of judgement (*epoche*), doubt can remedy the malignant wounds inflicted by the unfounded pretences of philosophy and restore our peace of mind.

The therapeutic moral of Sextus is very clear throughout his *Outlines of Pyrrhonism.*[15] "The originating cause of scepticism is, we say, the hope of attaining quietude".[16] This tranquility of mind follows the act of suspension of judgment and is attained "as if by chance"[17], as in the amusing story of Apelles the painter that Sextus tells.[18] The final aim of the sceptic is to heal:

> The Sceptic, being a lover of his kind, desires to cure by speech, as best as he can, the self-conceit and rashness of the Dogmatists.[19]

A similar tendency to emphasize the therapeutic aspect of the sceptical endeavor can be found all through Nāgārjuna's writings. Take, for example, his insistence (mentioned earlier) that he has no thesis to submit, no doctrine to defend, and hence cannot be charged with inconsistency.[20] It is evident that the monumental body of arguments and counter-arguments found in his writings is therapeutic in intention. Nāgārjuna does not want to increase confusion or debate by the useless addition of still more philosophical positions. On the contrary, Nāgārjuna's only purpose is to cure the disease that is philosophy. He means to do this by pointing out the problematic nature, absurdity, and pointlessness of each and all of the philosophical positions. By doing so, Nāgārjuna believes he will cure the philosopher, whom he sees as searching obsessively for non-existent final answers to useless questions. Nāgārjuna never tires of emphasizing that all his enterprise is a kind of activity or performance by which he tries to prevent his adversaries from continuing to err and to suffer. As an example of such a performance Nāgārjuna suggests[21] a delusive woman that some lusting man mistakes for a real woman. When seen as real, the woman causes pain. But then comes the healer, who does nothing but show the lusting man that the woman for whom he longs is unreal. In other words, he deters him from seeing her as a real

---

13 Naess (1968), p.4.

14 See, for example, Nāgārjuna (1970), Chapter 24, Verse 7 and Sextus (1933), I.27.

15 See Hiley (1988), Chapter 1. See also Cohen (1984).

16 Sextus Empiricus (1933), I.12, p.9.

17 Ibid., I.29, p.21.

18 Ibid., I.28, p.21.

19 Ibid., III.280, p.511.

20 See Nāgārjuna (1978), Verse 29.

21 See Nāgārjuna (1978), Verse 27.

person, negates the force of the lust and cures the man of his pain and anxiety. The crux of the whole matter is that this mysterious healer is himself an illusion. The exact status of his (the healer's) reality or unreality is, of course, irrelevant. In any case, the healing is effective.

The sole aim of the sceptical activity of Nāgārjuna is clearly practical, for his intention, as I have said, is to cure. Therefore there is no good reason to examine the theoretical standing of his arguments or the measure of their reality, whatever "reality" may be taken to mean. The process of curing that takes place, the curing of a perversion of *avidyā* or "ignorance"[22], is not bodily but spiritual. To Nāgārjuna, it is the function of the sceptic to cure the philosopher of this condition of ignorance-illness, but never by the addition of knowledge; never, that is, by the exchange of one assertion for another, presumably more correct one. Matilal proposes that we take the curative sentences that Nāgārjuna recommends not as assertions but as "empty utterances".[23] According to Matilal's interpretation, the sceptic does not negate statements - he simply pays no attention to their meaning, so that he does not negate propositions but negates the *illocutionary force* of the asserting, his act of negating being conceived to be an illocutionary act rather than a propositional negation.[24] To clarify what is meant, if the dogmatic philosopher argues, for example, that things have self-nature, the purpose of the sceptic is not to put the opposite proposition, which is "It is not true that things have self-nature", or even the indeterminate proposition, "It is not known whether or not things have a self-nature". The purpose of the sceptic is, instead, to prevent the proposition from being taken as genuinely asserted, that is to say, the sceptic tries to prevent the utterances from being taken as genuine illocutionary speech-acts of assertion. What the sceptic negates is the linguistic utterance "I assert that things have their self-nature". The sceptic shows "performance" to be impossible, and this demonstration of impossibility is presumed by Nāgārjuna to have a great therapeutic effect. Notice the similarity between the illocutionary act of the sceptic and what Gale calls the illocutionary act of a fictive use of language, which is that of disengagement - avoiding performing any other illocutionary act.[25] If we see Nāgārjuna's efforts in this light, it is clear that his activity of prevention cannot be refuted. Nāgārjuna argues explicitly that though the philosopher believes that he has refuted *śūnyatā*, his refutation is unable to show that the sceptic is mistaken [26] because the truth of the matter is that the refutation is not relevant to Nāgārjuna's "non-position". The philosopher assumes that he refutes scepticism as one among other philosophies, but scepticism is no more than a performance, a therapeutic activity, and as such cannot be refuted by directly philosophical arguments.

At least in its general aspects, this therapeutic aspect is common to both Sextus and Nāgārjuna. I do not mean by this that it is impossible to find differences, great and small, between the two philosophers. But because, in the context of the present article, the comparison between the two philosophers serves only as a methodical aid, it is enough to point out that the therapeutic aspect of scepticism is what I earlier called a *traditional aspect.*

---

[22]See Nāgārjuna (1970), Chapter 23, Verse 23.

[23]See Matilal (1986), p.48.

[24]Ibid., p.66.

[25]Gale (1971), p.335.

[26]See Nāgārjuna (1970), Chapter 24, Verse 13.

In order to understand Nāgārjuna and his place in Indian philosophy, we also have to understand what I have called the *original aspect*, that in which Nāgārjuna is different from Sextus. As I see it, the original aspect is the way in which Nāgārjuna sees the phenomenal world. I say nothing new if I add that what he means by the existence of the phenomenal world is, for the most part, the unceasing daily activity of human beings in the context of this world. Taken in this sense, existence might seem to be problematic to sceptics. One of the usual attacks on the sceptic, an attack we find both in the West and in the East, contends that if the sceptic's life is to be consistent with his philosophy, he is fated to complete inaction. The refusal of the kind of sceptic we are considering to take a position, his suspension of judgment, and the equality he finds between arguments pro and con, all might appear to make practical life impossible, for the consistent sceptic would seen to be denied the possibility of making any choices or judgments or of preferring one way over another. The anatogonist of scepticism therefore supposes that life in keeping with such a view is presumed to be impossible.

Both Sextus and Nāgārjuna are aware of this kind of attack. At first sight it appears that both give a similar and perhaps even identical answer. Sextus says specifically and clearly that he accepts appearances just as they are:

> Those who say that "the Sceptics abolish appearances", or phenomena, seem to me to be unacquainted with the statements of our School. For... we do not overthrow the effective sense-impressions which induce our assent involuntarily: and these impressions are "the appearances". And when we question whether the underlying object is such as it appears, we grant the fact that it appears, and our doubt does not concern the appearance itself but the account given of that appearance, - and that is a different thing from questioning the appearance itself.[27]

The acceptance of phenomena just as they are allows the sceptic to act as ordinary life requires. "Adhering, then, to appearances we live in accordance with the normal rules of life, undogmatically, seeing that we cannot remain wholly inactive."[28] The sceptic therefore accepts not only the so-called laws of nature and human instincts and desires, but also accepts the various social institution just as they are; that is, he accepts the traditional customs and laws and the activities of those who practice the various arts and professions.[29] As Hiley accurately puts it, Pyrrhonism "did not seek to call into question the appearances and customs of daily life but instead opposed the philosophical attempt to get behind those appearances and ground them in something foundational or ahistorical. Its goal in opposing philosophy was to live tranquilly in accordance with instinct, custom, and tradition; in that sense, its attack on philosophy aimed to restore the appearances of common life as guides for conduct."[30]

Nāgārjuna, too, emphasizes that he does not reject but accepts appearances as they are. His message is clear and exact: Without recourse to conventional reality or truth, nothing is possible, not even the sceptical activity itself.[31] Thus he explicitly admits

---

[27]Sextus (1933), I.19, p.15.

[28]Ibid., I.23, p.17.

[29]Ibid., I.24, p.17; I.231, p.143.

[30]Hiley (1988), p.9.

[31]Nāgārjuna (1978), Verse 28.

that he cannot state that all things are empty unless he takes recourse to ordinary human behavior.

It is therefore obvious that both Sextus and Nāgārjuna accept the world of phenomena and accept whatever results from their acceptance of convention. At this point, however, the difference between the two begins to appear. As I see it, Sextus accepts phenomena for common sense reasons. These reasons cause him to say explicitly that, "the Sceptic does not conduct his life according to philosophical theory (for so far as regards this he is inactive), but as regards the non-philosophic regulation of life he is capable of desiring some things and avoiding other."[32] In contrast, when Nāgārjuna states his conception of phenomena, he does not do so for common sense reasons but for opposite ones. When he explains what he takes phenomena to be, he relates his explanation to a concept that is problematic for all philosophers and even more so for the sceptic. We find in Nāgārjuna a kind of sudden, speaking metaphorically, explosive use of the theory of double truth. By means of this theory he reverses everything he has seemed to contend, because he accepts phenomena not for common sense reasons but for religious ones. In other words, Nāgārjuna is asked to answer the charge that scepticism leads to inactivity. The argument runs: If everything is empty, there will be no creation or destruction, no karmic fruits of action, no social institutions such as the *saṅgha*, and no truth in the sense of *dharma*.[33] In Nāgārjuna's answer to this accusation, he speaks of the acceptance of appearances, an acceptance taken within the completely religious context of his belief in two levels of reality.

This is the point that reflects what I have called the *original aspect* of Nāgārjuna's thought. Nāgārjuna here goes beyond the notion of the merely therapeutic value of scepticism. It is clear that Nāgārjuna is at one with Sextus in contending that the acceptance of the sceptical point of view releases the acceptor, and that suspension of judgment can lead the individual to peace of mind. But Nāgārjuna goes, in a sense, beyond Sextus. He proposes phenomenal reality as the framework within which the process of release occurs. In this way, he chooses phenomenal reality as the meeting ground of scepticism and religion. In what follows I would like to suggest a certain manner of reading Nāgārjuna, according to which this meeting ground is a possible one. I hope that my suggestion helps us to give a plausible interpretation of Nāgārjuna's thought and to make more visible some of the intricate connections between religion and philosophy in India.

Whoever reads Nāgārjuna will hardly be able to contend that what Nāgārjuna says about double truth are mere slips of the pen or merely incidental remarks. Furthermore, it is not reasonable to assume that his acceptance of double truth is merely lip-service to an already existing Buddhist tradition. Nāgārjuna points out explicitly and clearly that a distinction must be made between two quite different levels of reality, everyday or conventional reality (*saṃvṛti*) and the higher or absolute reality (*paramārtha*).[34] In order not to belittle the importance of the distinction, he adds that all those who cannot distinguish between the two levels do not really understand the principles of Buddha's doctrine.[35] Buddha himself is thus impressed

---

[32] Sextus (1936), *Ad. log*, 165, p.465.

[33] Nāgārjuna (1970), Chapter 24, Verses 1-6.

[34] Ibid., Verse 8.

[35] Ibid., Verse 9.

into service to show the extreme importance that Nāgārjuna attributes to the distinction. Furthermore, as if Buddha himself does not suffice to convince those who doubt or misunderstand the distinction, Nāgārjuna adds the warning that whoever does not understand the distinction correctly is like a man who seizes a snake by the wrong end.[36] We are thus evidently dealing with something that appears to Nāgārjuna of vital importance.

What is the point that Nāgārjuna is so eager to emphasize but is so concerned that others may misinterpret? I think that the answer to this question should direct us not to the distinction itself between the two levels of reality but to the connection between the two levels. Nāgārjuna puts the astonishing argument that unless one relies on everyday, phenomenal reality, ultimate reality cannot be achieved.[37] Because the understanding of the highest reality is an expression of the attainment of *nirvāṇa*, the genuine acceptance of phenomena as phenomena is itself the hoped-for release. This argument of Nāgārjuna sounded strange if not implausible to many of faithful readers, to the point that some of them preferred to explicate it through absolutistic spectacles.[38] According to such an explication, Nāgārjuna himself is represented as a particular kind of absolutist and the lower truth is represented as a particular *means* by which to reach the absolute reality. According to such an interpretation, the relations between *saṃvṛti* and *paramārtha* are represented as resembling those between *nirguṇa Brahman* and the world of representations (taken in the sense of *māyā*) in the thought of Śaṃkara. Such an interpretation is unconvincing because, for one thing, it does not take into account that when Nāgārjuna speaks of phenomenal reality he sees it as absolutely necessary for reaching the utmost truth. From his standpoint, it is therefore impossible to see the lower reality as a means alone because in the relations between means and ends it is not possible to see means as essential to the achievement of an end except if the rules that determine the end are constitutive rather than regulative; or the rules have at least to be contained within the definition of the end, in the sense that the means are already explicitly or implicitly defined within the end. If the phenomenal reality is essential for realization of the absolute reality, this conclusion must be present from the beginning in the very nature of *nirvāṇa*. If we take Nāgārjuna's words seriously and do not neglect his argument that without perceived reality we cannot reach absolute reality, the result is that we cannot see phenomenal reality as a ladder to be abandoned after we have used it. Furthermore, I find it hard to accept the schematic ladder argument as an adequate illustration of the sceptical endeavour. After all, if I use a ladder in order to climb up to somewhere, I must have some idea, however vague, concerning the somewhere, the destination of the ascent. In the absence of any idea of the destination, which is the step beyond the uppermost rung of the ladder, the ladder argument is nonsensical. To the best of my knowledge, neither the ladder nor any similar image is to be found in Nāgārjuna, so perhaps it may be presumed that he was aware of the weakness of the analogy. As I have already said, on this essential point Nāgārjuna is altogether different from Sextus.

It is all the more evident that we cannot accept the interpretation according to which the two-truths doctrine of Nāgārjuna is only a practical device meant for the vast majority of humanity, which is unable to realize the truth directly.[39] (Such a

---

[36]Ibid., Verse 11.

[37]Ibid. Verse 10.

[38]See, for example, Murti (1955).

[39]See, for example, Santina (1987), p.177.

distinction, which is social or sociological, between two kinds of truths, each directed at a different population, is found in Candrakīrti in his interpretation of *Madhyamaka-kārikā* Ch. 18, but it does not apply to the present discussion.)

What then is Nāgārjuna's meaning when he says that relying on conventional truth is necessary for attaining release or *nirvāṇa*? It seems to me that the answer to this question is given by Nāgārjuna himself, when stating the very possibility of *nirvāṇa*: There is no specifiable difference between *saṃsāra* or everyday reality and *nirvāṇa*. Nāgārjuna says this in an even more radical fashion: There is not even the slightest difference between the two realms.[40] Put differently, he seems to be telling us that if, in the attempt to understand, we imagine *saṃsāra* and *nirvāṇa* to be two different fields, these cannot be merely congruent fields but for all purposes identical.

We therefore are faced by a group of statements that, to be just to Nāgārjuna, we have to try put together into a harmonious whole. I put these arguments into four brief sentences:

(a) Knowledge in the usual sense is impossible.

(b) Therefore one should not defend any doctrine - all doctrines are symptoms of illness and result in suffering.

(c) Yet the acceptance of (b) does not require any reduction of or change in everyday activity, which is essential for the attainment of *nirvāṇa*.

(d) Everyday reality is not at all different from release.

What can we do with this group of statements? How can we understand this connection between radical scepticism and the belief in the phenomenal as essential to release? What shadow falls here between idea and reality? Among the four statements I have stated, the first two represent what I earlier called the *traditional aspect*, while the two latter ones represent what I called the *original aspect*. The difficulty here is to show the compatibility of these two aspects when they occur in the thought of the same sceptic. There is a strong temptation to say that we have come upon a contradiction and to suggest a solution that will single out some of the statements at the expense of the others (an apposite example is Murti's absolutistic representation of Nāgārjuna). But it seems to me that before we choose such desperate remedies, we should see if there is no way to understand all the four statements above as an intellectually coherent unity.

I will now try to show how the unity can be understood. To show this, I propose four simple statements, parallel to those I have put for Nāgārjuna. The parallel statements are all quoted from Ecclesiastes:

(a*) "Vanity of vanities! All is vanity" (1.2). "...He has put the world into man's minds, yet so that he canot find out what God has done from the beginning to the end" (3.11).

(b*) "However much man may toil in seeking, he will not find it out; even though a wise man claims to know, he cannot find it out" (8.18). "What is crooked cannot be made straight, and what is lacking cannot be numbered" (1.15).

---

[40]Nāgārjuna (1970), Chapter 25, verses 19-20.

(c*) "For everything there is a season and a time for every matter under heaven..." (3.1). "So I saw that there is nothing better than that a man should enjoy his work, for that is his lot" (3.22).

(d*) "Let your garments be all with white; let not oil be lacking on your head. Enjoy life with the wife whom you love, all the days of your vain life which he has given you under the sun" (9.8-9).

It is of course possible to see all these passages from Ecclesiastes as an eclectic collection of apothegms that lack any unifying thread. To my mind, however, such a thread exists. I do not want to be misunderstood when I say this. Nāgārjuna is a sophisticated philosopher, hard, no doubt, to interpret exactly, but able to think as sophisticatedly as a contemporary philosopher. In contrast, Ecclesiastes (or his compilers) express what is essentially folk wisdom, which is not by nature on a high level of abstraction and which does not extend its scepticism to epistemology or metaphysics. I do contend not that Ecclesiastes was a philosopher in the sense that Nāgārjuna was one, but that latent in Ecclesiastes there is a mode of thinking that, when drawn out by ourselves in the form of abstractions, resembles that of Nāgārjuna - one might consider it a Nāgārjunian latency or potentiality. In any case, I am using Ecclesiastes only to help me express what I take to be Nāgārjuna's position. This is because, to my mind, the core of the arguments that are involved is easier to reveal in Ecclesiastes than in Nāgārjuna. The core is this: A radical change of the condition of man in the world is possible not as a change of essence - a basic change in the world or a move from the world to another level of being - but only as a change of *status*. In Ecclesiastes there is an explicit leitmotif of "vanity" which appears and reappears during the whole course of the book. According to the usual interpretation, this "vanity" is an expression, leading, perhaps, to nihilism, of the futility or emptiness of the world. To me it seems that such an interpretation cannot explain the presence of "vanity" not only in statements of type (a*) and (b*), but also in statements of the (c*) or (d*) type. The implicit message in all these mentions of "vanity" is, I think, the therapeutic recommendation to demote our ordinary human goals, whether biological, social, or spiritual, and, instead, to concentrate our attention on "vanity". The sense of vital importance or of authenticity is then transferred from what we ordinarily take to be real to what is, as we now recognize, only "vain". So you can really enjoy life with the wife whom you love, as long as you realize all your enjoyment is taking place within the days, so to speak, of your vain life which was given you under the sun. Generally put, everything remains in fact just as it was except for our assessment of its status.

What is the meaning of such a change in status? I think that a description of several instances of the conferring of status will suffice for an answer. In his discussion of art, Dickie suggests a number of examples that can serve us as well.[41] A change of status can be, for example, a matter of legal action, as when a king confers knighthood on someone, a grand jury indicts, the chairman of an election board certifies that someone is qualified to run for office, or a minister pronounces a couple man and wife. The conferring of status can also be a non-legal matter, as when a university confers a Ph.D. degree on someone, or as when the church declares an object to be a recognized relic, or as when one acquires the status of wise man or of

---

[41] Dickie (1974), pp.34-35.

village idiot. Still another example of the conferring of status can be brought from a quite different field. Take the suicide of a certain woman, towards the end of the nineteenth century, under the wheels of a train in some station or other. If we were to read the description of the death of this woman in the weekend edition of a newspaper, it would be clear that the woman in question was one of flesh and blood. But if, after we finished reading the newspaper, we turned to Tolstoy's novel and discovered this very story in it, it would this time be clear that the novel dealt with the "heroine" Anna Karenina, a fictional figure created by the imagination of the author. What is the difference between the two accounts we have imagined? Is the difference an essential one? The plot in both instances might be identical down to its smallest details. Is the difference semantic in that the propositions that appear in the newspaper have a fixed truth value (are true or false), while the propositions that appear in the novel are neither true nor false because they speak of a person who exists only in the sense of existing within the novel, a fiction? Possibly so. This is the opinion of a number of those who have dealt with the problem of the definition of fictions.[42] In any case, for this semantic difference to be effective we must know in advance what distinguishes the factual from the fictional account. To my mind, the primary difference is one in status. When we call a group of propositions *fiction*, we do not change anything within the propositions themselves; we simply grant them a different status. As Macdonald puts it, "characters play a role while human beings live a life."[43] The difference between these two I take to be one of status. To put it crudely, in contrast to reality, fiction makes no claim to be either real or unreal. I cannot now enter into everything related to the definition of fictions (I am dealing with this elsewhere). For our purpose, it is enough if I say that in the thought of Ecclesiastes and the philosophy of Nāgārjuna we are faced with still another example of the conferring of status - a change that changes nothing within the propositions themselves and yet has far-reaching results on both the semantic and pragmatic levels.

In my interpretation, therefore, if there is a central point in Ecclesiastes, it is the recommendation to change the status of "reality" in the mind of the reader and to recognize the overriding importance of "vanity". I may have exaggerated in my interpretation of Ecclesiastes; but if I return to Nāgārjuna, it seems to me that we should see his scepticism and the relation between his scepticism and his religious position in the light of what has been said of changes of status. That is, I suggest that we see the terms *śūnya* and *vanity* as analogous, from the standpoint of the *use* made of them. Nāgārjuna adopts a wide-ranging radical, destructive scepticism, destructive in that when he is finished there is not a single philosophical argument that remains as it was before. At the end of the process of Nāgārjuna's sceptical assessment, the non-sceptical philosopher is faced with the destruction of all his arguments. However, the word *destruction* applies only to a certain kind of status - the philosophical status that required the non-sceptical philosopher to arrive at the truth. The destruction is, one might say, of the status of the *svabhāva*, the very self-nature of Indian philosophical arguments. Scepticism does not destroy the arguments as such but only their status. It gives them a different status, one that Nagarjuna calls *śūnya*. Nāgārjuna recommends that we see experience as lacking a reality of its own, lacking *svabhāva*, lacking the status of own-being or independent existence. The transition from *svabhāva* to emptiness may remind us of the transition from real life to fiction.

---

[42] See, for example Macdonald (1954); Margolis (1965); Gale (1971); Lewis (1978); Crittenden (1981).

[43] Macdonald (1954), p.176.

The status of *śūnya* is therefore that of conventional so-called reality, in the absence of which we cannot arrive at *nirvāṇa*. Conventional so-called reality is the *saṃsāra*, the realm of which is not in the least different from that of the realm of *nirvāṇa*. The difference between *saṃsāra* and *nirvāṇa* is not metaphysical or psychological. The only thing that is different is the status of *saṃsāra*. When the philosopher ceases to search for the fixed and stable, *saṃsāra* remains *saṃsāra* just as before, but ceases to cause suffering.

The difference between Sextus and Nāgārjuna can be clarified further. Sextus advised a therapy based on the suspension of judgment: He neither affirms not denies anything and so he indicates that the philosophical interpretation he makes of the objects that appear to him are equal in the degree of their credibility and incredibility.[44] He uses the casting of doubt and the suspension of judgment as a means to achieve inner tranquility. However, Nāgārjuna, who also preaches the suspension of judgment, sees this suspension not as a means but as a "performance" of a change of status. It is this performance which is release: To make *nirvāṇa* possible, there is no reason to assume the existence of anything except this performance. In other words, Sextus prefers a willed ignorance, whereas Nāgārjuna prefers to destroy ignorance.

A few words of caution. When I point out the differences between Sextus and Nāgārjuna, I do not mean to imply that the two are moving in quite different directions, but that the differences are in the end cultural ones. Each of these philosophers taught in a very different cultural environment. Within the Buddhist framework of Nāgārjuna's life, it was not possible, on the one hand, to pronounce one's faith in Buddha (I take Nāgārjuna to have been quite sincere in this) and, on the other hand, to further a state of affairs or state of belief in which *nirvāṇa* would be more difficult or even impossible to attain. Nāgārjuna develops his scepticism deep within his Buddhist faith and life. His philosophical enterprise is not meant to destroy his Buddhist heritage but to restore it to its original state. Like Sextus, Nāgārjuna manifests an inherently conservative stance.[45] But Nāgārjuna, unlike Sextus, cannot simply accept phenomena as they are, but must, in his cultural milieu, relate them to the possibility of attaining *nirvāṇa*. Nāgārjuna's great power results from the ability he demonstrates to relate phenomena to *nirvāṇa*. He does not go beyond the basic presuppositions of Indian religious thought as, for example, the Lokāyata do. If he had been as radical as the Lokāyata, it would be easier to see him, as the Lokāyata were seen, as more or less peripheral to Indian life. But Nāgārjuna (like the Pyrrhonist sceptics) acts within philosophy. It is therefore impossible for philosophers to succeed in declaring him to be an outsider. To use somewhat allegorical language, his scepticism allows him to be a kind of inner voice of Indian philosophy. To put it differently, his scepticism is a realization of the readiness of the Indian philosopher to take the possibility of *nirvāṇa* seriously. To my mind, he reopens the relations in India between philosophy and religion. Even if we forget the superlative in the statement, "It was the Mādhayamika which had the greatest impact on the religious culture of India,"[46] it is possible to see Nagarjuna's scepticism as central to Indian views of religious salvation, much as medieval European theology is central to European views of religious salvation. The likeness is structural: Each culture justified its view of salvation in its own way, the Indian (as exemplified in Nāgārjuna) by an open, combative scepticism; the European usually by a partly Aristotelian, partly Neoplatonic theology that meant to be in a sense

---

[44]See Sextus (1933), I.196, p.115.

[45]See Hiley (1988), p.12.

[46]Santina (1987), p.173.

positive and in a sense negative. Nāgārjuna claims to have destroyed ignorance by causing false beliefs, *viparyāsa*, to cease - false beliefs about the nature of the world and about the position of human beings within it.[47] As I have in effect argued, it is possible to see Nāgārjuna as someone who watches because, like the watchman in Kafka, someone is needed to watch, "someone must be there."

REFERENCES

Cohen, Avner (1984). "Sextus Empiricus: Skepticism as a Therapy" *Philosophical Forum* 15: 405-424.

Crittenden, Charles (1981). "Everyday Reality as Fiction - A Mādhyamika Interpretation" *Journal of Indian Philosophy* 9: 323-333.

Dickie, George (1974). *Art and the Aesthetic: An Institutional Analysis*. Ithaca: Cornell University Press.

Gale, Richard M. (1971). "The Fictive Use of Language" *Philosophy* 46: 324-340.

Hiley, David R. (1988). *Philosophy in Question: Essays on a Pyrrhonian Theme*. Chicago: University of Chicago Press.

Hume, David (1948). *Dialogues Concerning Natural Religion*, ed. H.D. Aiken. New York: Hafner.

Hume, David (1962). *Treatise of Human Nature*, ed. D.G.C. Macnabb. Glasgow: Fontana/Collins.

Lewis, David (1978). "Truth in Fiction" *American Philosophical Quarterly* 15: 37-46.

Macdonald, Margaret (1954). "The Language of Fiction" *Proceedings of the Aristotelian Society Supplement* 28: 170-184.

Margolis, Joseph (1965). *The Language of Art and Art Criticism*. Detroit: Wayne State University Press.

Matilal, Bimal Krishna (1971). *Logic, Epistemology and Grammar in Indian Philosophical Analysis*. The Hague: Mouton.

Matilal, Bimal Krishna (1986). *Perception: An Essay on Classical Indian Theories of Knowledge*. Oxford: Clarendon Press.

Murti, T.R.V. (1955). *The Central Philosophy of Buddhism*. London: Allen & Unwin.

Naess, Arne (1968). *Scepticism*. London: Routledge & Kegan Paul.

Nāgārjuna (1970). *Madhyamakakārikā*. In Kenneth Inada, *Nāgārjuna: A Translation of his Mūlamadhyamakakārikā with an Introductory Essay*. Tokyo: Hokuseido Press.

Nāgārjuna (1978). *Vigrahavyāvartanī*. In Kamaleswar Bhattacharya, *The Dialectical Method of Nāgārjuna*. Delhi: Motilal Banarsidass.

Russell, Bertrand (1948). *Human Knowledge: Its Scope and Limits*. London: Allen & Unwin.

Santina, P.D. (1978). "The Madhyamaka Philosophy" *Journal of Indian Philosophy* 15: 173-185.

Sextus Empiricus (1933). *Outlines of Pyrrhonism*, trans. R.G. Bury. Cambridge, Mass.: Harvard University Press.

Sextus Empiricus (1936). *Against the Ethicists (=Adv. log.)*, trans. R.G. Bury. Cambridge, Mass.: Harvard University Press.

---

[47] Nāgārjuna (1970), Chapter 23, Verse 23.

SOME VARIETIES OF MONISM[1]

Peter Forrest

University of New England

In this paper I explore a position, Monism, of which we have an initial, pre-reflective, understanding, but which stands in need of further clarification. The initial understanding is that to be a Monist is to deny that (in reality) there are any differences, and/or to assert that (in reality) all is one. The qualification "in reality" already hints at a potential weakening of the Monist position, based on an appearance/reality distinction. But, for the moment, let us ignore this qualification. Then we have two slogans. The slogan of Negative Monism is "There are no differences", where this is taken as the denial of difference rather than the assertion of non-difference. The slogan of Positive Monism is "All is One".

My task in this paper is that of making sense of such slogans. While positivists might have denied that these slogans made *any* sense, I confess to having the opposite problem. There are *too many* ways of understanding them. The task I have set myself is that of displaying some of the variety of Monist positions, without, I hasten to say, providing an exhaustive list.

What is the point of such a taxonomy of varieties of Monism - and an incomplete taxonomy at that? I provide it in the hope that it will be of assistance to those engaged in the hermeneutic task of understanding what mystics and others mean when they say things like "All is One". For it sometimes helps to supplement the question "What does he or she mean?" with the question "What could someone have meant by those words?" Conceptual analysis is a prophylactic against a too narrow hermeneutics.

Similarly, some grasp of the range of possible Monist positions is of help when evaluating metaphysical arguments for Monism. What might well be a good argument for a rather weak version of Monism could be mistaken for a poor argument for a stronger version.

Finally, there is a question of interest in Philosophical Theology concerning whether belief in a transcendent God is compatible with Monism, or whether Monism and Theism together lead inevitably to Pantheism. Here again, some understanding of the varieities of Monism could well prevent excessively crude or swift arguments.

---

[1]I gave a seminar with this title at the University of New England. I would like to thank all who participated, especially Fred D'Agostino, Robert Elliot, Dick Franklin, Jeff Malpas and Gordon Stanley.

R. W. Perrett (ed.), Indian Philosophy of Religion, 75–91.

As a preliminary, I make some fairly standard remarks about experience in order to introduce an appearance/reality distinction. This will be a stipulated distinction, but one within the limits set by tradition. In the next three sections I discuss, in order of decreasing strength, three basic varities of Descriptive Monism. I call these Radical Monism, Spinozistic Monism and Primitive Unity Monism. Each of these has versions which need discussing. In passing I also note some sub-monist positions, by which I mean positions similar to varieties of Monism. It does not matter if you think they are genuine varieties of Monism. The important point is that we should be aware of these positions, which could be mistaken for stronger ones. Finally I consider whether Monism could be taken as a non-descriptive thesis, for instance as one concerning evaluation.

The following table summarises the main distinctions in the taxonomy:[2]

I DESCRIPTIVE MONISM

A. Radical Monism			
(i)	No Differences	(a) Strong Advaita Monism	(+)
		(b) Strong Mādhyamika Monism	(+)
(ii)	No Real Differences	(a) Weak Advaita Monism	(+,-)
		(b) Weak Mādhyamika Monism	(-)
B. Conservative Monism			
(i)	Spinozistic Monism	(a) One Aristotelian Substance	(+)
		(b) One Humean Substance	(+)
		(c) One Aristotelian-cum-Humean Substance	(+)
		(d) No Humean Substance	(-)
		(e) No Aristotelian-cum-Humean Substance	(-)
(ii)	Primitive Unity Monism	(+)	
(iii)	Disjunctive Monism	(+)	

II OTHER MONISMS

A. Ultraradical Monism		(-)
B. Non-descriptive Monism		
(i)	Evaluative Monism	(+)
(ii)	Identificational Monism	(+)

III SUB-MONIST POSITIONS

A. No Aristotelian Substance
B. Realism about Relations
C. Interconnection Thesis
D. Organic Unity

---

[2]The signs + and - denote whether the Monist position is primarily positive (i.e. asserting that all is one) or negative (i.e. denying that there are any differences).

I

There are at least four ways of providing an appearance/reality distinction. One is ontological and concerns various grades of *being*. Some items are thought of as more *real* than others because they have more being. Thus there is a tradition among Christian theologians of thinking that God is the one truly real being, or the one most real being (*Ens Realissimum*). The highest grade of reality might then be reserved for a necessary being, and contingency taken as the mark of (comparative) unreality.[3]

I shall not make the appearance/reality distinction in that fashion. My reason is that if we do, then we could quite reasonably say that *strictly* any being with less than the highest grade of being is mere appearance. In that case Monism is too cheap. It is an interesting question whether belief in God as the unique most real being is even *consistent* with Monism. But it should surely not *entail* Monism.

Another way of understanding the distinction between the real and the unreal is to consider the phenomenology of *bādha* - sublation, or as Deutsch calls it, subration. As he puts it:

> *Subration* is the mental process whereby one disvalues some previously appraised object or content of consciousness because of its being contradicted by a new experience.[4]

I do not dispute the accuracy of this as a description of the process by which a person comes to judge unreal what was previously taken to be real. But I shall not follow Deutsch in his characterisation of Reality as "that which cannot be subrated by any other experience".[5] For, I am concerned here with a conceptual analysis of Reality. And such an analysis should leave it an open question whether Reality may be identified with an experience at all. It is more natural to conceive of Reality as *prima facie* something which might be the object of experience, leaving it as an, initially startling, further development to suggest that Reality is the experience itself.

Reality might be characterised in terms of sublation by saying that unless the sublation is itself illusory, the new experience is (of) something more real than the object of the old experience. Sublation, then, provides us with a way of characterising Reality more directly. For sublation is partly a growth in *knowledge* and partly a change of *evaluation*.

Reality, then, has ontological and evaluational aspects. The phenomenology of sublation should no doubt make us cautious in separating the two. But for an analytic exercise like this one, itself perhaps ultimately fit for sublation, it is necessary to distinguish the descriptive from the evaluative. Emphasis on the latter leads us to Evaluative Monism. But I shall for the most part concentrate on Descriptive Monism. I shall first explicate the descriptive concept of reality and then defend its

---

[3]Given a theory of grades or degrees of reality, it becomes a matter of some delicacy, no doubt reflecting a judgement of value, where the line is drawn between the real and the unreal. I suspect that an emphasis on the Will, that is, on human freedom and responsibility, and an emphasis on the importance of the Incarnation, have prevented Christian theologians from denying the reality of the created world.

[4]Deutsch (1969), p.15.

[5]Ibid., p.18.

appropriateness. The explication will be thoroughly familiar. The real is explicated as that which is independent of experience.[6]

The basic idea is that an object of experience is real if it exists *independently*[7] of the experience. It it does not exist then it is *illusory*, while if it exists but depends on the experience, then it is *ideal*. So appearance covers both the ideal and the illusory.

Since I allow illusory objects of experience I do not require experience to be veridical. A fortiori, I do not require it to be infallible. As a result I am entitled to resist the narrowly empiricist position that experience is just the having of sensations. I shall use the term *experience* quite widely, although I take the paradigm of experience to be perception.

In order to explain more fully what I mean by experience and by the object of experience I shall note four *features* of experience:

(i) In experience it *seems* to the subject that he or she is passive. Experience is experienced as something happening to the one having the experience.

(ii) The subject has a natural tendency to acquire or reinforce various beliefs and/or attitudes as a result of the experience.

(iii) The subject has a natural tendency to justify those beliefs and/or attitudes by appealing to the experience itself rather than to other beliefs and/or attitudes.

(iv) The experience has an intentional object, that is it is *about* something. And the beliefs which naturally arise are beliefs about that something.

Some remarks on these four features are in order. Firstly the passivity. It is widely held that we supply something to that which we experience. But that is not how it *seems to us* as we experience.[8] Moreover this passivity is quite compatible with the experience being part of an observation, which is itself partly active. For the experience is the part of that process of observation which seems to the observer to be passive. This passivity is also quite compatible with the widely-accepted thesis that our prior beliefs and attitudes to some extent condition the nature of our experience.[9]

---

[6]For a representative analysis of reality as independence of experience, see Hirst (1967), p.77. Because of the current emphasis on language in Anglo-Saxon philosophy, this has been transformed into assertibility-independence. But the underlying theme of independence remains.

[7]To say that *X depends on Y* is to say:
(i) That it is impossible for *X* to exist without *Y*
and (ii) That *X* exists because *Y* exists.
The first condition is not enough. For nothing can be vermilion without being red, yet *being vermilion* does not depend on *being red.*

[8]In the West this position is associated with Kant. Among Indian thinkers, Śaṃkara is an example of someone who treats ordinary experience as the result of our superimposing something on reality. Thus, in the *Brahmasūtrabhāṣya*, he says: "... it is wrong to superimpose upon the subject ... the object ... and vice versa .... In spite of this it is on the part of man a natural procedure ... not to distinguish the two entities ... but to superimpose upon each the characteristic nature of the other." (Deutsch and van Buitenen (1971), p.152.)

The next two of the features which I listed concern our natural tendencies. We can *resist* these, as when we learn that the bend in the stick half-immersed in water is usually illusory. Likewise we could be sceptical about whether the beliefs which arise from the experience are justified. I am here merely noting the tendencies.

Finally, about the intentionality of experience: We need not judge, at least not at the outset, whether this is reducible or explicable in terms of something less mysterious. It suffices that there *is* such intentionality. Moreover, in some cases, for example the experience of pain, we may be prepared to say that the experience is about itself. I do not exclude such reflexivity.

The intentional object of experience is what the experience is *about*. If the experience is illusory then the intentional object does not exist. How is it possible for there to be an intentional object which does not exist? A difficult question. But we should not deny that experience has intentionality and that the intentional objects might fail to exist, simply because this question is difficult. This is not the place to discuss answers to the "How is it possible?" question. I shall press on, assuming that intentionality, however puzzling as a topic in its own right, will not confuse or mislead us when discussing Monism.

The intentional object of an experience is *real*, then, if it exists and is independent of that experience. If it exists but is dependent on that experience, then it is *ideal*. If it does not exist, then it is *illusory*. Therefore, when we contrast *appearance* with *reality*, both the ideal and the illusory count as appearance.

Notice that if items *a* and *b* are the intentional objects of experiences *A* and *B*, respectively, they could be ideal even though the differences between them is *real*. For the difference is ideal only if the difference is dependent on the experience of difference, which is not the same as the difference between experiences. This prevents the idealist thesis that all objects of experience are ideal from entailing Monism. While Monism and Idealism often go together, I do not think that one should entail the other.

In distinguishing the ideal from the real I have relied on the concept of dependence. A possible complication here is that dependence could be *partial*[10], or admit of degrees. This raises the possibility of various partial Monisms. But for simplicity I shall ignore such partial dependence and hence ignore partial Monisms.

However, there is a rather different complication which should not be ignored. The real/ideal/illusory contrast applies primarily to what is experienced. Hence it is often appropriate to restrict Monist positions to what is experienced, or at least what *can* be experienced. If Monism is explicitly restricted I call it Limited Monism. But it is also often appropriate to put forward an unrestricted position, which I call Unlimited Monism. To say, for instance, that all differences are ideal can be construed either merely as saying that all the differences we experience are ideal, or as saying, in addition, that there are no other unexperienced differences. The former is Limited Monism, the latter Unlimited Monism.

One reason for introducing the Unlimited/Limited distinction is that it is all too easy to forget about what has not been experienced. In a mystical experience someone may well experience the unity of all that he or she is capable of experiencing. That

---

[9]This is the thesis of the theory-laden character of experience. While I insist that experience has a core which is invariant under possible changes of theory and concept, I concede that the quality of the experience is influenced by theories and concepts. For a discussion of theory-laden perception, see Hanson (1958).

[10]In the simplest case *X* partially depends on *Y* if some part of, or aspect of, *X* depends on *Y*.

person could then carelessly state this as the experience that *all* is one, that is, as a version of Unlimited Monism. But it would be more properly stated by saying that all he or she can *experience* is one, that is, as a version of Limited Monism.

Having provided an explication of a descriptive concept of reality, and of the ideal/illusory distinction, I shall now defend this explication by arguing that it is appropriate given the phenomenology of sublation. First, if an object depends entirely for its existence and nature on someone's experience of it, then we may reasonably judge that any value or significance the object has derives from that of the experience on which it depends.[11] There are two cases here. If the object does not exist, even as a dependent entity, then we judge it to have no value at all. But if it does exist, then it may have value, although only a value dependent on the value of our experience. Hence the real, the ideal, and the illusory have values in agreement with those implicit in sublation.

Second, if our consciousness or experience is not itself dependent on the experience of some other conscious being, then it is real. (Experience depends on experience in the trivial sense of not being able to exist apart from experience. But that is not the sense of experience-dependence I have explicated.)

Thirdly, sublation need not be the recognition of a straightforward misperception.[12] I submit that, when sublation is not the recognition of misperception or some other mistaken experience, then the loss of former significance which is part of sublation is comparative, not absolute. In those cases what is sublated is not lessened in value, for it is ideal, not illusory, and so does exist. Rather it ceases to be of concern because its value, although genuine, is seen to be dependent on the value of the experience itself. By contrast, if we make a mistake, what we thought existed is seen to be of no value at all, because non-existent.

I have made a case, therefore, for the appropriateness of the appearance/reality distinction which I have explicated. The recognition of the unreality of that previously taken to be real is an adequate account of the non-evaluative component of sublation, and, moreover, provides grounds for the evaluative component.

It might be objected that my explication of the appearance/reality distinction is too Western to be appropriate to the discussion of versions of Monism of Indian origin. In reply to this, I note that my aim is not primarily hermeneutics, but the statement of philosophically interesting positions which may have hermeneutic relevance. I also note that alternative explications tend to "domesticate" Monism. If it is to be an interesting topic, Monism should be initially startling. So we should avoid any explication of the real as, say, the non-contingent.[13]

---

[11]This inference is neither trivial, nor entirely conclusive. First, it needs to be pointed out that there can be a mode of dependence in which *X* depends on *Y* because *X* cannot exist without *Y*, even though the nature of *X* is not determined by *Y*. (An example might be a creature with free will who is, to a limited extent, the author of her/his nature, while being dependent on the creative power of God.) The reasoning behind the inference in question begins with the assumption that the dependence is not of this sort, but one in which the dependent item *X* both depends on *Y* and has its existence and nature determined as a result of this dependence. In that case, we tend to judge that the value of *X* itself derives from the value of *Y*. However, it should be noted that there is no strict inconsistency in saying that, although *X* depends on and is determined by *Y*, the value which *X* has is not derived from that of *Y*.

[12]The recognition of the illusory character of what was previously taken to be real is a special case of sublation. It *is* the recognition of an experiential error.

[13]Cf. "All this amounts to little more than saying that the phenomenal world ... is ... what we in the West usually call 'contingent being'." (Zaehner (1962), pp.76-77).

II

The Negative/Positive distinction among Monist positions is reflected in typical expressions of Monism. As such it is an important distinction. But it is not suitable for a taxonomy. For the assertion of unity is compatible with the denial of difference. Moreover, if the oneness or unity which is asserted is sufficiently significant, then the differences will tend to seem insignificant by contrast. Therefore there will be a psychological tendency to deny their reality. Because of this complication, I shall treat the positive or negative character of a Monist position as one of emphasis.

For purposes of taxonomy a related distinction is more suitable. This is the Radical/Conservative distinction. Radical Monism is negative in the sense of denying those differences which we ordinarily seem to experience. More accurately, a version of Monism is *radical* if it involves a more-than-ordinary rejection of ordinary experience. Conservative Monism does not require any *special* rejection of experience. That is, the Conservative Monist will reject experience as illusory only for the usual common-sense/scientific reasons, as when we reject the experience of the bend in the stick immersed in water.

To make this more precise, let us note two presumptions. There is the Presumption in Favour of Veridicality, and the Presumption in Favour of Reality. The latter tells us that there is a burden of argument on anyone who treats the intentional object of experience as *non*-real. The former tells us that there is a further burden of argument on anyone who insists these intentional objects are not merely non-real but *illusory*. Because the case I have most in mind is the experience of the differences between things, let me be quite explicit. The intentional object of experience is to include parts of the object, and any apparent relations between those parts, such as distinctness or difference.

I accept both presumptions. And I consider both to be too fundamental to need further justification.

Both presumptions are overcome in the case of ordinary perceptual illusions. So, to take our traditional example, if a straight stick is put in water at an angle it looks bent. Hence the intentional object of experience is a bent stick. But this bent stick does not exist.

I classify varieties of Monism into the Radical and the Conservative, depending on whether they do or do not conflict with ordinary experience. Conservative Monism requires no *special* overcoming of either of the two presumptions. By contrast, Radical Monism does require that the Reality Presumption be overcome in ways not due to the ordinary perceptual illusions. It might come as a surprise that Conservative Monism is possible. And this surprise is itself significant. For perhaps some thinkers have ignored the possibility of Conservative Monism, and so assumed a version of Radical Monism unnecessarily.

In the remainder of this section I shall consider Radical Monism. The most extreme version of it is the thesis that differences are straightforwardly illusory. Rashly perhaps, I refer to this as Strong Advaita Monism.

I call it this because it is a *reconstruction* of a tenet of the Advaita Vedānta. That it bears some resemblance to a position held by Advaitins could only be established by an examination of whole texts, which is beyond the scope of this paper. But, for what it is worth, the early Advaitin Gauḍapāda seems more explicit on this point than Śaṃkara. Thus Gauḍapāda says: "As dream and illusion or a castle in the air are seen (to be unreal), so this whole universe is seen by those who are wise in Vedānta".[14] And: "As in the dream state so in the waking state, the objects seen as insubstantial because of their being perceived. The difference between them is only that the objects of dreams are confined within the body."[15] Surely dreams are paradigms of the illusory.

Advaita Monism has three variants. There is Unlimited Strong Advaita Monism, which states that there are no differences. And there is Limited Strong Advaita Monism, which states that all the differences which we experience are illusory. In addition, there is Intermediate Strong Advaita Monism, which not only says that all differences which we experience are illusory, but also says that there are no differences between the experiencer and the experienced. I introduce Intermediate Strong Advaita Monism because the non-difference between the experiencer and the experienced is essential to Advaita. Furthermore, since it is controversial whether we experience ourselves *as* experiencers, this Intermediate position is not an obvious consequence of Limited Advaita Monism.

Exactly parallel to the three versions of Strong Advaita Monism are the corresponding versions of what I call Weak Advaita Monism, the position that differences are ideal (i.e. that they depend on the experience of difference), rather than illusory. All six versions of Advaita Monism could be expressed by saying that there is precisely one reality, where the context would indicate whether the claim was in any way limited in its scope. And all six versions are both positive and negative. They both deny differences and assert unity.

Is the Advaita Vedānta closer to Strong or to Weak Advaita Monism? I have already mentioned Gauḍapāda, who inclines, it seems, to Strong Advaita Monism. However, in spite of the widespread use of the word "illusion" to translate "*māyā*", there is some reason to interpret Śaṃkara as holding a position closer to Weak Advaita Monism. For he is a quasi-theist in that he believes penultimate reality to be Īśvara, the Lord. Ultimately Īśvara is Himself *māyā*. However, Śaṃkara shows considerable devotion to Him, which is neither rational nor psychologically plausible if He is believed to be an illusion. I conclude that, in the writings of Śaṃkara, the term "*māyā*" is better translated as "appearance".

I now turn to the versions of what I call Mādhyamika Monism, in which the emphasis is on negative Monism. I call it this because the Mādhyamika, as formulated by Nāgārjuna, emphasises that strand of Buddhist thought in which both thesis and its negation are denied.[16] In particular it is denied that Reality is many, but also denied that Reality is one. This is part of a more general insistence that Reality transcends all our categories of thought.[17]

Mādhyamika Monism is, then, the denial that multiplicity is real, without any assertion that Reality is one. Thus Weak Mādhyamika Monism differs from Weak Advaita Monism in that while the latter states that we impose a purely ideal difference on the one reality, the former would simply say that the differences are ideal, without

---

[14] Deutsch & van Buitenen (1971), p.120.

[15] Ibid.

[16] As are any attempts to disjoin or conjoin the thesis and its negation.

[17] A typical Mādhyamika statement capable of interpretation this way is the introductory verse to the *Mūlamadhyamakakārikā* by Nāgārjuna: "I pay homage to the Fully Awakened One, ... who has taught ... the blissful cessation of all phenomenal thought constructions. (... every event is 'marked' by): non-destruction, non-permanence, non-identity, non-differentiation ...". (Inada (1970), p.39.)

saying anything about the underlying reality. As has been noted,[18] it is reminiscent of Kant's account of the things in themselves which, prior to the imposition of categories on them by the understanding, are quite unknowable. (Hence there is no question of "them" being one or many.) The difference between Strong and Weak Mādhyamika Monism is that the latter grants, but the former rejects, some status as existing (but ideal) to the apparent differences imposed upon reality by our categories of understanding. Kant's own position would then be closer to the weak version.

Mādhyamika Monism comes only in unlimited versions. For it is not the claim that all is one, which could well be limited to what has been experienced. Rather it is the claim that the intellectual distinction between one and many has no basis in reality. This cannot reasonably be limited to what is experienced. For it is absurd to suggest that our categories fail to apply to what is experienced, but by some amazing metaphysical coincidence apply to some other reality.

One significant difference between Strong Advaita and Strong Mādhyamika Monism would be that, according to the Strong Advaita Monist, to assert that differences are real would be *plain false*. However, according to the Strong Mādhyamika Monist, such assertions have a false presupposition and so are not plain false.[19] The presupposition in question is that the concept of difference is properly applied to Reality.

The above remark could be taken as a reason for treating Strong Mādhyamika Monism as more plausible than Strong Advaita Monism. I for one find it more plausible that beliefs based on ordinary experience should be tainted with false presuppositions rather than straightforwardly false.

III

I now turn to Conservative Monism. I contrast it with Radical Monism because it is compatible with the Presumption in Favour of Reality. However this contrast should not be over-emphasized. A Mādhyamika monist could well think as follows:

> I have experienced the underlying ineffable reality which is neither one nor many. Hence I recognise the distortion which results by the imposition of our categories when we describe reality in a discursive fashion. Nonetheless such a distorted description has its place. And my distorted description, for what it is worth, is a version of Conservative Monism.

In this section I shall discuss what I call Spinozistic Monism. This is one attempt to explicate the positive assertion that there is one reality in a way which is compatible with the Presumption in Favour of Reality. I shall produce a rather different attempt, which I consider preferable, in the next section.

Consider again the slogans "There are no differences" and "All is one". These could be interpreted as "There are no differences between *things*" and "There is only one *thing*".

---

[18]Especially by Murti (1957), pp.293-301.

[19]A statement with a false presupposition is not straightforwardly false, for its negation will also have the false presupposition. We could say that it is neither true nor false, or we could say it is false, but not straightforwardly so. Alternatively, influenced by the Buddhist tradition we could deny any truth status to it.

Now the term "thing" is notoriously elastic. In a sense anything is a thing, even a non-existent intentional object of experience. But the term "thing" can be used in a more restricted sense. Typically philosophers have used the technical term "substance" to mean "thing in a restricted sense". Hence one version of Monism is One Substance Monism, which I call *Spinozistic* Monism. I call it this because Spinoza was quite explicit that the One Substance had an infinity of attributes. So he was not denying the reality of all distinctions, but only of distinctions between substances.[20]

Spinoza calls the one substance "God or Nature". Hence his intention is to state an Unlimited Monism. However we can also consider Limited Spinozistic Monism, according to which all we ordinarily experience consist of attributes of one substance. This would be quite compatible with the existence of a God which is separate from Her/His creation. The latter - or the portion of the latter we experience - would be a single substance.

We can also distinguish various versions of Spinozistic Monism by considering different concepts of a substance. Thus I shall distinguish between Aristotelian substances, Humean substances and Aristotelian-cum-Humean substances. An Aristotelian[21] substance is something which could instantiate properties or relations but is not itself a property or relation. A Humean substance is that which does not depend for its existence on other entities. Finally an Aristotelian-cum-Humean substance is an Aristotelian substance which is also an Humean substance.[22]

These are indeed different concepts of substance. For, on the one hand, if properties can exist uninstantiated, then they could be Humean substances, but they could be neither Aristotelian substances nor Aristotelian-cum-Humean substances. On the other hand, if everything depends for its existence on God[23], then there could well be Aristotelian substances other than God but no Humean substance could be separate from God.[24]

What is the number of substances? The interesting answers are "None", "One", and "More than one". And we have three concepts of a substance. This gives us nine positions. Three are clearly varieties of Monism, namely the theses that there is precisely one Aristotelian substance, precisely one Humean substance, and precisely

---

20In Spinoza's *Ethics*, Prop IX, he says: "The more reality or being a thing has, the greater the number of its attributes." (Spinoza (1884), p.50.) Thus Spinoza is opposed *a priori* to both Advaita and Mādhyamika Monism.

21"Substance" is ambiguous in translations of Aristotle. Consider this passage from *Metaphysics Delta* (1017b):

> It follows, then, that "substance" has two senses, (A) the ultimate substratum, which is no longer predicated of anything else, and (B) that which, being a "this" is separable. (McKeon 1944, p.761.)

I am taking an Aristotelian substance to be, roughly, a substance in sense (A).

22Spinoza's definition of a substance as that "which is in itself and is conceived through itself" would suggest that he meant an Humean substance. But his emphasis on the attributes of the one substance suggest that he might be thinking of an Aristotelian-cum-Humean substance.

23Depends, that is, in the strong sense that it could not continue to exist without God, not in the weak sense that God caused it to come into existence.

24An Humean substance would then consist of God together with various parts of Creation.

one Aristotelian-cum-Humean substance respectively. But what of the No Substance Theses? We might argue that these theses are Monist ones because they deny any differences between substances. Let us first consider why there might be no Aristotelian substance. This could be because we believe there is an infinite regress of properties or relations being instantiated by properties or relations. This seems a coherent metaphysical thesis. In that case there would be no Aristotelian substances and, a fortiori, no Aristotelian-cum-Humean substances. Yet this thesis would not, I submit, be a characteristically Monist one. I shall call it a sub-Monist position, the No Aristotelian Substance Thesis.

Let us now turn to the thesis that there are no Humean substances. How could that be? It would occur if both of the following hold:

(i) Every item depends on other items for its existence.

(ii) There is no whole, of which these items are parts.

The second clause would reflect the quite plausible thesis that there is no such thing as the sum total of things, just as in standard set-theory, there is no such set as the union of all sets. This I consider to be a version of Monism. It differs from One Humean Substance Monism only in that it denies the existence of the sum total of things.[25] We could also have a version of the No Aristotelian-cum-Humean Substance Thesis which was similarly Monistic in spirit. Thus, in some cases the No Substance Thesis is Monistic, but in others it is not. Clearly No Substance Monism is more negative in emphasis than One Substance Monism. Yet I am claiming it as a Conservative Monism. This is another way in which the Radical/Conservative distinction fails to coincide with the Negative/Positive distinction.

Finally we may distinguish the thesis that there is only one Aristotelian substance from the thesis that there is only one *real* Aristotelian substance. My definition of an Aristotelian substance does not exclude ideal substances. The ideal must depend on the experience whose intentional object it is. It does not follow that it is a property of that experience. If I see an after-image, then the after-image depends on my seeing it. The thesis that to see an after-image is just to have an experience with a certain kind of property, while initially attractive, may reasonably be denied.[26]

A Humean substance (and hence an Aristotelian-cum-Humean substance) cannot be ideal. For the ideal is by definition dependent. So we cannot distinguish between versions of One (or No) Humean Substance Monism by considering whether there are many ideal Humean substances. We can, however, distinguish versions of One (or No) Humean Substance (or Aristotelian-cum-Humean substance) Monism by considering different ways in which items may fail to be independent of other items.

First, we could claim that any property or relation depends on that which it is a property or relation of. In that case there might be only one Humean substance precisely because there is only one Aristotelian substance.

Or again, we could claim that there is only one Humean substance because various Aristotelian substances are related by means of *essential* relations. Call this Essential Relations Monism. It is often claimed that an individual human being could not have

---

[25]If the No Humean Substance Thesis is restricted to what is ordinarily experienced, or indeed to everything but God, then it is compatible with the thesis that the only Humean substance is God, without entailing Pantheism.

[26]For some difficulties with this thesis, see Jackson (1977).

existed without being human. Likewise, according to Essential Relations Monism, nothing could have existed without being related as it is to everything else. In that case nothing less than the sum total of things could be a Humean substance. I call this Essential Relations Monism.

Yet again, One (or No) Humean Substance Monism could be supported by the thesis that there are no contingencies. This leads to what I call Necessitarian Monism. It is stronger than Essential Relations Monism. For on the latter, though not the former, there could have been a totally different system of essentially related items.

There are two sub-monist positions which could be mistaken for Essential Relations Monism. One is merely Realism about Relations. Monism is often contrasted with Atomism, which is sometimes taken to mean that in reality there is nothing but a number of totally unrelated substances. The reality of relations between substances is incompatible with Atomism thus described. Hence Realism about Relations might be taken for a version of Monism. But I do not think it should, for it is merely the rejection of a position at the extreme opposite to Monism. Another sub-monist position worth noting is the (Limited or Unlimited) Interconnection Thesis. This is the thesis that any two substances are connected by a chain of real relations.[27] Although stronger than mere Realism about Relations this hardly seems a Monist position. But here the verbal dispute is of little significance. Call it Monism if you will.

I have described a number of varieties of Spinozistic Monism. Perhaps it is worth supplementing the taxonomy by listing four representative varieties (each of which has limited and unlimited versions):

(i) There is only one Aristotelian substance.

(ii) There is only one real Aristotelian substance.

(iii) All relations are essential.

(iv) There are no contingencies.

It remains to discuss whether these are indeed versions of Conservative Monism. That some items are properties of others, and that some items are relations between others, may be part of the content of ordinary experiences. But it is not, I submit, part of the content of ordinary experiences that various items are not themselves properties or relations of other items. We simply *fail to experience*, say, the cup as a property. It is not that we experience the cup as a non-property.[28] Hence various forms of One Aristotelian Substance Monism are compatible with ordinary experience. The situation is a little different with One Humean Substance Monism. I suspect that there are experiences which are relevant here. In particular some of us might experience the *contingency* of things, which would be evidence against Necessitarian Monism. But I

---

[27] A notable denial of the Unlimited Interconnection Thesis is David Lewis' Realism about Possible Worlds. See Lewis (1986), pp.1-5.

[28] I am not denying *all* experience of absences. All I am claiming is that we do not experience the absence of the status of being a property.

do not consider this to be *ordinary* experience.[29]

IV

Spinozistic Monism was an attempt to express Positive Monism. Its chief failing is that it is more heavily laden with metaphysical theory than I would like. In this section I state another version of Positive Monism, which I call Primitive Unity Monism. This emphasizes the claim that there is a special *unity* in things, a claim which I take to be central to Positive Monism.

Primitive Unity Monism, which comes in limited and unlimited versions, is based on the distinction between a unity which is *natural* and one which is not. The thesis of Unlimited Primitive Unity Monism is that the sum total of things has an irreducible natural unity. The thesis of Limited Primitive Monism is that everything ordinarily experienced is either identical to, or part of, something which has irreducible natural unity.

First let me explain what a natural unity is.[30] I begin by noting that given any predicate which applies to at least one thing which exists, there is an aggregate, or sum, of all things which exist and to which the predicate applies. For example, if the predicate is "is either round or identical to Nāgārjuna or vermilion" then there is an aggregate or sum of all things which exist and which are round, identical to Nāgārjuna or vermilion.

How do I know there is such an aggregate? I know it because there is, by definition, nothing more to the existence of a sum or aggregate than the existence of its parts. That follows from what I *mean* by a sum or aggregate. So provided the concept of an aggregate is coherent, the existence of sums or aggregates is ensured by the existence of the things which make them up.

Notice that a sum or aggregate is not the same as a set or a class. Suppose *a, b* and *c* are three peas in a pod. Then $(a+b)+c = a+(b+c)$, where "+" denotes aggregation. Indeed $(a + b) + c$ is just the sum or aggregate of the three peas in the pod. By contrast $\{\{a,b\},c\}$, $\{a,\{b,c\}\}$ and $\{a,b,c\}$ are three different sets. As this example illustrates, a sum is a simpler, although perhaps less familiar concept, than that of a set or a class. The sum of various things is always a single thing, a unity. But it is quite often an artificial or unnatural unity. The intuitive idea here is that the unity is artificial if it is *just* a sum with no *further* claim to being a single item. This intuition is reflected in the common enough reaction that there is something *silly* about saying that there is an entity which is the sum of everything round, Nāgārjuna and everything which is vermilion.

The natural/artificial distinction is similar to, but not quite the same as, the reality/appearance distinction. It is similar in that the unity or oneness of an artificial unity depends on our individual or collective treatment of it as a unity, and so is, in that way, mind-dependent. However, there is a difference in that, as I have presented it, the

---

[29] In addition, we may well have *moral experience* which, if veridical, requires a freedom of action which is incompatible with Necessitarian Monism. This is a borderline case between ordinary and extraordinary experience.

[30] The distinction between a natural and an artificial unity owes something to Duns Scotus' theory of the grades of unity (see Grajewski (1944)) and to Hume's remarks in *Dialogues Concerning Natural Religion*, Part IX: "I answer that the unity of these parts into a whole, like the uniting of distinct countries into one kingdom ... is performed merely by an arbitrary act of the mind, and has no influence on the nature of things" (Hume (1969), p.59). But my chief debt is to David Lewis' distinction between natural and artificial properties. (Lewis (1983); Lewis (1984); Lewis (1986), pp.59-61.)

reality/appearance distinction concerns the intentional objects of *experience*. But we do not experience an artificial unity as a single thing. Rather we *think of* it as a single thing.

There are various different ways in which aggregates can have natural unity. It might be because the aggregate is made up of parts which are related in some way, but which are not related in this way to that which is not part of the aggregate. In that case the aggregate forms a natural *system*. Or it might be that the parts of the aggregate are properties, and that the aggregate is the sum of all the properties of a given item. Or, again, it might be that the parts of the aggregate are all the items to which a given property belongs. At the other extreme, an item has a natural unity if it has no proper parts. I submit that these are all different ways in which an item can have a natural unity. I further submit that the phrase "natural unity" is univocal. It is not that I ambiguously call various different ways of being a unity *natural*, it is rather that they are all different ways in which a unity can have a single quite striking characteristic. If you grant this univocity, then I am entitled to speculate that there could be a unity which, although natural, cannot be further explained or analysed. It is not the unity of a natural system, nor that of a sum of all the properties of a single item, not that of the sum of all the items with a single property. But neither is it the unity of that which is indivisible into parts. Such a unity I call a *primitive* unity. To say that various different things form a primitive unity is to say that they form a single thing, that the unity or oneness of the thing they form is not artificial, and yet there is no further account of *why* they form a unity. They just do.

Let me emphasize that Primitive Unity Monism is a metaphysical rather than an epistemological or hermeneutic thesis. I am not saying that to know or to understand we require some grasp of the sum total of things. That is a holistic thesis concerning the unity of knowledge or understanding. By contrast a primitive natural unity is a natural unity of what there is. It concerns *being* rather than *knowledge* or *understanding*.

Examples of a primitive natural unity would, no doubt, be useful. But there are no non-controversial examples. For what they are worth, here are two controversial ones. The first is the diachronic unity of a person. Think of a person as a temporally extended item which is an aggregate of person-stages. Then, presumably, this aggregate is a natural unity. Various reductionist accounts of personal identity would tell us that the unity of this aggregate is not a primitive one. But those of us who reject all such reductions, while still allowing of a distinction between person-stages, assume that the unity is primitive.

My other example is that of aesthetic unity. To be impressive a work of art has to have, among other things, an aesthetic *unity*. Is this unity merely the unity of a system? To be sure a painting, say, can be considered as a system of patches of colour. But it is not preposterous to suggest that supervenient on this system is an unanalysable primitive natural unity, and that we respond aesthetically to this unity. In that case, one of the functions of the artist is either to create or to reveal a (natural) unity. In this respect the artist is akin to the mystic, if the latter is taken to experience unity.

Primitive Unity Monism has one disadvantage and two advantages as an expression of Monism. Its disadvantage is that a primitive unity is mysterious, and mysteries are not to be multiplied more than is necessary. One advantage is that it, like Spinozistic Monism, is a Conservative Monism. For ordinary experience does not contain an experience of the lack of primitive unity. The other advantage is that, unlike Spinozistic Monism, it is an expression of Monism in terms of unity itself. It is thus rather closer to the slogan of Positive Monism, the assertion that all is one.

Finally I note what might be called Disjunctive Monism. This is the position that *some* version of Descriptive Monism is correct. But it is not specified which is. Since several of the disjuncts are themselves versions of Conservative Monism, it is itself a version of Conservative Monism. And clearly it is a weaker position than any other version. So *if* the pressure to accept Monism is merely due to the experience that in some sense all is one, then Disjunctive Monism would be the position to hold.

V

Thus far I have considered Monism to be a descriptive thesis expressing a purely theoretical, non-evaluative, belief. That is not to say that Descriptive Monism, combined with other premisses, might not have various implications regarding values. Typical of these extra premisses is the premiss that nothing which fails to exist can have (non-aesthetic)[31] intrinsic value, or the stronger premiss that nothing which is unreal can have (non-aesthetic) intrinsic value.

These extra premisses may either be extended to cover disvalue or restricted so as to concern value only. I suspect that it would be widely accepted that the non-existent cannot have (non-aesthetic) disvalue either. But there may be those who claim that the ideal can have disvalue but not value. This would provide motivation for the project of dissipating the ideal, so that only reality remains.

It should be noted that none of these consequences include the thesis that the one Reality is good. As far as the consequences of Descriptive Monism go, it might be indifferent or even bad. This ties in with my use of the term "sublation". I mentioned the disvaluation of what was previously valued. But I did not intend to imply that what was revealed as real would be valued. No doubt, in the vast majority of cases of sublation, the real is revealed as valuable. But that is a further feature, not part of the logic of sublation.

In addition to the evaluative consequences of Descriptive Monism, there are some versions of Monism which are not purely descriptive. First we may extend Madhyamika Monism to cover *all* intellectual distinctions including those of evaluations. I call this Ultraradical Monism. According to it the difference between the good, the bad and the indifferent would be due to our understanding, and so either ideal or illusory. This position could be expressed by saying that Reality is "beyond good and evil".[32]

Ultraradical Monism should not be confused with the thesis that the one reality has value-status, but a neutral one, neither good nor evil. Nor should it be taken for a stereotype Subjectivism. Furthermore, I suspect that it is more appropriate for the Ultraradical Monist to call the values assigned ideal, than to call them illusory. For surely they are still action-guiding, even for the Ultraradical Monist. But illusory values should not be action-guiding.

Ultraradical Monism is a descriptive-cum-evaluative thesis. I now turn to a much less ambitious thesis, which I call Evaluative Monism, which might well be conjoined with either a Spinozistic or Primitive Unity Monism. It is the thesis that only the sum total of things has intrinsic value. The parts then have value only because they are

---

[31] Kant claims that aesthetic value is independent of existence. See *The Critique of Judgement*, Part I, Section One (Kant (1952), pp.41-42).

[32] For example, Bradley writes "Goodness is an appearance, it is phenomenal, and therefore self-contradictory" (Bradley (1908), p.419).

required for the whole. This thesis should be distinguished from the weaker, sub-monist, thesis that the whole has an intrinsic value which is not simply the resultant of the intrinsic values of the parts. This sub-monist position I call the Organic Unity Thesis.

Evaluative Monism, while it could be based on Descriptive Monism, does not entail the latter. Admittedly, it is plausible that an artificial unity can have no value in addition to the value of its parts. This premiss and Evaluative Monism jointly entail that the sum total of things has a natural unity. Must this unity be primitive? I think not. A system could well have some special value over and above those of its parts and of the relations between parts, even without any unity other than that of a system. Compare, for example, a situation in which *A* and *B* love each other and so do *C* and *D*, on the one hand, with the situation in which *A* loves *B* who loves *C* who loves *D* who loves *A*, on the other. And ignore any value derived from the *awareness* of mutual love. Then it would be coherent, although controversial, to claim that the first situation has more value than the second, or even that the second has no value at all. In that case, although the occurrence of the relation of *mutual love* is nothing more than the appropriate occurrences of the relation of *love*, the value of the mutual love would exceed the sum of the value due to the occurrences of the relation of *love*.

There is another version of non-descriptive Monism which I call Identificational Monism. It is common enough for mystics to insist on the identity between themselves and what they experience. If this is intended as a report on an antecedently existing identity then it is indeed a descriptive thesis. But the concept of *self* is a slippery one, and perhaps there is a sense in which you are what you identify yourself with. For example, regardless of the precise metaphysical relation of the mental to the physical, people vary considerably as to the extent to which they *think of themselves* as bodies with a mental life, on the one hand, or as minds inhabiting bodies on the other. This is a matter of identification rather than identity. Yet again, it is possible to detach or disassociate yourself from pain, ceasing to think of it as a part or property of yourself.

There is, then, a position in which you identify yourself with the sum total of things. I am not sure whether it should be called a version of Monism or a sub-monist position. But, however it is classified, it is a possible construal of the claim that all is one. For by identifying myself with many things I unify those things - they become part of me. This unity is will-dependent. But that does not imply that it depends on the experience of the one who so identifies him or herself.

Other non-descriptive Monisms or sub-monisms could be developed. For instance, the *love* of the sum total of things could perhaps be called Agapic Monism. But I think that pointing to Identificationist and Evaluational Monism suffices by way of introducing some non-descriptive monisms.

To sum up: There are many ways of being one. And it is foolish to assume, unnecessarily, a stronger or more radical Monism than is required.

REFERENCES

Bradley, F.H. (1908). *Appearance and Reality: A Metaphysical Essay*. 2nd ed. London: Allen & Unwin.

Deutsch, Eliot (1969). *Advaita Vedānta: A Philosophical Reconstruction*. Honolulu: East-West Center Press.

Deutsch, Eliot & van Buitenen, J.A.B. (1971). Editors. *A Source Book of Advaita Vedānta*. Honolulu: University Press of Hawaii.

Grajewski, M.J. (1944). *The Formal Distinction of Duns Scotus*. Washington, D.C.: The Catholic University of America Press.
Hanson, N.R. (1958). *Patterns of Discovery*. Cambridge: Cambridge University Press.
Hirst, R.J. (1967). "Realism". In Paul Edwards (ed.), *Encyclopedia of Philosophy*. New York: Macmillan.
Hume, David (1969). *Dialogues Concerning Natural Religion*. New York: Hafner.
Inada, Kenneth (1970). *Nāgārjuna: A Translation of His Mūlamadhyamakakārikā with an Introductory Essay*. Tokyo: Hokuseido Press.
Jackson, Frank (1977). *Perception*. Cambridge: Cambridge University Press.
Kant, Immanuel (1952). *The Critique of Judgement*, trans. James Meredith. Oxford: Clarendon Press.
Lewis, David (1983). "New Work for a Theory of Universals" *Australasian Journal of Philosophy* 61: 343-347.
Lewis, David (1984). "Putnam's Puzzle" *Australasian Journal of Philosophy* 62: 221-236.
Lewis, David (1986). *On the Plurality of Worlds*. Oxford: Basil Blackwell.
McKeon, Richard (1944). Editor. *The Basic Works of Aristotle*. New York: Random House.
Murti, T.R.V. (1957). *The Central Philosophy of Buddhism: A Study of the Mādhyamika System*. London: George Allen & Unwin.
Spinoza, Benedict (1884). *Spinoza's Works*, Vol II. London: George Bell & Sons.
Zaehner, R.C. (1962). *Hinduism*. Oxford: Oxford University Press.

THE CONCEPTS OF SELF AND FREEDOM IN BUDDHISM

David J. Kalupahana

University of Hawaii at Manoa

Conception of Self

One of the most controversial views expressed by the Buddha is said to be that regarding the nature of the subject, the self or the human person who experiences the objective world. It is generally assumed that he, as a strong advocate of what is popularly known as the doctrine of "no-self" (*anattā*, *anātman*), is unable to give a satisfactory account of human action and responsibility, not to speak of problems such as knowledge and freedom. Such criticisms were directed at him by his contemporaries as well as by some classical and modern writers on Buddhism.

For some of his contemporaries, the continuity in the human personality can be accounted for only by the recognition of a spiritual substance different from the physical body (*aññaṃ jīvaṃ aññaṃ sarīraṃ*).[1] For some others, it required only a sensibly identifiable physical body (*taṃ jīvaṃ taṃ sarīraṃ*).[2] Those who opted for a spiritual substance could not depend upon the ordinary events or occurrences such as continuity in perceptual experience and memory in order to speak of a self because such events are temporal and changeable. Their search culminated in the conception of a permanent and immutable spiritual substance. Others who assumed the self to be identical with the physical body were not merely claiming that the self survives recognizably from birth to death and not beyond, but, like the behaviourists, also were denying the reality of conscious life. When the Buddha himself rejected the self as a spiritual substance, he was perceived as someone who, like the latter, advocated the annihilation of an existing conscious person.[3]

The Buddha had a difficult task before him, especially when he realized that the negation of a subjective spiritual entity will produce great anxiety in ordinary human beings.[4] However, he also felt that the appeasement of such anxieties had to be

---

[1]*Majjhima-nikāya* (abbr. *M*), 1.485 ff.

[2]Ibid.

[3]Ibid., 1.140.

[4]Ibid., 1.136.

R. W. Perrett (ed.), Indian Philosophy of Religion, 93–113.

effected without doing violence to critical thinking or without sacrificing significant philosophical discourse. The method adopted by him in dealing with the spiritualist as well as materialist views is evidently *analytical.* His teachings therefore came to be popularly known as a "philosophy of analysis" (*vibhajjavāda*). A truly analytical philosophy is generally believed to advocate no theories. Analysis is intended as a means of clarifying the meaning of terms and concepts without attempting to formulate alternate theories even if such theories were meaningful. However, the Buddha seems to have perceived analysis as a means, not a goal. It will be necessary to keep this in mind when we proceed to examine the Buddha's response to the Spiritualists as well as the Materialists. The response to the Spiritualists is more popular in the early discourses, for theirs was the more widespread view in pre-Buddhist India.

The Doctrine of Aggregates (*Khandha*)

To the question as to what constitutes a human person, the Spiritualists' answer was almost always: "There exists a spiritual self, permanent and eternal, which is distinct from the psychophysical personality." The Buddha therefore concentrated on the analysis of the so-called psychic personality in order to discover such a self. Every time he did so he stumbled upon one or the other of the different aspects of experience such as feeling (*vedanā*), perception (*saññā*), disposition (*saṅkhāra*) or consciousness (*viññāṇa*). If there was anything other than these psychic elements that constituted the human personality it was the body (*rūpa*).[5] Yet, none of these factors can be considered permanent and eternal. They are all liable to change, transformation and destruction. In brief, they are impermanent (*anicca*). As such, whatever satisfaction one can gain from them or through them will also be limited. Often such satisfaction can turn into *dis*satisfaction. Hence the Buddha looked upon them as being *un*satisfactory (*dukkha*).[6]

Arguing from the impermanence and unsatisfactoriness of the five aggregates, the Buddha was led to the conception of "no-self" (*anattā*) which represents the culmination of the analytical process. Even though his treatment is very analytical, its interpretation by some of the classical and modern scholars appears to take an absolutistic turn. Let us first examine the Buddha's conception of "no-self". His assertion regarding "no self" is presented in three separate sentences. Referring to each one of the five aspects of experience or aggregates (*khandha*) mentioned above, he says:

> "It is not mine. He is not me. He is not my self."
> (*N' etaṃ mama. N' eso aham asmi. Na m' eso attā*).[7]

All three statements do not necessarily refer to the aggregates. Only the first one does. Hence the subject is in the neuter form.

> "It is not mine." (*N' etaṃ mama.*)

What is denied in this first statement is the existence of a mysterious entity to

---

[5]*Saṃyutta-nikāya* (abbr. *S*), 2.3 ff.

[6]Ibid., 3.21 ff.

[7]Ibid., 3.19.

which each of the aggregates are supposed to belong. Thus, the Buddha's argument begins with the question of *possession* or *ownership*. The Buddha discovered that as a result of over-stretched emotions (*vedanā*), a natural process of sense experience gets solidified into a metaphysical subject that is henceforward taken to be the agent behind all experiences.[8] A feeling of possession arises not simply on the basis of one's interest, but as a result of one's desire. The Buddha is here arguing that in order to explain the functioning of body, feeling, perception, disposition and consciousness, it is not necessary to posit such a mysterious entity which is perceived as the *owner* of such experiences. Therefore, the statement that follows:

> "He is not me," (*N' eso aham asmi*),

refers directly to that mysterious owner negated in the first statement. This explains the use of the masculine pronoun (*eso*) instead of the neuter (*etaṃ*) of the previous sentence. It also makes a significant difference to his claim. He is not denying each and every conception of "I" (*ahaṃ*) which is associated with the aggregates but only the metaphysical presupposition behind the statement: "Such and such aggregate belongs to such and such self." The assumption that a certain term has one meaning only and no other was contrary to the Buddha's conception of language.[9] This is why the Buddha, after rejecting the *conception* of "I" adopted in the Brahmanical system, continued to use the very same *term* throughout his discourses.

Equally important for him was safeguarding the use of the term "self" without rejecting it altogether as absolute fiction. Hence the necessity for repeating the previous sentence replacing "I" (*ahaṃ*) with "self" (*attā*),

> "He is not my self," (*na m' eso attā*).

This accounts for the constant use of the term "self" (*attā*) in a positive sense in the discourses along with its negation, "no-self" (*anattā*). It seems appropriate to say that there are two different meanings or uses of the terms "I" and "self," one metaphysical and the other empirical. The metaphysical meaning cannot be accounted for by any one of the aggregates, and this is the thrust of his argument in the above context.

If a metaphysical self cannot be explained in terms of the aggregates, can a non-metaphysical or empirical self be accounted for by them? The general tendency among Buddhist scholars is to assume that the aggregates serve only the negative function of denying a metaphysical self. However, a careful reading of the early discourses will reveal that these five aggregates explained in terms of the principle of dependence (*paṭiccasamuppāda*) also perform a positive function of clarifying what an empirical self is. Thus, while the analytical process leads to the negative conception of "no-self", it is to be supplemented by the positive description in terms of dependence which provides meaning for the empirical conceptions of "I" and "self".

Body or material form (*rūpa*) is the first of the five aggregates. Since the theory of aggregates was intended to replace the spiritualist conception of "self", it is not surprising that the first of the aggregates listed is the body (*rūpa*). Allowing the physical personality such a prominent role, the Buddha was simply insisting upon the importance of *sensible* identity as one of the requirements for maintaining the identity of a human person, the "I" or "self". Of course this physical identity does not involve

---

[8]*M* 1.111-112.

[9]Ibid., 3.234-235.

any permanence even during the time the body survives, but it is a convenient way of individuating and identifying a person, even though it is not the only way, as it is for some modern philosophers.[10] In this connection it will be of interest to note that the early discourses do not speak of a human person without a body or material form (*arūpa*). *Arūpa*, the formless or the immaterial, is more often a state of contemplation that goes beyond the perception of materiality (*rupasaññānaṃ samatikkama*)[11] or a reference to one who has no idea of form (*arūpasaññī*).[12]

Feeling or sensation (*vedanā*) refers to the emotive content of human experience which is another important aspect or constituent of the personality. It accounts for emotions which are an inalienable part of a living person, whether he be in bondage or has attained freedom (*nibbāna*). Feeling consists of three types: the pleasant or the pleasurable (*manāpa, sukha*), the unpleasant or the painful (*amanāpa,dukkha*) and neutral (*adukkhamasukha*). Except in the higher state of contemplation (*jhāna*) characterized by cessation (*nirodha*) of all perception and the experienced or the felt, which is a non-cognitive state,[13] feelings are inevitable in experience. Such feelings can be twofold depending on how far they are stretched. In the most rudimentary form they can account for interest. If they are over-stretched they can produce continuous yearning or thirsting for the object.

Perception (*saññā*) stands for the function of perceiving (*sañjānātīti saññā*). As in the case of feelings, perceptions are also related to all other consituents of the human personality. Thus, they are not atomic impressions that are compounded into complex entities as a result of the activities of mind such as imagination. Each one of our perceptions constitutes a mixed bag of memories, concepts, dispositions as well as material elements. A pure percept undiluted by such conditions is *not* recognized by the Buddha or any subsequent Buddhist psychologist who has remained faithful to the Buddha. A pure percept is as metaphysical as a pure *a priori* category.

Dispositions (*saṅkhāra*) explain why there cannot be pure percepts. In the Buddha's perspective, this is *the* factor that contributes to the individuation of a person, and therefore, of his perceptions. Almost everything, including physical phenomena, come under the strong influence of this most potent cause of evolution of the human personality as well as its surroundings.

Indeed, the dispositions are responsible not only for the manner in which we groom our physical personality with which we are identified, but also in partly[14] determining the nature of a new personality with which we may be identified in the future. It is not merely the human personality that is moulded or processed by dispositions. Our physical surroundings, even our amenities of life, housing, clothing, utensils, and in a major way, our towns, cities, etc., our art and architecture, our culture and civilization, and in the modern world, even outer space come to be dominated by our dispositions. Karl Popper calls this the World Three.[15] For this very reason, the Buddha when describing the grandeur in which a universal monarch lived, with palaces, elaborate pleasure gardens and all other physical comforts, referred to all of them as dispositions

----

[10] Strawson (1959).

[11] *M* 1.174-175.

[12] *Dīgha-nikāya* (abbr. *D*), 2.110.

[13] *M* 1.175 where it is distinguished from *paññā* or wisdom.

[14] Ibid., 1.389.

[15] Popper and Eccles (1985), pp. 38ff.

(*saṅkhāra*).[16]

Epistemologically, the dispositions are an extremely valuable means by which human beings can deal with the world of experience. In the absence of any capacity to know everything presented to the senses, that is, omniscience, dispositional tendencies function in the form of interest, in selecting material from the "big blooming buzzing confusion" of sensible experience[17] in order to articulate one's understanding of the world. The total elimination of dispositions would therefore be epistemological suicide. Furthermore, the recognition of the importance of dispositions prevented the Buddha from attempting to formulate an ultimately objective *view* of the world.

Consciousness (*viññaṇa*) is intended to explain the continuity in the person who is individuated by dispositions (*saṅkhāra*). Like the other constituents, consciousness depends upon them for existence as well as nourishment. It is not a permanent and eternal substance or a series of discrete momentary acts of conscious life united by a mysterious self. Thus, consciousness, when separated from the other aggregates, especially material form (*rūpa*), cannot function. It is said to act with other aggregates if thoughts were to occur.

When consciousness is so explained, it is natural for someone to conclude that it is a substantial entity. This was the manner in which the substantialists responded to the Buddha. Buddha's response was that consciousness is no more than the act of being conscious (*vijānātīti viññāṇaṃ*).[18]

Thus, the analysis of the human personality into five aggregates is intended to show the absence of a metaphysical self (an *ātman*) as well as the presence of an empirical self that is dependently arisen.

The Theory of Elements (*Dhātu*)

While the theory of aggregates remains more popular in the discourses, there is occasional reference to the conception of a human person consisting of six elements (*cha-dhātu*).[19] The six elements are earth (*paṭhavi*), water (*āpo*), fire (*tejo*), air (*vāyu*), space (*ākāsa*) and consciousness (*viññāṇa*). Unlike in the theory of aggregates, here we find a more detailed analysis of the physical personality, and this may have served as a refutation of the Materialist view of a human person.

While it is true that the first four represent the basic material elements (*mahābhūta*) to which is added space, there is here no attempt to deal with them as purely objective phenomena. They are almost always defined in relation to human experience. Thus, earth represents the experience of solidity, roughness, etc.; water stands for fluidity; fire refers to the caloric; and air implies viscocity.[20] The Buddha recognized space as an element that is relative to the four material elements mentioned above. The fact that space is not generally included in the list of material elements led to much misunderstanding and controversy regarding its character. The scholastics, like some of the modern day scientists, believed that space is absolute, hence unconditioned (*asaṃskṛta*).[21] On the contrary, the early discourses recognized the conditionality of

---

[16]*D* 2.199.

[17]James (1979), p.32.

[18]*M* 1.292.

[19]Ibid., 3.239.

[20]Ibid., 1.421-423; see also Karunadasa (1967), pp. 16ff.

[21]See Karunadasa (1967), p. 93.

space, for the experience of space is dependent upon the experience of material bodies.[22] Just as much as the Buddha refused to recognize a psychic personality independent of the physical, he refrained from considering the physical personality independent of conscious life (*viññāṇa*) as constituting a complete human person.

Presenting an explanation of the physical personality in terms of material elements all of which are understood from the perspective of human experience, the Buddha was able to avoid certain philosophical controversies generated by a more objective physicalistic approach. Prominent among them is the mind-body problem. It is true that the Buddha spoke of the human person as a psychophysical personality (*nāmarūpa*). Yet the psychic and the physical were never discussed in isolation, nor were they looked upon as self-subsistent entities. For him, there was neither a "material-stuff" nor a "mental-stuff", because both are results of reductive analyses that go beyond experience. On a rare occasion, when he was pressed to give a definition of the physical and the psychic components by an inquirer who had assumed their independence, the Buddha responded by saying that the so-called physical or material (*rūpa*) is contact with resistance (*paṭigha-samphassa*) and the psychic or mental (*nāma*) is contact with concepts (*adhivacana-samphassa*), both being forms of contact.[23] Interestingly, such an explanation of the psychophysical personality where conscious or mental life is analysed in terms of concepts (for *adhivacana* literally means "definition") brings into focus the relationship between language and consciousness.

The description of the human personality in terms of the five aggregates as well as the six elements is an elaboration of the knowledge and insight referred to in the *Sāmaññaphala-suttanta*.[24]

> With his thought thus serene, made pure, translucent, cultured, devoid of evil, supple, ready to act, firm and imperturbable, he applies and bends down his thought to knowledge and vision. He comes to know: "This body of mine has material form, it is made up of the four great elements, it springs from mother and father, it is continually renewed by so much boiled rice and juicy foods, its very nature is impermanence, it is subject to erasion, abrasion, dissolution and disintegration, and there is in this consciousness of mine, too, bound up, on that does it depend.

The explanation of that insight in positive conceptual terms required the avoidance of two extreme views prevalent during his day. The negative conception of "no-self" discussed above referred to the views of the Spiritualists as well as the Materialists which were not only substantialist but also deterministic. While the Materialist view appears more like hard determinism, the Spiritualist version is a form of soft determinism with emphasis upon the knowledge of the eternal and strictly determined self as constituting freedom. In the backdrop of these different versions of determinism was a theory of indeterminism referred to as *yadṛcchā-vāda*.[25] The term *yadṛcchā*, which means "whatever way [it] falls on or happens", is generally translated

---

[22] *S* 2.150

[23] *D* 2.62.

[24] Ibid., 1.76.

[25] *Śvetāśvatara Upaniṣad* 1.2 (in Radhakrishnan (1953), p. 709).

as "chance occurrence". However, for the Buddha, whose philosophical explanation of events in terms of the principle of dependence (*paṭiccasamuppāda*) is based upon the experience of the "dependently arisen phenomena" (*paṭiccasamuppanna dhamma*), which in turn avoids any absolute guarantee of future events, the conception of "chance" is not something irrational and preposterous so long as it is not looked upon as something positive, comparable to the conception of "luck". The term *yadṛcchā* implied such a positive conception. However, in its Prakrit form, *yadicchā*, it could also mean "according to [one's] wishes", which, for the Buddha, did not necessarily mean indeterminism.[26] What was not acceptable to him was the positive conception of "chance" that implied indeterminism relating to the past as well as the present events. For this reason, he designated the conception of such occurrence as *adhicca-samuppanna* (lit. "that which has arisen, coming one on top of another", that is, causally unrelated).[27] Thus, the conception of the "dependently arisen" (*paṭiccasamuppanna*) is often presented as a middle standpoint between the fixed or the determined (*niyata*) and the undetermined (*adhiccasamuppanna*).

A human being who is dependently arisen is also referred to as a *bhūta* (literally, "become").[28] The Buddha refers to four kinds of nutriments that are essential for such human beings to remain human beings (*bhūtānaṃ vā sattānaṃ ṭhitiyā*) or for beings who are yet to come (*sambhavesīnaṃ vā anuggahayā*).[29] The four nutriments are as follows:

1. material food, gross or subtle (*kabaliṅkāro āhāro oḷāriko vā sukhumo vā*),
2. sensory contact (*phasso*),
3. mental dispositions or volitions (*manosañcetanā*), and
4. consciousness (*viññāṇa*).

These four nutriments, in fact, define what a human person is. The non-recognition of a human person independent of a physical personality is underscored by the Buddha's insistence that material food is the first and foremost nutriment. The second nutriment suggests that the human person is sensory-bound. Stopping of sensory contact for the sake of temporary rest, as in the state of cessation (*nirodha-samāpatti*), may be useful, but the elimination or suppression of it altogether would mean the destruction of the human person. The inclusion of mental dispositions or volitions or, what may be called, "intentionality" as a nutriment indicates the importance attached to the individual's decision-making or goal-setting capacity. It is this aspect of the human person that has led to much controversy among philosophers, and is generally known as the problem of the will. Tradition records that the Buddha abandoned the disposition to live (*āyu-saṅkhāra*) at a place called Cāpālacetiya almost three months before he passed away.[30] In other words, the continuity of human life is not a mere automatic process. The human disposition is an extremely relevant condition for its survival. Finally, consciousness, which is generally associated with memory (*sati*),[31] is needed to complete the human personality, for its absence will

---

[26] *Aṅguttara-nikāya* (abbr. *A*), 3.28.

[27] *Udāna* (abbr. *Ud*), 69.

[28] *M* 1.260

[29] Ibid., 1.261.

[30] *D* 2.118.

[31] Ibid., 3.134.

eliminate the capacity on the part of the human being to co-ordinate his life. Without it, the human being will be a mere "vegetable". These four nutriments are founded upon craving (*taṇha*), hence contributing to suffering, a process that is explained in the popular theory of the twelve factors (*dvādasāṅga*).[32]

The Theory of Twelve Factors (*Dvādasāṅga*)

Having rejected the *substantial* existence of an individual self, the Buddha did not remain silent so as to give the impression that the real person is beyond description. The discourse to Kaccāyana lays down in no unclear terms that the middle way adopted by the Buddha in explaining the human personality is "dependent arising" (*paṭiccasamuppāda*).[33] That process is outlined in terms of twelve factors. This twelvefold formula in its positive statement represents an explanation of a person in bondage, while the negative statement that immediately follows explains the process of freedom.

Enlightenment is a necessary precondition for freedom. Therefore, it is natural to begin explaining the life of a person in bondage as one who is engulfed in ignorance (*avijjā*).

As mentioned earlier, no concept becomes more important in a discussion of the human personality than the conception of dispositions (*saṅkhāra*). Following is the definition of dispositions available in the discourses:

> "Disposition is so-called because it processes material form (*rūpa*), that has already been dispositionally conditioned, into its present state." [This statement is repeated with regard to feeling (*vedanā*), perception (*saññā*), dispositions (*saṅkhāra*) and consciousness (*viññāṇa*).][34]

According to this description, while dispositions are themselves causally conditioned, they process each one of the five factors of the human personality thereby providing them with the stamp of individuality or identity. Thus, the most important function of individuating a personality belongs to the dispositions. The dispositions are an inalienable part of personality. They can function in the most extreme way, for example, in creating an excessively egoistic tendency culminating in the belief in a permanent and eternal self (*ātman*). This may be one reason why the Buddha considered the self (*ātman*) as a mere "lump of dispositions" (*saṅkhāra-puñja*).[35]

Thus, ignorance can determine the way human dispositions function (*avijjāpaccayā saṅkhārā*), either creating the belief in permanent existence (*atthitā*), or denying the value of the human personality altogether (*n'atthitā*).

The elimination of ignorance and the development of insight would therefore lead to the adoption of a middle standpoint in relation to dispositions. It has already been mentioned that the elimination of dispositions is epistemological suicide. Dispositions determine our perspectives. Without such perspectives we are unable to deal with the sensible world in any meaningful or fruitful manner. The Buddha realized that

---

[32] *M* 1.261 ff.

[33] *S* 2.17.

[34] Ibid., 3.87.

[35] Ibid., 1.135.

subdued dispositions provide for enlightened perspectives. Hence his characterization of freedom (*nibbāna*) as the appeasement of dispositions (*saṅkhāra-samatha*).

Thus the dispositions, while carving an individuality out of the "original sensible muchness",[36] also play a valuable role in the continuity of experiences. The development of one's personality either in the direction of imperfection or perfection rests with one's dispositions. These, therefore, are the determinants of one's consciousness (*saṅkhārapaccayā viññāṇaṃ*).

Consciousness (*viññāṇa*), wherein dispositions function by way of providing an individuality, determines the continuity (or the lack of continuity) in the individual's experiences. Therefore, it is sometimes referred to as the "stream of consciousness" (*viññāṇasota*).[37]

The Indian philosophical tradition in general, and the Buddhist tradition in particular, uses the term *nāmarūpa* to refer to the complete personality consisting of both the psychological and physical components. Although this psychophysical personality comes to be conditioned by a variety of factors, such as the parents, the immediate associates and the environment, the Buddha believed that among these various factors consciousness stands out pre-eminent (*viññāṇapaccayā nāmarūpaṃ*).[38] It is this perspective that induced the Buddha to emphasize the capacity of the individual to develop one's personality, morally as well as spiritually *in spite of* certain external constraints. Dispositions and consciousness, in combination, are referred to as "becoming" (*bhava*).[39] When a person, including one who has attained freedom, like the Buddha, is referred to as "become" (*bhūta*),[40] it explains the manner in which dispositions and consciousness function together in order to form his personality within the context of the physical environment. In this sense, neither the psychic personality or its achievements, like freedom, need be looked upon as being anomalous phenomena, as it was in the case of some of the pre-Buddhist traditions or with some of the more prominent philosophers of the Western world such as Immanuel Kant[41] or Donald Davidson.[42] The Buddha's is another way of resolving the determinism/free-will problem.

The next five factors in the twelvefold formula explain the process of perception and the manner in which an ordinary unenlightened person may react to the world of experience. As long as there exists a psychophysical personality and as long as its sense faculties are functioning, so long will there be contact or familiarity (*phassa*) with the world and feeling or emotive response (*vedanā*) to that world. These are inevitable. However, because of the presence of ignorance and, therefore, of extreme dispositional tendencies, the unenlightened person can generate craving (*taṇhā*) (or its opposite) for the object so experienced. Craving leads to grasping (*upādāna*) both for pleasurable objects and ideas. Grasping conditions becoming (*bhava*) and, if this process were to be continued, one would be able, depending upon proper conditions, to attain whatever status one aspires for in this life or even be reborn in a future life.

---

[36]James (1979), p.32.

[37]*D* 3.105.

[38]Ibid., 2.62-63.

[39]*A* 2.79.

[40]*D* 2.157.

[41]Kant (1985), p. 85.

[42]Davidson (1980).

This process of becoming (*bhava*), allowing for the possibility of achieving goals and satisfying desires, whatever they be, is not denied in Buddhism. Satisfaction (*assāda*) to be derived even from pleasures of sense (*kāma*) is admitted.[43] To begin with the lowest level of satisfaction, a person misguided concerning his goals may achieve the fruits (*attha*) of his action, say, by depriving another human being of its life. In his own small world, he may derive satisfaction (*assāda*) by doing so. But soon the unfortunate consequences (*ādīnava*) of that action could lead him to the greatest suffering and unhappiness. Instead of being a fruit (*attha*), it would now turn out to be "un-fruit-ful" (*an-attha*), hence bad (*a-kusala*).

At another level, a person may, without hurting himself or others, derive satisfaction from having a spouse, children, confortable lodging as well as being sufficient in food and clothing. These may be considered the satisfaction (*assāda*) derived from pleasures of sense (*kāma*). Indeed there is no unqualified condemnation of these satisfactions compared with the condemnation of the satisfactions derived from the destruction of human life mentioned above. However, the fact that these satisfactions are meagre and are not permanent and eternal and that they could eventually lead to dissatisfaction is recognized.[44] These are the satisfactions that one enjoys under great constraint. The nature of such constraints will be analysed in connection with the problem of freedom (*nibbāna*). The *final* result of all this is impermanence, decay and death, grief, suffering and lamentation. Constant yearning for this and that, thirst for pleasures of sense, as well as dogmatic grasping on to ideas - these are the causes and conditions of bondage and suffering. It is a life that will eventually lead to one's own suffering as well as the suffering of others, the prevention of which represents the highest goal of Buddhism.[45]

Through the understanding of this process, a person is able to pacify his dispositions and develop his personality (*nāmarūpa*) in such a way that, freed from grasping (*upādāna*), he would be able to lead a life not only avoiding suffering and unhappiness for himself, but contributing to the welfare and happiness of others as well. Getting rid of *passion* and developing a *dispassionate* attitude in life, the freed one will be able to cultivate *compassion* for himself as well as others. At the time of death, with ignorance gone and dispositions completely annihilated, his consciousness is described as ceasing without establishing itself in another psychophysical personality.[46]

Conception of Freedom

The analysis of freedom (*nibbāna*) and the happiness (*sukha*) associated with such freedom, independent of the conception of the human personality discussed above, as well as the problem of suffering, can lead to much misunderstanding. The first and the second noble truths relate to the problem of suffering and its cause, respectively. It is to be noted that even though all dispositions are considered to be suffering or unsatisfactory (*dukkha*), they are not looked upon as the cause of suffering. The cause of suffering is almost always referred to as lust (*rāga*), craving (*taṇhā*), greed (*lobha*), attachment (*ālaya*), grasping (*upādāna*) or hatred (*dosa*), aversion (*paṭigha*) and other

---

[43] *M* 1.85.

[44] Ibid., 1.85-87.

[45] Ibid., 1.341.

[46] *S* 1.122.

psychological tendencies.

Epistemological Freedom

The distinction between the first noble truth and the second is very crucial. It was pointed out that the dispositions are necessary conditions for human knowledge and understanding. Abandoning all dispositional tendencies is tantamount to committing epistemological suicide. It is a condition not only for knowledge and understanding but also for the continuity of the life process that began with birth. The reason for this is that dispositions are not purely mental (*mano*), they are physical (*kāya*), as well as verbal (*vacī*), that is, habitual bodily behavior and similarly habitual verbal behavior. Complete annihilation of these dispositional tendencies would be to stop the functioning of the physical organs and make it almost impossible for a human being to continue to respond to the world. The Jaina practice of not performing any new actions, except those mortifications intended to expiate for past actions,[47] would come closer to such an elimination of bodily and verbal responses. When such practices are carried out to their conclusions they can mean actual suicide.

Thus, allowing the dispositions to have complete mastery over one's knowledge and understanding will end up in dogmatism, while their annihilation is equivalent to epistemological suicide. Similarly, allowing dispositions to overwhelm one's behaviour can lead to bondage and suffering and annihilating the dispositions would mean complete inaction or even suicide. The middle standpoint recommended by the Buddha is the appeasement of all dispositions (*sabbasaṅkhārasamatha*), which is equivalent to freedom (*nibbāna*).[48] This would mean that freedom pertains to both human knowledge and understanding as well as human behavior. For the Buddha, the first form of freedom is a necessary condition for the second.

The term *nibbāna* (Sk. *nirvāṇa*) has a negative connotation. It conveys the same negative sense associated with the conception of freedom whenever the latter is defined as "absence of constraint". Epistemologically, a view or a perspective becomes a constraint whenever it is elevated to the level of an absolute (*parama*) or when it is looked upon as embodying the ultimate truth.[49] It is such absolutizing of views that contributes to all the contention in the world where one view is pitted against another, where one perspective is looked upon as superior and another as inferior.[50] The Buddha carefully avoided formulating any eternal truths (*saccāni ... niccāni*)[51] and provided a definition of truth that is non-absolutistic, thereby leaving room for its modification in the light of future possibilities. Yet the body of knowledge, the variety of perspectives that has remained functional, is respected as the "ancient tradition" (*sanātana dhamma*),[52] and is not discarded altogether. The Buddha was emphatic in stating that one cannot hope to attain purity either by clinging on to one view (*diṭṭhi*) or by having no-view (*adiṭṭhi*).[53] If he were to assume that there can

---

47 *M* 1.193.

48 Ibid., 1.167; *S* 1.136.

49 *Sutta-nipāta* (abbr. *Sn*), 796.

50 Ibid., 841.

51 Ibid., 886.

52 *Dhammapada*, 5.

53 *Sn*. 840.

be one view that will lead to freedom and purity, then only those who lived in India during the sixth century B.C. could attain such freedom, for that one view cannot be applied to any other context where the content of human knowledge will be different. Since he did not believe that there is one absolutely true view, he could claim that his conception of truth is not confined to any particular time or is atemporal (*akālika*).[54]

Freedom is sometimes referred to as a state of stability (*accutaṃ padaṃ*)[55] and one in which there is no fear from any quarter (*akutobhaya*).[56] These definitions have more epistemological than behavioural significance. How often is one's stability disturbed by a shattering of one's perspective cherished for a whole life-time? Whence can there be a greater fear than to think of the sun not rising tomorrow? Analytical knowledge intended to get rid of dogmatic views was symbolized in the form of a "diamond" (*vajira*).[57] The fear that is driven into the hearts of the dogmatic philosophers as a result of such analysis was symbolized as Vajrapāṇi, "the demon with the diamond in hand" (or the demon with the thunderbolt in hand).[58] Disruption of cherished views can bring instability and fear worse than what one experiences as a result of a loss of one's property or of those that are near and dear. It is for this reason that freedom is considered to be release from excessive involvement (*yogakkhema*).[59] With no such excessive involvement in perspectives and being able to modify them in the light of new information or different interests, a person can remain at peace (*khema*) and without fear (*appaṭibhaya*).[60] With fear gone one can enjoy unswerving happiness (*acalaṃ sukhaṃ*).[61] It is a stable happiness, not one that fluctuates.

Behavioural Freedom

In terms of behaviour, freedom as "absence of constraints" means the ability to act without being constrained by unwholesome psychological tendencies such as greed and hatred. It is not the ability to function without any regard for each and every principle of nature, physical, biological or psychological. While those physical, biological or psychological principles that are wholly determined by human dispositions (*saṅkhata*) can be brought under control as a result of the enlightened person's appeasement of dispositions, he still has to function within the context of a world where the principle of "dependent arising" (*paṭiccasamuppāda*) prevails. Thus, he may be almost immune to disease and ailments because of his healthy way of living. In the case of the historical Buddha, the only ailments he suffered seem to have been the after-effects of his severe self-mortification that he practised before enlightenment. Yet, the Buddha was unable to prevent the onset of old-age and decay and final death. The principle of dependent arising that brought about his death was

---

[54] *S* 2.58.

[55] Ibid., 3.143; *Sn* 1086.

[56] *A* 2.24; *Itivuttaka* (abbr. *It*), 122.

[57] *Thera-gāthā* 419.

[58] *D* 1.95; *M* 1.231.

[59] *M* 1.117, 347, 377, etc.

[60] *S* 4.175; *Sn* 454.

[61] *Therī-gāthā* 350.

initiated when he was born in this world over which occurrence he had no complete control. However, his recognition that if there were to be survival of the human person after death, and the individual's desire for survival (*bhava taṇhā*) being one of the contributory factors for such survival, compelled him to recognize the possibility of overcoming future rebirth. This is the result of his spewing out craving in the present life. It is primarily in the sense of being not reborn (*a-punabbhava*) that the conception of immortality (*amata*) is explained in the early Buddhist tradition.[62] Seen in the light of the above information, it would be necessary to reconsider the implications of the famous discourse in the *Udāna* used by almost every modern interpreter of Buddhism as evidence for an absolutistic conception of freedom (*nibbāna*). The discourse reads:

> Monks, there is a not-born, not-become, not-made, not-dispositionally conditioned. Monks, if that not-born, not-become, not-made, not-dispositionally-conditioned were not, no escape from the born, become, made, dispositionally-conditioned would be known here. But, monks, since there is a not-born, not-become, not-made, not-dispositionally-conditioned, therefore an escape from the born, become, made, dispositionally-conditioned is known.[63]

It is to be noted that the negations pertain to concepts referred to by the past participles *a-jāta*, *a-bhūta*, *a-kata* and *a-saṅkhata* indicating that they involve events that have already occurred. Their nominal forms: birth (*jāti*), becoming (*bhava*), making or doing (*kamma*) and dispositions (*saṅkhāra*) explain the world of bondage and suffering. Therefore, their negation is simply a negation of the bondage and suffering that a person experiences as a result of the process that has already taken place. Since part of that process involved human dispositions, the opportunity to restrain that process by the appeasement of dispositions is also recognized. In other words, it is an explanation of the possibility of freedom, not in an absolutistic sense, but in a limited sense of "absence of constraint". The fact that the passage refers only to those events which are predominantly conditioned by dispositions and not to those that are "dependently arisen" (*paṭiccasamuppanna*) seems to indicate that this is a reference to the freedom and happiness one can attain in the present life contrasted with bondage and suffering.

Behaviourally, freedom finds expression most clearly in the attitude one adopts towards life in the world. This is best illustrated by the simile of the lotus (*puṇḍarīka*).[64] Like a lotus that springs up in the muddy water, grows in it, and rises above it remaining unsmeared by it, so does one who has spewed out greed and hatred, even though born in the world, has remained in the world, yet is unsmeared by the world (*lokena anupalitto*). This world of experience is sometimes described in couplets: gain and loss, good repute and disrepute, praise and blame, happiness and suffering.[65] A person who has attained freedom is not overwhelmed by such experiences; hence he remains unsmeared by them, is freed from sorrow, is taintless

---

[62] *S* 1.174.

[63] *Ud* 80-81.

[64] *A* 2.37-39.

[65] *D* 3.260.

and secure.[66] This is not to say that he does not experience that world.

In order to remain unsmeared by the world of present experience (i.e., the third noble truth) by the elimination of the cause of suffering, which is greed or craving (i.e., the second noble truth), it is necessary to understand the problem of suffering (i.e., the first noble truth). Thus, the behaviour of the person who has attained freedom can be understood only in terms of the conception of suffering.

The Buddha's discussion of suffering focused on the immediate experiences without, at the same time, ignoring the past and the future. Therefore, his explanation of happiness should also concentrate on the immediate experiences without disregarding the past and the future. The general tendency, it was noted, is to look upon the birth of a human being as an event to be rejoiced over and the death as something to be bemoaned. However, the Buddha perceived both birth and death as suffering. Yet, the solution is neither to rejoice in both birth and death, nor to bemoan them both. The elimination of craving and the appeasement of dispositions enabled the Buddha to adopt a more sober attitude towards death. This attitude is expressed in the words of one of his chief disciples:

> Neither do I take delight in death nor do I rejoice in life. I shall discard this body with awareness and mindfulness. Neither do I take delight in death nor do I rejoice in life. I shall discard this body, like a hireling his earnings.[67]

It is possible to interpret this attitude as one of reckless abandon, bordering on pessimism. But the statement simply expresses fruitlessness of any attempt to avoid death when birth has already occurred. If death is unavoidable by a human being who has come to be born, either as a result of a previous craving for survival or due to circumstances beyond his control, what he ought do is neither to waste his time worrying about death and trying to find a way out of death in the present life nor to commit suicide, but rather to deal with the problem of immediate suffering with compassion for himself as well as others.

It is this attitude that is also reflected in the Buddha's advocacy of fearlessness in the service of humanity. Yet, it is necessary to distinguish this from conscious and deliberate self-immolation. Self-sacrifice or unrestrained altruism is neither a means nor a goal. However, if in the process of helping oneself and others to attain happiness, a person were to face unforeseen death due purely to circumstances, that is, due to dependent arising, and if it is *not something sought after (apariyiṭṭha)*, the Buddha's conception of life and death would allow for that form of death to be hailed as noble.[68] This qualification would necessarily rule out any decision on the part of someone to take a course of action knowing that it will certainly lead to death either of oneself or of others. This would be in complete contrast to the ideal presented in the *Bhagavadgītā*, as well as in some of the later Buddhist texts like the *Jātakas*[69] and the *Saddharmapuṇḍarīka-sūtra*.[70]

Thus, it is not only the abandoning of greed (*lobha*) and hatred (*dosa*) that

---

[66]*Sn*. 268.

[67]*Thera-gāthā*, 1002-1003.

[68]*S* 4.62.

[69]*Jātaka*, 3.51-56.

[70]*Saddharmapuṇḍarīka-sūtra*, XII.15.

constitutes freedom, but also overcoming confusion (*moha*). A clear understanding of the nature of life, even according to the limited sources of knowledge available to human beings, is a necessary condition for freedom and happiness. Thus, an enlightened person is one who has overcome the perversions of knowledge and understanding (*vipallāsa*).[71] The four types of perversions are mentioned and these pertain to perception (*saññā*), thought (*citta*) and views (*diṭṭhi*). They constitute the identification of

1. the impermanent with the permanent (*anicce niccan ti*),
2. the not unsatisfactory with the unsatisfactory (*adukkhe dukkhan ti*),
3. the non-substantial with the substantial (*anattani attā ti*), and
4. the not pleasant with the pleasant (*asubhe subhan ti*).

Here the subject represents the impermanent, the not unsatisfactory, the non-substantial and the not pleasant about which permanence, unsatisfactoriness, substantiality and pleasantness are predicated as a result of confusion. If the subject stands for what is experienced, and this would include the cognitive as well as the emotive aspects of experience, the so-called world of fact and value, bondage (*saṃsāra*) and freedom (*nibbāna*), then the predication that renders the identification a perversion (*vipallāsa*) would make it impossible for freedom (*nibbāna*) to be considered permanent, unsatisfactory, substantial and pleasant. Most interpreters of Buddhism would refrain from asserting *nibbāna* as a permanent and substantial entity at least as far as its cognitive aspect is concerned. However, often they would insist upon the permanence and substantiality of its emotive character. Thus, even if *nibbāna* is not an ultimate reality (*paramattha*) in an ontological sense, there is a tendency to look upon it as ultimate reality in the sense of permanent and eternal happiness, hence a sort of transcendental emotional experience that has nothing to do with the feelings and sensations of ordinary human beings.

The evidence that *nibbāna* does not constitute a permanent and eternal cognitive reality has been presented above. What remains to be discussed is the nature of the emotive experience, namely, the sort of happiness that is associated with the attainment of freedom or *nibbāna*.

Psychological Freedom

The term for happiness is *sukha* (etymologically explained as *su-kha*, meaning "having a good axle-hole", that is, a vehicle moving smoothly without any constraints). The early discourses refer to two forms of happiness. The first is worldly or material happiness (*āmisa sukha*); the term *āmisa* (derived from *āma*, meaning "raw") expressing the sense of raw sensual appetite.[72] The second is expressed by the negative term *nir-āmisa*,[73] hence understood as the mental or the spiritual happiness, which is to be contrasted with the happiness derived from the satisfaction of the five physical senses. For this reason there has been a general reluctance to associate this form of happiness with any feeling or sensation (*vedanā*) which is inevitable in sense experience.[74] The happiness of freedom is perceived as being outside the pale of sense

---

[71] *A* 2.52.

[72] *S* 4.235.

[73] Ibid.

[74] See de Silva (1987), pp. 13-21.

experience and, therefore, of any satisfaction relating to the senses. In this case the so-called worldly or material happiness (*āmisa-sukha*) becomes identical with whatever happiness is derived from following one's desires (*kāma-sukha*).

Yet, the Buddha does not seem to advocate the view that feelings (*vedanā*), and even sense experience (*saññā*), are necessarily evil and conducive to unhappiness. The suppression of all perceptions and whatever is felt (*saññā-vedayitanirodha*) was intended as a deconstructive method, never to be considered a goal in itself. Once the deconstruction process has taken effect, feelings and perceptions can serve their proper functions without running the risk of reifying either their cognitive content or their emotive component.

The fact that the person who has attained freedom continues to have experience through the same sense faculties that he possessed before, and that he continues to have agreeable (*manāpa*) and disagreeable (*amanāpa*) as well as pleasurable (*sukha*) and painful (*dukkha*) experiences is clearly admitted by the Buddha.[75] This means that there is no qualitative difference between the feelings of one who is in bondage and one who is freed. All that is asserted is that in the case of one who has attained freedom there is an absence of greed, hatred and confusion that is *generally* consequent upon sense experience. For this reason the distinction that is normally made between the material happiness (*āmisa-sukha*) and spiritual happiness (*nirāmisa-sukha*) needs to be reconsidered.

In fact, the Buddha does not appear to be condemning the so-called material happiness indiscriminately. The discussion of material inheritance (*āmisa-dāyāda*) and spiritual inheritance (*dhamma-dāyāda*) in the early discourses seem to support this view.[76] A disciple of the Buddha is represented as experiencing great physical discomfort as a result of fasting and refusing to eat some of the food left over by the Buddha, because he believes that a true disciple is one who should not be an heir to the material possessions of the Buddha. The Buddha does not consider this to be appropriate behavior. Material or physical comfort is not in itself to be abandoned nor condemned. Physical deprivation, according to the Buddha, is as disruptive of moral and spiritual development as is indulgence in physical comfort.

Thus, the so-called spiritual happiness (*nirāmisa-sukha*) need not be qualitatively distinct from material comfort or happiness. It is the cognitive and emotional slavery to the objective world that constitutes suffering and it is this slavery that is referred to as bondage, whereas freedom from such slavery constitutes the highest happiness (*paramaṃ sukham* or *nirāmisaṃ sukhaṃ*) that a human being can enjoy so long as he is alive.

To assume that this happiness is permanent and eternal would mean that there is a being, a person who is permanent and eternal who continues to have such experience. This is to admit a Supreme Being who, even if he is not the creator and preserver of the universe, is at least present during the past, present and future, for without him one cannot account for the experience of permanent and eternal happiness. The Buddha or his disciples cannot deny George Berkeley's conception of God and still continue to speak of permanent and eternal happiness. There cannot be the experience of such happiness unless one admits the existence of an experiencer who is permanent and eternal. All that he can assert without contradiction is that if a person were to follow such and such perspective and adopt such and such forms of behavior, he would be

---

[75] *It* 38.

[76] *M* 1.12-13.

able to experience such and such happiness comparable to that experienced by the Buddha and his enlightened disciples. The concepts of previous Buddhas and those of the future Buddhas can be meaningful only in such a context. Thus, non-substantiality (*anattā*) pertains not only to the world of bondage (*saṃsāra*) but also to freedom (*nibbāna*). The Buddhists were therefore prepared to admit that freedom as well as conception (*paññatti*) are undeniably non-substantial (*anattā*).[77] One of the discourses relating to freedom underscores this characteristic of freedom:

> Non-substantiality is indeed difficult to see. Truth certainly is not easily perceived. Craving is mastered by him who knows, and for him who sees there exists no something (*akiñcana*).[78]

Freedom is an experience. As an experience it can find expression in language, as any other human experience does. Hence it is a truth (*sacca*), or more specifically, a noble truth (*ariyasacca*), which also makes it a noble view (*ariyā diṭṭhi*).[79]

However, those who adopt a substantialist perspective regarding truth are prone to distinguish freedom from the person who experiences it. Attributing ultimate objectivity to freedom they create an elephant of enormous size about which they are unable to provide a reasonable description. Obsessed with their extremely restricted views and unable to touch the fringes, one person will explain the animal only as a huge pot and *nothing else*, for he has touched the animal's head. Another person insists that it is *none other* a winnowing basket, because he has felt only the animal's ear. Still another defines it as a plough share and *nothing else*, since he confined his experience to the animal's tusk. The search for ultimate objectivity has blinded them completely.[80] After creating something *more* they struggle with their descriptions whereupon language fails them. The inevitable result is the assertion that freedom is beyond linguistic description. The Buddha was striking at the root of the problem when he insisted that freedom, as any other phenomenon, is non-substantial (*anattā*).

Unanswered Questions

There are two sets of unanswered questions relating to the person who has attained freedom. One relates to the living person and the other pertains to the dead person. In both cases the term used is *tathāgata*, meaning the "thus-gone one". Unfortunately, it is this notion of the "thus-gone" that led to the emergence of many metaphysical issues relating to the conception of freedom because it is when a freed person is so described that questions such as "Where did he go?" can arise. It raises questions regarding the destiny of a person who has attained freedom. If he is living, then his life must be different from that of anyone else. If he is dead and is not reborn like anyone else, then he must be surviving in a totally different form of existence.

The two sets of questions are posed in the form of six propositions to which the Buddha does not provide answers. They are:

1. The soul is identical with the body. (*Taṃ jīvaṃ taṃ sarīraṃ.*)

---

[77] *Vinaya Piṭaka*, 5.86, *nibbānañ c'eva paññatti anattā iti nicchayā.*

[78] *Ud* 80.

[79] *D* 3.246.

[80] *Ud* 66-69.

2. The soul is different from the body. (*Aññaṃ jīvaṃ aññaṃ sarīraṃ.*)
3. The *tathāgata* exists after death. (*Hoti tathāgato parammaraṇā.*)
4. The *tathāgata* does not exist after death. (*Na hoti tathāgato parammaraṇā.*)
5. The *tathāgata* both exists and does not exist after death. (*Hoti ca na ca hoti tathāgato parammaraṇā.*)
6. The *tathāgata* neither exists nor does not exist after death. (*N'eva hoti na na hoti tathagato parammaraṇā.*)[81]

The first two propositions are generally considered to be references to the metaphysical notions of self (*ātman*) and not in any way related to the problem of the *tathāgata*, whereas the last four propositions refer specifically to the *tathāgata* "after death" (*parammaraṇā*). However, Sāriputta, one of the leading disciples of the Buddha, in response to the questions raised by a monk named Yamaka regarding the dead *tathāgata*, raises further questions and these relate to the first two propositions. They are as follows:

1. Is the *tathāgata* identical with the body? (This question is repeated in regard to the other aggregates, feeling, perception, disposition and consciousness.)
2. Is the *tathāgata* different from the body. (Same with regard to the other aggregates.)
3. Is the *tathāgata* in the body? (Same with regard to the other aggregates.)[82]

These questions, of course pertain to the living *tathāgata*. Yet the inquiry is not regarding the ordinary conception of *tathāgata*, but relating to one who exists in truth (*saccato*) and reality (*thetato*). In this latter sense, the explanation of the *tathāgata* goes beyond normal objectivity. It is an ultimately real *tathāgata*, one who is beyond change and impermanence, one who is permanent and eternal, that is sought for. In that sense, the *tathāgata* is not different from the soul or self (*ātman, jīva*) of the Brahmanical thinkers who believed that it is different from the ordinary human personality. The denial of such a *tathāgata* would be similar to the notion of self posited by the Materialists for whom the self is identical with the body.

Thus, the assumption of a metaphysical, yet living *tathāgata* is not radically different from the supposition of a *tathāgata* after death. For the Buddha, these are theories based upon the transcendence of all human perspective, hence views from nowhere. There is no way in which questions relating to them can be answered from the point of view of the human perspective. Therefore, he was not willing to make any statement, for any statement would commit him either to an assertion or to a negation relating to the content of the question. If the content of the question is such that it can neither be asserted nor negated, the Buddha finds the question itself to be metaphysical in the sense of being meaningless.

There is a belief that the Buddha observed "silence" on all these matters, the silence indicating his reluctance to make any statement because these are matters that transcend linguistic expression. While it is true that "whereof one cannot speak, thereof one must be silent", such silence is justified only if these questions continue to be raised in spite of the reasons given for not answering or explaining them (*a-*

---

[81] *M* 1.426.

[82] *S* 3.109-115.

vyākata). However, it must be noted that the Buddha was not simply silent when such questions were raised. In fact, he was vehemently protesting against raising such questions, because the questions themselves were meaningless, let alone the answers. Not only are they epistemologically meaningless and unanswerable,[83] but pragmatically irrelevant, for answers to these questions do not in any way help to solve the problem of immediate human suffering.[84]

What then is the Buddha's own conception of the living *tathāgata*? This is the conception of freedom with substrate left (*sopādisesa-nibbāna*). The description runs thus:

> Herein, monks, a monk is a worthy one who has destroyed the defiling impulses, lived the [higher] life, done what has to be done, laid aside the burden, achieved the noble goal, destroyed the fetters of existence, and is freed through wisdom. He retains his five senses, through which, as they are not yet destroyed, he experiences pleasant and unpleasant sensations and feels pleasure and pain. His cessation of craving, hatred and confusion is called the freedom with substrate left.[85]

The Buddha recognized the possibility of the survival of human beings, the condition for such survival being the excessive craving and grasping for life. Therefore, when he spoke of fredom as the absence of constraints such as craving, hatred and confusion, the Buddha was compelled to explain what happens to the *tathāgata at* death, even though he was reluctant to answer the question regarding the *tathāgata after* death. The description of freedom without substrate (*anupādisesa-nibbāna*) is intended for this purpose.

> Herein, monks, a monk is a worthy one who has destroyed the defiling impulses, ... [as in the passage quoted earlier], is freed through wisdom. Monks, all his experience [lit. things he has felt], none of which he relished, will be cooled here itself. This is called freedom without substrate.[86]

Speculation regarding the after-life of a freed person is dominant among those who are still obsessed with survival in one form or another but not among those who have attained freedom. Unsmeared by such speculations the freed person leads a life conducive to the welfare of as many people as possible including himself, and through compassion for all the world.

A controversy between a monk named Udāyi and a carpenter named Pañcakaṅga recorded in a discourse called "Multiple Experiences" (*Bahuvedanīya*)[87] throws light on the Buddha's conception of happiness. The carpenter believed that the Buddha spoke of two kinds of feelings or sensations: pleasant and unpleasant (happy and unhappy, *sukha* and *dukkha*). He included neutral feelings under the category of the pleasant or happy. However, the monk argued that the Buddha spoke of three

---

[83] *M* 1.438-489.

[84] Ibid., 1.426-432.

[85] *It* 38.

[86] Ibid.

[87] *M* 1.396-400.

varieties: pleasant or happy (*sukha*), unpleasant or unhappy (*dukkha*) and neutral (*adukkhamasukha*). When the matter was reported to the Buddha, he found fault with both for rejecting each other's views because both were right. In some instances, the Buddha has spoken of two categories, sometimes three, sometimes five, and so on up to one hundred and eight categories. These are all contextual (*pariyāya*).

The Buddha begins his explanation by referring to the normal forms of pleasant feelings or sensations, namely, the five strands of sense pleasure (*pañca kāmaguṇa*), for example, a material object cognizable by the eye, desirable, pleasant, liked, enticing, associated with the pleasures of sense and alluring. Yet the Buddha was not willing to accept these as the highest form of pleasantness or happiness (*sukha*). There are other forms that are more excellent and exquisite. He then proceeds to enumerate them one after another. These include the happiness or pleasant sensations associated with the higher comtemplations (*jhāna*) including the state of cessation of perception and what is felt (*saññā-vedayita-nirodha*). At this stage the Buddha anticipates that other teachers would recognize the state of cessation as "happiness in itself" and continue to speculate as to what it is and how it is. The Buddha was not prepared to identify happiness with one particular feeling or sensation. For him, happiness is contextual. Wherever (*yattha yattha*) it is obtained, through whatever source (*yahiṃ yahiṃ*) it is obtained, he was prepared to recognize happiness. In other words, he was not willing to speak of happiness in an abstract way. This was his anti-essentialist approach.

REFERENCES

Aṅguttara-nikāya (1885-1900). Ed. R. Morris and E. Hardy. London: Pali Text Society.

Davidson, Donald (1980). "Mental Events". In Ned Block (ed.), *Readings in Philosophy of Psychology*, Vol.1. Cambridge, Mass.: Harvard University Press.

de Silva, Lily (1987). "Sense Experience of the Liberated Being". In David J. Kalupahana & W.G. Weeraratne (eds.), *Buddhist Philosophy and Culture*. Colombo: N.A. Jayawickrema Felicitation Volume Committee.

Dhammapada (1900). Ed. V. Fausboll. London: Pali Text Society.

Dīgha-nikāya (1890-1911). Ed. T.W. Rhys Davids and J.E. Carpenter. London: Pali Text Society.

Itivuttaka (1889). Ed. E. Windish. London: Pali Text Society.

James, William (1979). *Some Problems of Philosophy*, ed. F. Burkhardt. Cambridge, Mass.: Harvard University Press.

Jātaka (1895-1907). Ed. V. Fausboll. London: Pali Text Society.

Kant, Immanuel (1985). *Foundations of the Metaphysics of Morals*, ed. Robert Paul Wolff. New York: Macmillan.

Karunadasa, Y. (1967). *Buddhist Analysis of Matter*. Colombo: Department of Cultural Affairs.

Majjhima-nikāya (1887-1901). Ed. V. Trenckner. London: Pali Text Society.

Popper, Karl R. & Eccles, John C. (1985). *The Self and its Brain*. New York: Springer.

Radhakrishnan, Sarvepalli (1953). *The Principal Upaniṣads*. London: George Allen & Unwin.

Saddharmapuṇḍarīka-sūtra (1912). Ed. H. Kern and B. Nanjio. St. Petersburg: Imperial Academy of Sciences.

Saṃyutta-nikāya (1884-1904). Ed. Leon Feer. London: Pali Text Society.

Strawson, P.F. (1959). *Individuals*. London: Methuen.
Sutta-nipāta (1913). Ed. D. Anderson and H. Smith. London: Pali Text Society.
Thera-therī-gāthā (1883). Ed. H. Oldenberg and R. Pischel. London: Pali Text Society.
Udāna (1948). Ed. P. Steinthal. London: Pali Text Society.
Vinaya Piṭaka (1903-1913). Ed. H. Oldenberg. London: Pali Text Society.

REFLECTIONS ON THE SOURCES OF KNOWLEDGE IN THE INDIAN TRADITION

Ninian Smart

University of California at Santa Barbara

The various ideas about the sources or instruments of knowledge in the different schools or *darśana-s* in the Indian philosophical tradition suggest questions to those raised in the Western tradition. The fact that there is a considerable overlap of theory and argument should not blind us to the ways in which certain key notions are so diversely conceived. The *pramāṇa-s*, which I shall here translate as "sources of knowledge" (Potter, though, for instance, prefers "instruments of knowledge"), not only include perception and inference, but also interesting variants such as negative perception (that is, the perception of the absence of something) and analogy or perceptual recognition based in part on prior verbal testimony. The most striking difference from typical Western treatments of epistemology is the inclusion of this last.

The inclusion of testimony or *śabda* is especially relevant to the philosophy of religion, because typically it refers to testimony about matters transcendental. It typically, that is, refers to *śruti* or authoritative utterance. It can thus be likened to the appeal, in the West, to revelation. Of course, "scripture" is rather differently conceived in the Indian tradition. For one thing, it is handed down orally. It is the words of the Veda as uttered rather than as written. Because in modern times we are accustomed to finding printed texts and to have been softened up by that compendious title "Sacred Books of the East", it is easy to forget that the idea of *śruti* is of a body of knowledge handed down by brahmins, specially trained in, among other things, the transmission of the Vedic lore. This is one reason why there emerges from times to time deep speculation about the nature of sound, as in the thought of Abhinavagupta. All this gives the idea of *śabda* a social placement which differs somewhat from notions of scriptural revelation in the West (though we may note that the Qur'ān is something recited as well as written and gaining something of its power from its heard impact). It is thus a bit misleading to think of *śabda* as involving scripture, with that expression's reference to writing. But for ease of language I shall use the term scripture and verbal testimony to refer to *śabda*.

The comparative or crosscultural treatment of philosophy already poses a deep question to the usual forms of the philosophy of religion. With the exception of a handful of scholars, such as William Christian, John Hick, Charles Hartshorne and myself, the philosophy of religion in the West still tends to get pursued in blithe

----

R. W. Perrett (ed.), Indian Philosophy of Religion, 115–123.

indifference to the challenges of other religious traditions, notably Hindu and Buddhist, but also Taoist, Confucian and others. The agenda is still dictated by liberal Protestantism, which has also deeply penetrated Roman Catholic thought in the last twenty-five years since Vatican II. In many ways this liberal tradition is fine. The strength of liberal Protestantism is that essentially it had certain things right. You cannot step back into a precritical phase. Even if you fashionably espouse post-modernism, this is by no means premodernism. But the danger of its Protestant roots and of its Enlightenment flower is ethnocentrism: an intellectual tribalism, in sort.

Now Indian discussions of the role of *śabda* are interesting, and can be connected up to some Western debates about revelation. Already there was deep division from quite early times in India over whether *śruti* was necessary. This in part turned on the verbal character of *śruti*. For the brahmins who transmitted the Veda the sanctity and power of the actual sounds were woven into their daily ritual existence. They experienced the performative nature of the Sanskrit. They were immersed in what might be called J.L. Austin with magic. Moreover, the efficacy of what they uttered in part depended on the meticulous mode of transmission. It is obvious to us that at some stage somebody must have put together the Vedic hymns and the Upaniṣads, for instance. But once the brahmanic social control had taken its grip, and once the words were seen as pristine and of indefinable antiquity, it was easier to think of them as authorless, *apauruṣeya*. It was possible to conceive of *śruti* as something quite without development. From this it followed that novelty of thinking was not really a good idea. The brahmin was there primarily to perform rites which in turn depended on the unerring transmission of scripture. The world of the orthodox or *āstika* was in important ways the opposite of our world. Our apparatus of learning and artistic endeavour implies that it is a virtue to change, that even old classics must be reinterpreted, that hermeneutics itself is creative, that genius does not arise from mere faithfulness to tradition. Perhaps such attitudes might be more prevalent among Buddhists (and we shall come to the *nāstika-s* in a moment): but they surely were not the attitudes of Hindu thinkers. It is true that in fact there came to be many variations in Vedanta, from Śaṃkara to Rāmānuja, and from Bhedābheda to Dvaita. This is testimony to the vitality of the tradition. But commentarial excellence itself implied the acceptance of that which was to be interpreted.

Fortunately, too, the *āstika-s* had the *nāstika-s* to contend with. A critical approach to the brahmin doctrine of *śruti* parallels the major problems of the appeal to revelation in the Christian or other Western traditions. Suppose we have arguments for the existence of an author of the world and of revelation, then there still remains the conceptual gap between this Author and the particular God of your tradition, such as Christ, or rather the Trinity. How does one bridge that gap? Then again, it may be that because of adherence to a belief in the unique and exclusive saving power of God you cannot appeal to the arguments of natural theology (one thinks here of Rāmānuja and Barth), why should you stick to one *śruti* rather than another? Does not the embracing of the New Testament or the Veda mean a mere arbitrary dogmatism?

It is obvious that reliance on scripture must depend on the thesis that in regard to transcendent matters - that is, matters which belong to a transcosmic sphere - knowledge must derive from some source other than ordinary perception or inference. So there may be some good argument that we need revelation. Even so, there still remains the important question as to which one of the putative revelations on offer is the true one.

The chances of a Barthian position seeming at all reasonable is in a cultural milieu where one religious tradition is dominant, and where the living alternative is some kind of non-religious atheism or agnosticism. In such a tribalistic environment, you can perhaps persuade others that some revelation is necessary if the Absolute is to intervene in human affairs, and there is basically only one revelation to offer. Likewise in the later development of Indian philosophy the *nāstika* possibilities could perhaps be ignored. Moreover, since verbal testimony or *śabda* typically referred to the Brahmanical scriptures, the Buddhists did not make appeal to *śabda* as a separate source of knowledge. This meant that the debate was pitched in somewhat different terms from those of a straight rivalry between revelations.

Now in order to adduce reasons for one revelation rather than another it becomes necessary to appeal to such criteria as the following: internal consistency or coherence; the good fruits of heeding the virtues and spiritual practices commended by one, compared to the fruits of following another path; the consistency of scripture with other knowledge, of history and science, and the relative inconsistency of other scriptures; the capacity of one revelation rather than another to resolve spiritual problems; the coherence of one rather than another with the nature of the ultimate as established on other grounds; and so on. Mostly these reasons involve going outside the putative revelations. In the case of moral fruits we are relying on intuitions as to the good (and we cannot confine ourselves to the virtues or fruits commended by one tradition rather than another, for in this case we would be comparing apples with oranges, and this does not resolve the further query as to which kind of fruit is superior). In the case of consistency with other knowledge, tautologically we go outside revelation to judge it. It is a common play: consider how fundamentalists are keen to claim that Biblical records have been confirmed by historical and archaeological evidence, etc. In the case of establishing the existence of the ultimate by other means (e.g. natural theory, philosophical argumentation, etc.) again it is tautological that we go outside of revelation. Now the fact that we have to go outside of revelation is significant from the following point of view: however we may hold that truths guaranteed by scripture are certain, we have to acknowledge that the arguments for the authoritative nature of scripture are not probative. They may impress, but they cannot be sure. The so-called proofs for God's existence are notoriously opposed by equally cogent reasonings. History can confirm something in scripture but nohow can it prove the spiritual or transcendental meaning of historical events. Fruits can commend a faith and with its revelation, but they cannot be clinching evidence. In fact, it seems to be the nature of worldviews that they cannot be proved. Given one worldview, we may have strong grounds, even proof: but of the worldview itself there is no proof. Another way of putting this is to say that the grounds for worldviews are soft. Soft grounds may be hospitable to certitude in the sense of committed sureness, but not public certainty.

I am assuming that worldviews are in some respects incompatible. They might not, after all, be rivals. There are those who think that all religions point to the same truth. This was a position powerfully presented by Swami Vivekananda and developed by others in the modern Hindu tradition. Similar positions can be found in the writings of Guenon, John Hick, Aldous Huxley and others; and it is a position which is attractive. Now this position could go with a worldview, such as Buddhism, which did not rely upon *śabda*, in that the confirmation of the truth or rightness of the *darśana* would derive ultimately from spiritual experience. In brief, experience could confirm, but not falsify, a worldview. Such a position might come from a standard, but not universal, Indian thesis, that *śabda* is a source of knowledge when one is being told about something by an *āpta* or expert. In this case the *āpta* would be an expert in spiritual matters. Now suppose that an *āpta* is an expert within the framework of treading a certain path or exercising his or her spiritual faculties within a given tradition of community. Then his expertise would relate to his supernormal perceptual powers -

his *yogipratyakṣa* for instance. Such perception by the expert would be grounds for accepting a certain account of the ultimate. But it would not be a ground for rejecting the deliverance of some other *āpta*, with a different training and religious milieu. In short, it would be a situation where *śabda* would confirm a proposition but not falsify it.

This would be a situation where all positions might thus be held to be true and from this it would follow that they were not contradictory. This form of argument is what perennialism usually uses, mystics being taken as the *āptas*, from their differing traditions.

This eirenic universalism has its discomforts, however; since often differing *darśana-s* involve contradictory imperatives. One does not escape contradiction by emphasizing the performative character of much of religious language. In fact it is notorious that however alike Jewish and Islamic ideas of God may be, the Torah and the Sharī'a are not entirely consonant, and thereby mandate different instructions. In so far as these regulations are laid on the different groups of people, peaceful coexistence becomes possible. But at least one side regards its injunctions as potentially universal. Similarly, the Mīmāṃsaka-s cannot escape contradictions with, say, the Buddhists, not only because in fact there are some limited factual claims which Mīmāṃsā needs to make in order to render appropriate their whole analysis of the Veda in terms of injunctions; but also because their imperatives on the front of the sacrificial are contradicted by the Buddhist rejection of the sacrificial mode of acting.

From the epistemological thesis about the softness of the grounds of worldviews and from the thesis that not all worldviews are compatible, we would derive a position which we dub "soft non-relativism". This assumes of course that we do not despair and let go of all worldviews, attempting perhaps some heroic blend of Habermas and Nāgārjuna.

There is, however, another reflection about the philosophy of religion which we might stimulate from the way in which Śaṃkara and the Advaitins treat of *śabda*. There are differing views which might be taken of the relation between language and experience. One might be described as the engineering relationship: that is, the language used might not be essentially descriptive in intent but rather designed to bring about a certain experience. This view can be found in various places, e.g. in Rinzai Zen and well brought out in Alan Watt's *The Way of Zen*, and in Ian Ramsey's theory propounded in *Religious Language*. Such a theory helps to make sense of the role of language in the case of the four great sayings of the Vedic revelations - *ahaṃbrahmāsmi, prajñānaṃbrahma, tattvamasi* and *ayamātmābrahma*. These cannot be construed literally, and they each employ distinctions between terms, such as *aham* and *brahman* and *tat* and *tvam*, which in the nature of the case is misleading. But because they convey in various modes the thought that two are one, a kind of monism is asserted; and this shakes up our intellectual grasp. We rise immediately (if suitably prepared) to "see" the higher truth. That seeing is not something dual: it is an immediate conscious experience. So we may think of the formulae of the four great utterances as having a kind of engineering function. As the Zen *koan* shakes us into *satori*, so the great sayings induce in us that immediate realization which is salvation: in the light of this self-luminous consciousness the world of ordinary experience is falsified. The great sayings point us to the higher state: and yet no change has occurred, since we only thereby realize what was true all along. So on this interpretation the higher truth of the Vedas turns out to be a kind of immediate experience.

Of course some important questions remain. Why should we be saddled with the baggage of the *karmakāṇḍa*? Why should we be saddled with the Veda? Why have to learn Sanskrit and listen to Brahmins? What if some other formulae could do the same trick? And if the final "truth" is ineffable, why hitch to it the language of Brahman? Negatively: why not go for the *śūnyavāda* of Nāgārjuna? In short, Śaṃkara's whole procedures start from the assumption of the revealed and authoritative nature of the *śruti* (and *smṛti*): and yet in the long run he destroys the authority of *śruti*.

If we do not take the relation between language and experience to be an engineering one, but think that experience is somehow descriptive of some reality, then somewhat different problems arise. For it is clear that even if we confine ourselves to mystical or contemplative experience (and presumably this is what *yogipratyakṣa* refers to) there are wide divergences of systems of ideas of reality. How do we account for the divergent shapes of the differing versions of Vedānta? One possibility is to find at least a partial answer through the weight attached to non-mystical forms of religion, most notably *bhakti* religion. Then Rāmānuja's Viśiṣṭādvaita becomes intelligible. For while he was loyal to tradition, which undoubtedly contained the scriptural endorsement of some kind of non-dualism, he was anxious that Tamil *bhakti* life (and poetry) should not be sacrified. This is what he saw Śaṃkara's non-dualism doing. In the last resort, non-dualism destroys the meaningful gap between heaven and earth which supplies the ambience of *bhakti*. The loving Lord disappears in the light of non-dual realization. Likewise Dvaita was keen to stress the religion of Viṣṇu (though Madhva got over the problem of the great sayings by rewriting them with a buried - or rather elided - negation). *Atat tvam asi* was an interesting way of reading the text. So we could explain the variation of intepreting Brahman through a differing weighting of the importance of *bhakti*. Though Śaṃkara supposedly wrote devotional literature he was not in the end loyal to it as the ultimate relationship to the ultimate. And to add to the nuances, there was also the religion of the Brahmins to take into account - a religion of sacrifice and ritual technique. We can, for instance, understand that the main religious position which Rāmānuja wished to express was a devotional one, but see, too, that he wished to make room not just for the Hindu contemplative tradition but ritual orthodoxy as well.

Now this suggests an implication of the concept of *śabda* which we would do well to bear in mind: much of *śabda* was, as we have noted, imperatival. Rituals were its typical consequence as well as being the home which the sacred sounds most comfortably occupied. So *śruti* was after all orthopraxy. Right ritual conduct was implicit in accepting *that* form of revelation. In fact the very word "revelation" which is most often used to translate *śabda* is misleading, in that it suggests the self-unveiling of the ultimate: a performance with cognitive effects. *Śruti* has primarily pragmatic effects. It is summed up in *Om*, and *Om* is a reverberation and a mini-ritual in itself. We can of course speculate as to why Rāmānuja wished to make South Indian piety orthodoxly brahminical, and to wed the Āḷvāras to the sacred rituals. He need not have made this synthesis. It was a heroic errand which he ran, and given his social milieu it was very constructive and part of the whole process of Sanskritization in South India. Rāmānuja did not seriously attempt to defend his procedures outside of the milieu of Brahmanical debate. By then the Buddhists had evaporated and the Jainas were not what they had been.

Despite their grammatical wizardry Indian thinkers had not attained to modern critical scholarship. Theologians such as Rāmānuja had to accommodate to the nitty-gritty of the Vedic revelations and indeed *smṛti* too. Coherent accounts of the *Gītā* had to be given. Now we are more cavalier: for liberal scholarship has undermined the old revelatory holism. To some degree interpretation of scripture becomes a matter of free-ranging choice. We do not expect consistency from documents put together by various hands. Scriptures cease to have the old authority but become source-material to be used by us in varying fashions: necessary, perhaps for knowledge of ancient religion, but not dictating what we ought to believe. That at least is a common view among moderns and Westerners especially. Under this disintegration of minute authority, adherence to the main messages of the tradition means bringing a number of tests to scripture. They become sources of certain ancient insights, repositories of ancient history, treasuries of putative wisdom, and often more in need of backing from outside than of influencing what lies outside them. They import authority rather than export it.

Of course *śabda* could also mean ordinary verbal testimony without special reference to that which is transcendent. This is a suggestive notion. For it points to something that has somewhat skewed much Western epistemology. In some classical writings on the subject the assumption has been that knowledge is something belonging essentially to the individual. How does the individual know that his senses are not deceiving him? But though individual knowledge is of some interest it is not from a practical point of view anywhere nearly so important as public knowledge. It is obvious that much of the philosophy of science, especially since it took a sociological turn, is concerned with the cooperative and large scale development of science. Naturally, we are interested in individuals as discoverers of solutions to problems that the progress of science generates: but such individuals have their significance within the wider framework. Given then that knowledge is a communitarian enterprise, then some role could be played in its development by *śabda*. Verbal testimony is the complex deposit of more or less established knowledge and outstanding problems with which a person working in a given field is confronted. The way in which knowledge is represented as simply depending on *anumāna* and *pratyakṣa* does not cater for the communitarian aspect of knowledge. So it is an advantage that India has taken *śabda* seriously.

I have tried to place it in the context of science, which at any one time presents us with a growing and complex tradition posing certain problems: it is at this interface between the past, presented by communitarian *śabda*, that discovery takes place. It is also the tradition as it stands at any one time which is presented as knowledge, in textbooks and lecture-theatres. Now, of course, what is *śabda* is falsifiable, or subject to *bādhitva*, to use an Indian term, in the light of controlled perception, viz., experimental evidence. The sources of knowledge cannot be regarded as absolute, but subject to correction by one another.

We might now look at the religious cases in the light of the example of science. Do we have, in religions, a rather different form of communitarian tradition? As I have already pointed out, Brahmanical tradition particularly does not in theory allow of genuine innovation, and the *śruti* is to be handed down absolutely word-perfect. If there are apparent innovations - such as new varieties of Vedānta, they have to be justified as presenting the essence of what is ancient. Even in the Buddhist case, there is the attempt by Mahāyāna innovators to present their new doctrines as flowing originally from the mouth of the Buddha himself. That famous formula at the start of discourses, *evam me sutam*, suggests deep continuity to the voice of the Buddha himself. The *sutam* seems uncommonly like *śruti*.

Does this imply that it is not possible to have a critical tradition? This is a famous topic in Karl Popper's *Conjectures and Refutations*. It seems to me that there are two ways to vary a tradition, one of which is both liberal and conservative at the same time. One way is to use analogy: if *X* was the teaching in context *C1*, what should be the teaching in context *C20?* Presumably some great adaptation of *X*. Such analogical application of the idea of the original intention of the tradition is summed up under the notion of *upāya* in the Buddhist tradition - the skill in means which adapts the teaching to changed psychological and social conditions. (This, by the way, is sometimes connected to the concept - prominent in one way or another in all the traditions of the Subcontinent, that the message gets progressively obscured, and the human condition therefore deteriorates, the further we get from the source of revelation.) The project of varying the formulation and practice of a tradition in accordance with change reflects the fact that hermeneutically an utterance which literally stays the same in a changed context changes its meaning: so the only way to stay the same is to change the utterance. This perception means that a liberal interpretation may be the most conservative one, provided it has got its analogy right. But such a case of *upāya* is not really available if you think of sacred sound as everlasting and changeless, with meaning intrinsic to it. So a major assumption of Hindu *śabda*, in the sacred context at least, is something which we would have to reject today, now that we have had a clearer grasp of the evolution of language.

The other way to vary a tradition is to accept frankly that there is an evolution of doctrine, a building up of ideas which leads to a richer knowledge of the Ultimate. In practice the analogical method and the evolutionary model are not clearly distinguished. Both involve a degree of revisionism in the formulation of the tradition. Indeed it could be that pieces of the tradition are dropped simply because they are seen to rest on false assumptions, e.g. in cosmology or as to the point of punishment. So perhaps it is best to think of both kinds of variation of tradition as being revisionary. The Popperian question as to whether it is possible to have a critical theory of tradition can be answered affirmatively: yes, we can view our tradition as something to be critically revised. This is a great limitation upon the acceptance of *śabda* simply as a source of knowledge.

I noted earlier that the *evam me sutam* formula in Buddhist sutras is close to the notion of *śruti*. If we appeal to someone's authoritative *yogipratyakṣa*, as in the Buddhist tradition, we still have to make use of words, and so surely *śabda* as a source of knowledge ought to be accepted in the Buddhist schools. It is interesting that Zen or Ch'an or Dhyāna Buddhism actually has what may be an ancient idea, that transmission is by direct transmission of experience from master to pupil, in an historical chain, going back to the Buddha himself. This notion takes the repudiation of *śabda* very seriously, and links up too with Buddhist traditions about the distorting character of language. There is throughout Buddhism a deep ambivalence about the nature of the Dharma - as to whether it can really be put into words: yet, of course, it was a main task of the Saṅgha to maintain the integrity of the Dharma seen as something which could be recited in words. If Zen direct transmission is what is operative, then the Dharma as spoken is part of the conventional and social apparatus which engineers the conditions for attaining enlightenment.

Different religions have different roles for historical facts to play. Obviously, where history is regarded as important, as in the Christian idea of salvation history (which, of course, goes beyond the facts of history, but yet depends on them in some degree), verbal testimony is the primary source of knowledge. Indian texts do not say much about historical knowledge. The notion of collective memory (e.g. that the Irish or the Armenians have long memories) really incorporates *śabda*, since no one literally remembers the Battle of the Boyne, but the "memory" is handed down by verbal transmission. This represents another vital context for thinking seriously about *śabda* as a source of knowledge. Critical history might then be regarded as a modern sophisticated mode of sifting *śabda* so that we are not deceived by the confusions and falsehoods which are often bound up with verbal transmission. Naturally, in all this wider metaphysical or valuational elements cannot simply be regarded as acceptable, though such elements are vital to the interpretation of history as revelatory.

In view of my earlier argument for soft non-relativism, it would seem that appeal to tradition, e.g. historical tradition, can be regarded at best as affirming what may be called a hypothetico-deductive position, which we may adopt in order to test its fruits, etc. Since the role of a worldview is typically to sketch a map of the world which will help you to navigate to the haven of liberation, a degree of pragmatism must surely enter into the testing of positions.

The basis of the Buddhist drawing on the *evam me sutam* is that the Buddha himself had abnormal, superior knowledge, through his capacity for perceiving the truth existentially and for reasoning about the nature of the world in the light of his inner experience. As with Zen, we have an appeal to experience. And this raises issues about *pratyakṣa* or perception. It is clear that the idea of common perception is stretched here, beyond the five (or counting *manas* the six) senses. There is a question as to whether in counting merely the five senses, Western empiricism has not imposed too tight a restriction. What about religious experiences, such as that of the numinous (as in Rudolf Otto's classic work) and mystical or inner experience (written about by a number of writers lately, particularly in the volumes edited by Steven Katz)? Or is it that the crucial sort of religious experience is a case of seeing as (a view followed by such writers as John Hick and James Richmond)? The Jain query as to whether experience of God is brought about by the belief or the belief by the experience is pertinent here. In the Indian case the chief understanding of stretched experience, beyond the senses, is that of the mystical or inner type. There are other kinds of experience, e.g. shamanistic, conversions and so on.

The notion of "seeing as" is obviously important, but it has the same limitations as *śabda*: it may be traditional to see the world as displaying God's handiwork, and that handiwork then becomes grounds for belief in God. But it is easy to think how a given slant on the world is subjective, even if collectively so. The greater challenge to a humanistic interpretation of the world is the range of religious experience which does not seem so indebted to a tradition in the way it is seen to confirm a position. It should be noted, however, that the modern model of perception gives the brain an active role, and so we as perceiving animals impose order upon the world around us, programmed no doubt by a long evolutionary process. Is cultural conditioning so very far removed from evolutionary conditioning?

I shall not in this paper reflect on Indian accounts of inference; but enough has been said to show that some interesting questions are raised by Indian epistemology, because India has carved the cake rather differently from the West. Particularly in the philosophy of religion there are challenges and yet also parallels to more traditional ways of doing things in the West. The notion of *śabda* in particular is one which is deserving of further exploration and evaluation.

REFERENCES

Almond, Phillip (1984). *Rudolf Otto: An Introduction to his Philosophical Theology.* Chapel Hill: University of North Carolina Press.

Baillie, John (1956). *The Idea of Revelation in Recent Thought.* New York: Columbia University Press.

Barth, Karl (1955-59). *Church Dogmatics*, trans. G.W. Bromley & T.F. Torrance. 4 vols. Edinburgh: T. & T. Clark.

Dasgupta, S.N. (1922-55). *A History of Indian Philosophy.* 5 vols. Cambridge: Cambridge University Press.

Dumoulin, Heinrich (1963). *A History of Zen Buddhism.* New York: Pantheon.

Eliade, Mircea (1964). *Shamanism.* London: Routledge & Kegan Paul.

Guenon, René (1925). *L'Homme et son Devenir Selon le Vedānta.* Paris: L'Editions Traditionelles, 1981.
Hick, John (1983). *Philosophy of Religion.* 3rd ed. Englewood Cliffs: Prentice-Hall.
Katz, Steven T. (1978). Editor. *Mysticism and Philosophical Analysis.* London: Sheldon Press.
Larson, Gerald J. & Bhattacharya, R.S. (1987). Editors. *Sāṃkhya: A Dualist Tradition in Indian Philosophy.* Princeton: Princeton University Press.
Otto, Rudolf (1928). *The Idea of the Holy*, trans. J.W. Harvey. Harmondsworth: Penguin, 1959.
Popper, Karl (1963). *Conjectures and Refutations.* London: Routledge & Kegan Paul.
Potter, Karl H. (1977). Editor. *Indian Metaphysics and Epistemology.* Princeton: Princeton University Press.
Potter, Karl H. (1981). Editor. *Advaita Vedānta up to Śaṃkara and His Pupils.* Princeton: Princeton University Press.
Proudfoot, Wayne (1985). *Religious Experience.* Berkeley: University of California Press.
Ramsey, Ian T. (1957). *Religious Language.* London: SCM Press.
Richmond, James (1970). *Theology and Metaphysics.* London: SCM Press.
Smart, Ninian (1964). *Doctrine and Argument in Indian Philosophy.* London: Allen & Unwin.
Wainwright, William J. (1978). *Philosophy of Religion: An Annotated Bibliography of Twentieth-Century Writings in English.* New York: Garland.
Watts, Alan (1957). *The Way of Zen.* New York: Pantheon.
Zaehner, R.C. (1961). *Mysticism Sacred and Profane.* London: Oxford University Press.

OMNISCIENCE IN INDIAN PHILOSOPHY OF RELIGION

Roy W. Perrett

Massey University

The concept of omniscience is prominent in both Western and Indian philosophy of religion. A comparison of the different treatments accorded the notion in each tradition reveals some interesting parallels and divergences. I begin with the traditional Western treatments of omniscience as one of God's attributes and then go on to offer a general characterization of the concept. Utilizing this characterization, I discuss some traditional Indian arguments and theories about omniscience (*sarvajñatva*) and try to locate them in their religio-philosophical context.

I

What is it for a being to be omniscient? Recent Western treatments of the concept have tended to focus on omniscience as one of the attributes of God, for the traditional Biblical belief that God is all-knowing is often expressed as the claim that he is omniscient.[1] But to present an acceptable definition of divine omniscience is a rather more difficult task than it might at first appear. Consider, for example, the following candidate:

(1) *A* is omniscient at *t* if and only if for every proposition *p*, at *t A* knows that *p*.

This is inadequate because if *p* is a false proposition, then nobody can *know* it. It might seem easy enough to rectify this defect by introducing:

(2) *A* is omniscient at *t* if and only if for every true proposition *p*, at *t A* knows that *p*.

However this definition fails to exclude the possibility of an omniscient being believing many false propositions in addition to all the true ones. We can eliminate that possibility by the reformulated definition:

---

[1]Recent discussions include: Geach (1977), Ch.3; Swinburne (1977), Ch.10; Kenny (1979), Chs. 2-4; Davis (1983), Ch.2; Kvanvig (1986).

R. W. Perrett (ed.), Indian Philosophy of Religion, 125–142.

(3) *A* is omniscient at *t* if and only if for every true proposition *p*, at *t A* knows that *p*; and for every false proposition *q*, at *t A* does not believe *q*.

Even then a further refinement may still be needed. For suppose it is the case that (as certain philosophers argue) the truth-value of some propositions changes over time. This would mean that the facts an omniscient being knows would also change over time. Perhaps the simplest way to handle this possibility is to modify the definition to:

(4) *A* is omniscient at *t* if and only if for every proposition *p* that is true at *t*, *A* knows *p* at *t*; and for every proposition *q* that is false at *t*, *A* does not believe *q* at *t*.[2]

Let us suppose for the moment that omniscience can be defined by (4) or even (3). Two questions now present themselves: (i) can the concept thus defined be instantiated; and (ii) can the concept thus defined be instantiated *by God*? Firstly, consider the following argument for the impossibility of omniscience.[3] Let *X* be an omniscient being and *Y* be the totality of facts (which *X* would have to know fully in order to be omniscient). Now in order to be omniscient *X* has to know that he is omniscient. But to know that he is omniscient *X* has to be certain there are no facts beyond those he knows. That is, he needs to know something besides *Y*: viz. *Z*, which is the truth of the negative existential statement, "There are no facts unknown to me". Is it possible to know *Z*?

Apparently not. True, in limited factual situations we can know the truth of some negative existential statements (e.g. "There is no elephant in this room at present"). But *Z* is a rather different sort of statement, for it makes an existential claim that is completely uncircumscribed, spatially and temporally. Knowing *Z* is more like knowing it is true no centuars exist *anywhere*, at *any time*. Now if *X* is to know he is omniscient he has to ascertain that the limit of the known is the limit of the factual. All he can do, however, is arrive at the limit of the known; he cannot ascertain that no further facts exist beyond this limit. Moreover, it is entirely conceivable that there may be such facts. Thus *X* cannot know that he is omniscient and hence cannot be omniscient. That is, there can be no such thing as an omniscient being.

It is obvious that this argument depends crucially on the claim that *Z* cannot be known (even if *Y* can). And the argument for that claim in turn rests upon the supposition that *Z* is *something besides Y*. But this latter supposition is unfounded. For if it is true that *X* knows *Y*, then it is a fact that *X* knows *Y*. Hence if *X* is omniscient and knows all the facts, *X* knows that *X* knows *Y*. In other words, *Z* is *included in Y*. Nor will it help to argue instead that *X* can know neither *Y* nor *Z* on the grounds that to do so *X* would have to set a limit to the knowable. In order for *X* to be omniscient all that is necessary is that there *are* no facts unknown to him; not that it is *inconceivable* to *X* that there are facts unknown to him.[4] This argument for the logical impossibility of an omniscient being, then, fails.

However, even if it is logically possible for an omniscient being to exist it still remains to be shown that God could be such a being. In particular, it may be that some of God's traditional attributes are incompatible with omniscience. Consider, for

---

[2]This is essentially the form of definition favoured in Davis (1983), p.37.

[3]Cf. Puccetti (1963).

[4]Cf. Davis (1983), p.38.

instance, the divine attribute of omnipotence. Suppose God is both all-powerful and all-knowing. His omniscience presumably includes knowledge not just of the past and present, but also of the future. But if he knows the future then surely the future is already determined. And if the future is determined, then surely nobody has free will. But if nobody has free will, then nobody is omnipotent. Thus God cannot be both omniscient and omnipotent.

Various responses to this argument are possible. Firstly, one might deny the inference from determinism to lack of free will by embracing compatibilism. Secondly, one might argue that God is timeless and hence it is not the case that he *fore*knows anything. Rather he knows it as it happens, but there is no moment at which he does not know it. Thus he is omniscient in the sense that all things are present to him, simultaneously, as they happen. Thirdly, one might deny that there are any true propositions about future contingents and hence assert there is nothing for God to foreknow. Finally, one might deny that omniscience involves knowledge of those things which are not yet fixed, which depend on the future free actions of free agents. Hence an omniscient being can know all the possible futures that may develop, but which particular future will be actualized is not a candidate for knowledge.

Each of these options has its supporters and its critics. Thus the literature on compatibilism, theological and non-theological, is vast; there is a venerable tradition for the thesis that God is timeless; and anti-realism about the future has its distinguished advocates, both ancient and modern. Common ground to these first three approaches, however, is an acceptance of the unrestricted scope of divine omniscience. On such a conception of God's omniscience if it is granted that there are truths about the future, then God must indeed have complete knowledge of all future events. Given this premise, the problem is how to avoid the conclusion that no omnipotent being can exist. This is done by denying that God's foreknowledge of future events entails lack of free will, even if such events are determined; or by denying that a timeless God's knowledge of the future is *fore*knowledge; or by denying that there are truths about the future to be known.

The fourth approach to the problem is more radical in that it denies the assumption that God's omniscience is unrestricted in scope. On this account, even if there are present truths about the future, it may be that God's omniscience does not entail that he knows such truths. In particular, propositions about future free actions can be true or false now, even though they cannot be *known* to be true or false until the occurrence of the future events which are their truthmakers.[5] For this to provide a satisfactory solution to the problem of reconciling God's omnipotence and omniscience we need the truth of both of two distinct theses: (i) that knowledge of future free actions is impossible; and (ii) that such a restriction on what can be known is compatible with the existence of an omniscient being.

One argument for the first thesis begins from a libertarian conception of freedom such that free agents are genuinely able to do otherwise than they actually do. On this account if a being has beliefs about what a free agent will do, then the truth of those beliefs depends upon what that agent chooses to do. Thus if the agent chooses to act in accord with those beliefs, then those beliefs are true; if the agent chooses to act contrary to those beliefs, then those beliefs are false. Now on such a view of free agency it could happen that God might have beliefs about all the future actions of free agents and that all of those beliefs turn out to be true. But such a God could only be omniscient if no free agent chose to make God's beliefs false. Since *ex hypothesi* free

---

[5]See Swinburne (1977), pp.175-178 for such a modified account of omniscience.

actions are not necessitated by anything external to the agents themselves, the fact that God's beliefs about these actions turn out all true would be purely fortuitous. Surely, however, the theist will want to resist the consequence that God is omniscient by sheer good luck. Moreover even if all God's beliefs about the future did turn out true in this way, this would not amount to *knowledge* of the future, for God would have no justification for holding his beliefs about the future actions of free agents.[6]

If this line of argument is sound then it seems to clash with any account of divine omniscience which implies that God knows all true propositions. To ensure that the unknowability of future free actions is compatible with the existence of an omniscient being it will be necessary to modify the traditional doctrine of omniscience and restrict the scope of God's knowledge. Perhaps the following definition of omniscience will suffice to do this:

(5) *A* is omniscient at *t* if and only if for every true proposition *p* about *t* or an earlier time, at *t A* knows that *p*; and for every false proposition *q* about *t* or an earlier time, at *t A* does not believe *q*; *and* for every true proposition *r* about a time later than *t*, such that what it reports is causally necessitated by some cause at *t* or earlier, at *t A* knows that *r*; and for every false proposition *s* about a time later than *t*, such that the falsity of what it reports is causally necessitated by some cause at *t* or earlier, at *t A* does not believe *s*.

In other words, God is omniscient if he knows about everything but those future states and their consequences which are not causally necessitated by the past; and if he knows that he does not know about those future states.

The obvious objection is that such an attenuated sense of divine omniscience is philosophically ad hoc and theologically unacceptable. It is by no means clear, however, that this is so. Consider the other divine attribute mentioned earlier: omnipotence. Attempts to define omnipotence encounter analogous difficulties to those with attempts to define omniscience and a satisfactory account of divine omnipotence also has to restrict God's powers in various ways.[7] Take, for instance, the obvious first candidate for a definition of omnipotence:

(6) *A* is omnipotent if and only if for any state of affairs *s*, *A* can bring about *s*.

In fact this is a very strong definition of omnipotence: so strong that most philosophers and theologians have rejected it. This is because it fails to exclude contradictory states of affairs as being beyond the power of an omnipotent being to bring about. But any definition which entails this is surely incoherent. Thus it is usual to favour a more restricted definition of omnipotence that does not require of an omnipotent being the ability to perform impossible tasks. One such candidate might be:

(7) *A* is omnipotent if and only if for any logically possible state of affairs *s*, *A* can bring about *s*.

But even this weaker definition of omnipotence is unsatisfactory. For the act of

---

[6]Ibid., pp.170-172.

[7]On the definition of omnipotence see: Geach (1977), Ch.1; Swinburne (1977), Ch.9; Kenny (1979), Ch.7; Davis (1983), Ch.5.

making a table that God did not make is a logically possible act, but one that God cannot perform. Hence on definition (7) God cannot be omnipotent.

Perhaps we can evade these sorts of difficulties by abandoning the attempt to define omnipotence and concentrating instead on an explanation of the statement that God is omnipotent. Consider:

(8) God is omnipotent if and only if for any logically possible state of affairs *s* which it is logically possible for a being with the attributes of God to bring about, God can bring about *s*.

The first thing to note about (8) is that (as already conceded) it is not a definition of omnipotence, but rather an explication of divine omnipotence. Secondly, in order for the account offered to be non-vacuous it is necessary to understand by "attributes" those properties of God that are not themselves powers (e.g. goodness, immutability etc.). Finally, on this account divine omnipotence must be something rather more restricted in scope than total omnipotence. But this is as we should have expected, for traditional theism denies to God a number of powers that it is logically possible to possess including the power to change, to sin, and to die.

The claim is, then, that just as there are implicit limits to the scope of divine omnipotence, so too are there comparable limits to the scope of divine omniscience. These limits are not an arbitrary restriction on God's powers, but rather are entailed by certain fundamental philosophical and theological beliefs about the nature of God and of the world.

II

Of course, some will find unpersuasive any argument for restricting the scope of divine omniscience that proceeds from an analogy with similar restrictions on divine omnipotence. After all, if the former restriction is held to be ad hoc, then the latter will also be held to be ad hoc. Presumably what underpins scepticism about such restrictions on God's powers is the feeling that God so described is no longer *all*-knowing or *all*-powerful. But it is not at all clear that this feeling is justified. For it is arguable that it is often the case that uses of quantifiers presuppose implicit restrictions of scope which are supplied by the context in which the sentence occurs.

Consider, for example, sentences like these:

(9) John hates everyone.
(10) Charles admires someone.
(11) Fred is cleverer than anyone of his generation.

The following are quite natural interpretations of these sentences:

(9*) John hates everyone, except possibly John himself.
(10*) Charles admires someone else.
(11*) Fred is cleverer than anyone of his generation other than himself.

The naturalness of such interpretations of (9)-(11) together with the fact that rather more restrictive construals of the same sentences are also available highlights the point that the bound variables of quantification admit of two different sorts of interpretation. Hintikka has called these "exclusive" and "inclusive" interpretations.[8] On the *inclusive* interpretation of variables we presuppose a particular way of using variables such that no coincidences of the values of different variables are excluded. Hence the value of a variable may in fact concur with an individual specified in some other way. Sentence (11), for instance, comes out false on such a construal, for it is not true that Fred is cleverer than himself. On the *exclusive* interpretation of variables we try to exclude these sorts of coincidences, basically by allowing a bound variable to range over all individuals except those whose names occur within the scope of the variable. (This is the sort of interpretation that gives us (9*)-(11*) as plausible construals of (9)-(11).) Now in certain contexts the inclusive reading of variables (or expressions with similar functions) is the natural one. But then again in other contexts speakers presuppose, more or less consciously, an exclusive interpretation of variable-like expressions. The fact is, however, that someone who is confronted by an occurrence of an English sentence typically has to rely on the context of utterance in order to determine which interpretation is the appropriate one. There is nothing in just the utterance itself that decides the intended scope of uses of terms like "all".

Again, think of the familiar possible worlds explication of logical necessity. On such an account to say a proposition is *logically* necessary is to say that it is true in all possible worlds. The form of this definition then allows us to explicate other forms of necessity. Thus a proposition is *physically* necessary if and only if it is true in all physically possible worlds; a proposition is *morally* necessary if and only if it is true in all deontically possible worlds; a proposition is *epistemically* necessary if and only if it is true in all possible worlds compatible with the conjunction of the agent's beliefs; and so on for other modalities. The important point for our purposes is that the various non-logical modalities are not defined just in terms of truth in all possible worlds, but rather in terms of truth in all possible worlds *of a certain type*. That is, once again uses of the quantifier "all" can quite naturally involve implicit restrictions of scope.

The point of these examples is that there is nothing in the use of the term "all" such that to describe a being as "all-knowing" or "all-powerful" in itself entails that there can be no limitations on the powers of such a being. The quantifier might well be being used with an implicit restriction of scope. Indeed we can build upon this point in order to offer a general account of degrees of omniscience.[9] Thus a claim that a being is all-knowing is more precisely understood as a claim that a being is all-ϕ-knowing, where ϕ is a class of propositions. Omniscience is really ϕ-omniscience and a being is ϕ-omniscient if it knows the truth-value of every proposition in ϕ. Specifying the class ϕ then enables us to differentiate various sorts of omniscience: *logical* omniscience is where ϕ is the class of logical truths; *total* omniscience is where ϕ is the class of all propositions; *inevitability* omniscience is where ϕ is the class of determined propositions; and so on. We can also ask of the class ϕ whether it is closed under deduction. If it is, then ϕ-omniscience entails logical omniscience. Hence we have a spectrum with total omniscience at one end, where ϕ is the full class of all propositions, and logical omniscience at the other end, where ϕ is the class of logical truths. The former is the strongest sort of omniscience, the latter the weakest sort. In between would be inevitability omniscience, where ϕ is the class of determined propositions. Thus the thesis that God's omniscience does not include knowledge of future free actions is the thesis that God is inevitability-omniscient, but not totally omniscient.

----

[8]Hintikka (1956); (1973).

[9]As suggested to me by Graham Oddie.

III

This account of degrees of omniscience provides a useful general framework for understanding Indian conceptions of omniscience (*sarvajñatva*).[10] Since the Sanskrit term here (*sarva*, all + *jñatva*, knowing) is clearly cognate with the Latinate "omniscience", it is particularly interesting to note the differing restrictions of scope Indian thinkers imposed upon the quantifier "*sarva*". Although the Vedic deities like Agni and Varuṇa were believed to be all-seeing and all-knowing, it is in the Upaniṣads that we first encounter the term "*sarvajña*" (he who knows everything).[11] Thus in the *Muṇḍaka Upaniṣad* (1.1.9) it is used for the absolute Brahman. In the *Māṇḍūkya Upaniṣad* (6), however, it is used of Īśvara and this usage is continued both in the philosophical schools of Yoga and Nyāya-Vaiśeṣika and in the Purāṇas. In this theistic tradition the term is given unrestricted scope: divine omniscience involves total knowledge, understood as infinite in content and acquired through direct perception, independent of mind and body.

But the Upaniṣads also employ the term *sarvajña* as a synonym for *brahmajña* or *ātmajña*, the knower of the eternal Self. In the search for what the *Chāndogya Upaniṣad* (6.1) calls "the One thing by the knowledge of which all this is known", the Upaniṣadic monists assert that the knower of Brahman knows all and becomes all. Thus the *Praśna Upaniṣad* (4.10) says of he who has come to know the pure Imperishable: "He, knowing all, into the All has entered." The latter usage of "*sarvajña*" is distinct from the former usage, for it is not intended here that the aspirant is unrestrictedly omniscient in the way Īśvara is supposed to be. Śaṃkara's commentary on the *Praśna Upaniṣad* verse makes this clear: "the aspirant was previously the knower of the finite on account of his *avidyā*, but with the removal of the latter he now becomes the All."[12] The Hindu theistic tradition, then, reserves the unrestricted sense of "*sarvajña*" for divine beings only. However the tradition also recognizes a weaker sense of "*sarvajña*" such that by knowing the nature of the one essential entity one can attain knowledge of the basic truth regarding all things. This restricted sense of "all-knowing" features not only in the Upaniṣads, but also in Buddhism. Thus Āryadeva's *Catuḥśataka* (8.16): "He who realizes the nature of one thing is known to realize the nature of all, for *śūnyatā* (essencelessness, Void) is universally found, it is the very nature of all entities."[13]

It is unsurprising that the theistic tradition would be inclined to deny unrestricted omniscience to anyone but a divinity, for otherwise such a *sarvajña* would be on a par with the deity. Moreover the severest Indian critics of the possibility of omniscience are all atheists: the Cārvāka materialists, the Ajñānavādin sceptics, and the Pūrva-Mīmāṃsā exegetes. However it is a curious fact that some of the strongest supporters in the Indian tradition of the possibility of an omniscient being are also atheists, for the non-theistic religions of Jainism and Buddhism claim for their great saints Mahāvīra and Gautama Buddha the status of omniscient beings.

The Jaina view is particularly interesting in that it is both atheistic and committed to a very strong account of omniscience.[14] In the Jaina scriptures all emancipated

---

[10] A review of Indian treatments is available in Solomon (1962). See also Singh (1974).

[11] Cf. Jaini (1974), pp.71-72.

[12] Ibid., p.72.

[13] Solomon (1962), p.39.

[14] On Jaina views see Jaini (1974); (1979), pp.258-259; Singh (1974).

souls, both ordinary *arhats* and great *tīrthaṅkaras* like Mahāvīra, are said to be endowed with the quality of omniscience. The usual Jaina term used for this quality is "*kevalajñāna*", knowledge isolated from karmic interference; sometimes they use instead "*anantajñāna*", infinite knowledge. The favoured image is of a mirror in which every one of the innumerable existents, in all its qualities and modes, is simultaneously reflected. Moreover the soul just directly perceives these knowables; there is no activity of the senses or mind involved on the part of the knower.

Obviously omniscience so understood is a supermundane affair. In fact the Jaina conception of omniscience is very similar to the Indian theistic schools' conception of divine omniscience. According to the Jainas, however, this cosmic attribute is an attribute of certain (highly developed) human beings. No other Indian school makes quite so bold a claim for the possible scope of human knowledge. (Later Buddhism refers to the Buddha as *sarvajña* but, as we shall see, generally has a rather more restricted conception of omniscience.) And yet despite the extremity of the claim Jainas have not felt any obligation to produce apologetics for the doctrine. Rather it is accepted as a consequence of certain fundamental Jaina metaphysical doctrines about karma and the nature of the soul.

According to Jainism knowledge is a distinctive quality of the soul (*jīva*). In the state of bondage that is *saṃsāra* this innate quality of the soul is obstructed by the force of karma, much as the reflecting quality of a mirror is obstructed by a covering of dust. Indeed the Jainas conceive of karma as a special kind of subtle matter which accumulates on a soul so that there is a direct relationship between the density of the karmic matter and the degree of development of the sensory and mental faculties. Since knowledge (*jñāna*) is the innate nature of the soul then, given proper conditions, the soul must be able to cognize the whole mass of knowables. As karma is destroyed by purifying ascetic activity, so the innate purity of the soul is regained and with it a corresponding increase in the range of knowledge. The total elimination of karma by an *arhat* entails perfect purity of that soul and hence total omniscience with the soul, now completely independent of the senses and the mind, directly and simultaneously mirroring the whole range of knowables. But though the emancipated soul thus knows all existents at once, these external objects are known in an indirect way. In fact the soul *perceives only itself*, but the absence of karmic obstructions in the liberated soul means that all external objects will be reflected therein. The omniscient being in Jainism, then, is really one who has complete *self*-knowledge.

Clearly this view of omniscience depends heavily on a certain metaphysics of the soul. Hence it is not surprising that Buddhism, committed as it is to a "no-self" doctrine, rejects the Jaina account of the omniscience of the perfected human being. The early Buddhist scriptures, for instance, attach more importance to the knowledge of *dharma* than to the knowledge of all; indeed when the term "*sarvajña*" is used of the Buddha it is understood in the sense of "knower of the *dharma*", i.e. knower of the truth that leads to liberation.[15] In other words, early Buddhism imposes implicit restrictions on the scope of the quantifier "*sarva*": the Buddha's omniscience is understood to be equivalent to his knowledge of the class of truths conducive to enlightenment.

But the influence of the strong construal of omniscience favoured by the Jainas seems to have led the Theravādin school to compromise this earlier understanding of the nature of the Buddha's omniscience. Reluctant to have the Buddha seem less great than Mahāvīra but also committed to an entirely opposed metaphysics of the self, the

---

[15] On early Buddhist views of omniscience see Jaini (1974); Jayatilleke (1963), pp.376-381.

Theravādins sought to restrict the scope of the Buddha's omniscience in a different way than that of the early scriptures. The scriptural warrant for this is located by them in the *Kaṇṇakatthala-sutta* of the *Majjhima-nikāya*. There the king Pasenadi of Kosala, a benefactor of the Jainas and a devotee of the Buddha, asks the Buddha about his reported denial of the existence of all-knowing beings. The Buddha says the report misrepresents his view and he restates what he in fact means:

> I, sire, claim to have spoken the words thus: There is neither a recluse nor a Brahman who *at one and the same time can know all*, see all - this situation does not exist.[16]

The Theravādin commentators put considerable weight on this passage. They construe "all" (*sabbaṃ*) to mean "the whole past, present and future" and take the expression "*sakid eva*" to mean "with one 'adverting' (of the mind), one thought, one impulsion". In other words, they define the omniscience of the Buddha as an ability to know *all* objects, but only one object at a time. The Buddha's omniscience, then, involves a sequential, one-at-a-time knowledge of existents; only the continued knowledge of all things of all times simultaneously is denied. The Buddha can know about anything by attending to it, but he does not know about it otherwise. (This harmonizes with the Buddhist denial of the soul: an omniscient being's knowledge must be a function of the flux of mental processes, not an attribute of a permanent self.) A classic statement of this Theravādin view is to be found in the *Milindapañha* (IV, 1, 19) when the king Milinda asks if the Buddha was omniscient. The Venerable Nāgasena replies:

> Yes, O king, he was. But the insight of knowledge was not always and continually (consciously) present with him. The omniscience of the Blessed One was dependent on reflection. But if he did reflect he knew whatever he wanted to know.[17]

This position, however, is not very satisfactory. The Theravādin view rejects the possibility of knowing everything at once but allows for the possibility of knowing anything sequentially. One reason for this is perhaps the feeling that while a finite mind cannot know an infinite set of propositions all at once, the possibility of a finite mind knowing any finite set of propositions at any particular time is perfectly admissible.[18] But the Theravādins go on to claim that the omniscient Buddha can know *all* objects one at a time. Now since the universe is beginningless in Indian philosophy, the Theravādins are committed to an actual infinity of objects. It seems impossible, however, that a finite mind could exhaust the infinite objects by knowing them one at a time for it seems impossible that an actual infinite can be formed by a process of successive addition.[19] But this is just what the Theravādin account implies.

In fact later Theravādin treatments of the Buddha's omniscience abandon the position previously outlined. Thus the commentator Dhammapāla (6th century A.D.)

---

[16] *Majjhima-nikāya*, II, 127; Jaini (1974), p.82. The Pali is: *natthi so samaṇo vā brāhmano va yo sakideva sabbaṃ ñassati, sabbaṃ dakkhiti, netaṃ thānam vijjatiti.*

[17] Rhys Davids (1890), p.154.

[18] Jayatilleke (1963), p.204.

[19] Cf. Craig (1979), pp.102-105. See also Śāntarakṣita's *Tattvasaṃgraha*, 3250.

gives up on attempts to restrict the scope of the Buddha's omniscience in any of the ways previous commentators had proposed:

> Whatever the Lord wishes to know, whether the whole or a portion of it, of that the Lord has knowledge by direct perception, for there is no obstruction to the operation [of his mind]. And in the absence of any disturbances (*vikṣepa*), attentiveness is also ever present in him .... Even his knowing of past and future objects should be considered an act of direct perception, as it is not dependent upon inference, scripture or reasoning .... [The] Buddha, whether he wishes to know the objects all together, or separately, all at once or one by one, knows them all as he wishes. Therefore he is called *sammā-sambuddha*.[20]

In defence of his position, however, Dhammapāla can do nothing but appeal to (apparently incompatible) passages from the scriptures.

Buddhist accounts of omniscience, then, begin by being sharply opposed to the Jaina conception of total omniscience: the Buddha is not held to be unrestrictedly omniscient in the way Mahāvīra is supposed to be. This is unsurprising for the Buddhist "no-self" doctrine cannot support the kind of account of total omniscience that the Jaina metaphysics of the soul underwrites. Hence the early Buddhist view is that the Buddha's omniscience is implicitly restricted in scope: he knows all the truths conducive to enlightenment. But the Theravādin school goes on to reject this acount and maintains instead that the Buddha (like Mahāvīra) knows all existents. However in order to square this with the Buddhist account of the self they too have to place some restrictions on the scope of omniscience. This time instead of restricting the scope of the Buddha's omniscience to the class of all truths conducive to liberation, they instead impose a restriction on the way in which the Buddha can come to know all truths. Unlike the Jaina *arhat*, he can only know them sequentially. But this way of restricting omniscience while conceding also that it involves knowing *all* truths is inherently weak. Hence eventually the Theravādin tradition lapses into asserting the totally unrestricted omniscience of the Buddha, despite this being apparently incompatible with other fundamental scriptural tenets.

The writings of the Mahāyāna Buddhist philosophers present a reconsideration of the problem, at least partly in response to the vigorous attack on the possibility of omniscience by the Mīmāṃsaka philosopher Kumārila.[21] Kumārila's arguments in the *Ślokavārttika* are to the effect that the existence of an omniscient being cannot be established by any of the sources of knowledge (*pramāṇas*) recognized by Mīmāṃsā epistemology. He also indicates certain implausibities that attach to the claim that there exists a totally omniscient being.[22] The motivation for these objections is provided by the fundamental Mīmāṃsā view that knowledge of *dharma* (merit, good) and *adharma* (demerit, evil) is only possible through the Vedas. Neither ordinary perception nor inference will provide such knowledge and the Mīmāṃsā rejects the possibility of supersensuous perception (*yogipratyakṣa*) admitted by some other schools. Mīmāṃsā also rejects the idea that the Vedic revelation is the creation of an

---

[20]Jaini (1974), p.85.

[21]The influence of Kumārila is particularly evident in Śāntarakṣita's *Tattvasaṃgraha* which cites passages from Kumārila's *Ślokavārttika* verbatim.

[22]*Ślokavārttika*, II, 110-115. For reviews of some of the Mīmāṃsā argumentation see Solomon (1962), pp.40-50; Singh (1974), Ch.8.

omniscient deity; instead the Vedas are held to be eternal and authorless (*apauruṣeya*). Obviously the admission of an omniscient being would compromise these central tenets.

The Mahāyāna philosophers sought to respond to this Mīmāṃsaka challenge. Moreover since their metaphysics was not realist in the manner of the Theravādins, they were unimpressed by a purported ability to know "the all". Instead there is a return to the earlier position of the Pali scriptures: the Buddha's omniscience is once again restricted in scope to the class of truths necessary for salvation. Thus the demand that an authoritative teacher be unrestrictedly omniscient is disparagingly rejected in Dharmakīrti's *Pramāṇavārttika* (7th century):

> People, afraid of being deceived by false teachers in the matter of directing the ignorant, seek out a man with knowledge, for the sake of realizing his teaching. What is the use of his wide knowledge pertaining to the number of insects in the whole world Rather, enquire into his knowledge of that which is to be practised by us. For us, the most desired authority is not the one who knows everything [indiscriminately]; rather, we would have a Teacher who knows the Truth which leads to prosperity in this world, as well as to the insight into things to be forsaken and things to be cultivated. Whether he sees far or whether he sees not, let him but see the desired Truth. If one becomes an authority merely because of seeing far and wide, let us worship these vultures who can do it better![23]

Śāntarakṣita, writing a couple of centuries later, expresses a similar view in his *Tattvasaṃgraha*:

> If the attempt were made to prove that one has the knowledge of the details of all individuals and components of the whole world, - it would be as futile as the investigation of the crow's teeth.... By proving the existence of the person knowing only *dharma* and *adharma*, whom the Buddhist postulates, - one secures the reliability and acceptability of the scripture composed by him; and by denying the said person, one secures the unreliability and rejectability of the said scripture. Thus when people [e.g. the Jainas] proceed to prove the existence of the person knowing all the little details of the entire world, they put themselves to the unnecessary trouble of writing treatises on the subject and carrying on discussions on the same.[24]

Śāntarakṣita, however, does not actually deny that total omniscience is possible.[25] Moreover he tries to show that the Mīmāṃsaka arguments against this possibility are inconclusive. But what he does insist on is that a totally omniscient being is not required to guarantee the trustworthiness of scripture. In doing so he highlights the problem of revelation which motivates most of the Indian discussions of omniscience.

---

[23] *Pramāṇavārttika*, II, 32-35; Jaini (1974), pp.86-87.

[24] *Tattvasaṃgraha*, 3138-3141; Śāntarakṣita (1939), pp.1397-1398.

[25] Cf. *Tattvasaṃgraha*, 3309 and especially Kamalaśīla's commentary thereon; Śāntarakṣita (1939), p.1463.

IV

Since classical Indian philosophy is overwhelming religious in its avowed orientation, it is not surprising that most schools accept the authority of certain scriptures. This is obviously the case in Hinduism where the acceptance of the authority of the Vedas is the mark of orthodoxy, extraordinary divergences between the different schools of Hindu philosophy in other respects notwithstanding.[26] Buddhism and Jainism reject the Vedas and are hence heterodox (*nāstika*) but they both appeal instead to their own bodies of scripture. Moreover since they do so reject the authority of the Hindu scriptures, they are obliged to justify the authority of their own scriptures.

The arguments used by the different schools in support of the authority of scriptural revelation are worth attending to. Perhaps the simplest (to be found, for instance, in both Sāṃkhya and Bhartṛhari) goes like this.[27] Certain fundamental beliefs (like the customary Indian confidence in the law of karma, the efficacy of religious practices and the possibility of final release from the cycle of rebirth) cannot be justified on the basis of ordinary experience or inference. However, they are discussed in the scriptures. Hence it is scripture that justifies those beliefs which fall outside the sphere of matters justifiable by ordinary means. Obviously this justifactory strategy begins by isolating a domain of supersensible objects (*atīndriyāṇi*) concerning which the scriptures are said to have special authority; virtually all Indian philosophers (except the Cārvāka materialists) accept this, though they disagree on precisely what belongs to this domain. But even if this move is conceded, the argument is circular. It proceeds by nominating a set of commonly held beliefs, asserts those beliefs are true and then asserts that whatever states those beliefs (viz. scripture) is thereby a source of truth. In other words, the truth of the original beliefs is justified by appeal to scripture and the appeal to scripture is in turn justified by appeal to the truth of the original beliefs.

In addition to this threat of a vicious circularity in their reasoning, the defenders of the Brahmanical scriptural tradition faced other difficulties. The Cārvākas were particularly vociferous in this context. Firstly, they argued that the scriptural assertions, dealing as they supposedly do with the realm of supersensibles, are incapable of any independent verification. Believing in them, then, is just irrational. Secondly, they urged the inconsistency of various Vedic statements with each other. Hence even if we cannot know which of the Vedic claims about the supersensible are true, still we can know that some Vedic statements must be false. Thirdly, they questioned the integrity of the priestly transmitters of the Vedic texts, who clearly had a vested interest in preserving ritual practices: "the three Vedas themselves are only the incoherent rhapsodies of knaves ... [the] means of livelihood for those who have no manliness nor sense."[28]

The force of the first objection is dependent upon the acceptance of a narrowly empiricist epistemology which would be challenged by most other Indian schools. The other two objections, however, require a different response. The early Nyāya philosophers, upholding Brahmanical orthodoxy, responded to the charge of scriptural

---

[26] For a brief introduction to Hindu treatments of revelation see Biderman (1978). For a full-length study, with particular reference to Advaita Vedānta, see Murty (1959).

[27] Cf. Hayes (1984), p.650.

[28] Madhava, *Sarvadarśanasaṃgraha*; Radhakrishnan & Moore (1957), p.230.

inconsistencies by arguing that such inconsistencies were only apparent and a proper hermeneutics could resolve all seeming contradictions. As for the challenge to the integrity of the priestly transmitters of the Vedas, the early Nyāya philosophers responded by arguing that the authors of the scriptures were also the authors of the earliest medical texts. Thus the altruism and reliability evidenced by the latter texts makes it reasonable to trust the former texts. For early Nyāya, then, the authority of the Vedas derives not from their congruity with common belief, but from their being written by trustworthy persons (*āpta*).[29]

According to this account the Vedas are as reliable as any other texts composed by well-intentioned experts. But the obvious problem with this is that such experts can be wrong on at least some occasions. Later Nyāya remedies this flaw by making God (*Īśvara*) the author of the Vedas. Since he is both omniscient and benevolent, the reliabilty of the scriptures is thus justified. Of course, to avoid circularity here we need to be supplied with independent grounds for believing in the existence of God. But Nyāya does offer such grounds, most famously in the form of the various causal arguments in Udayana's *Nyāyakusumāñjali*.[30] Further arguments, however, are required for the thesis that God is omniscient. Udayana offers two. Firstly, in the *Ātmatattvaviveka* he argues from the principle that an agent must have an adequate knowledge of all the different causes he utilizes in producing an effect. The causal arguments establish that God is the agent or maker (*kartā*) of this universe. Thus he too must have an adequate cognition of all the different causes he utilizes: i.e. a knowledge of all the causes of the universe and of the categories of reality. Such a being must be omniscient (*sarvajña*).[31] Secondly, in the *Nyāyakusumāñjali* he argues that if God is the author of the sacred scriptures then he must be omniscient. For the scriptures speak of the realm of the supersensible

> ... but if their speaker (*vaktā*) is trustworthy, how can it be that he does not see their objects? If he perceives objects that are beyond (the perception of) the senses, how can he be non-omniscient?[32]

Neither argument is overwhelming. The first rests upon a highly contentious Nyāya epistemic principle that knowledge of an individual belonging to a class entails knowledge of all the individuals of that class comprehended under that generic character. The second is threatened by circularity. True, as an argument against the Mīmāṃsakas, who accept the trustworthiness of the Vedic scriptures but deny their divine authorship, it is non-circular. But if one is sceptical about the trustworthiness of the Vedas one will not be reassured by the claim that they are the product of an author whose omniscience is supposed to follow from the trustworthiness of the Vedas.

Nyāya represents one popular Hindu strategy for defending the reliability of the scriptures: viz. attribute them to an omniscient author. Not surprisingly, this view is by no means unique to Nyāya and is espoused by various of the theistic schools. The other major Hindu strategy is more radical. It is defended by the Mīmāṃsā school and by Advaita Vedānta. The central thesis is that the Vedas are authorless (*apauruṣeya*). Indeed their authority derives from precisely this property, for if they did have an

---

[29]Cf. Hayes (1984), p.652.

[30]On these see Chemparathy (1972).

[31]Cf. Chemparathy (1972), pp.166-169.

[32]Ibid., p.170.

author they would be fallible (as are other authored texts of our acquaintance). However since they do not have an author, they must be infallible because their falsity could have no possible cause (the possibility of falsity always depending on some person or other). Mīmāṃsā concedes that there is no positive proof of the validity of the Vedas, for this would require the assumption of something prior or external to the eternal revelation. However, this is epistemically untroublesome for Mīmāṃsā since it holds a negative theory of confirmation according to which no theory can be positively proved true. Non-falsification is the criterion of truth and every statement is assumed true unless contradicted by another statement.[33] (This theory of the self-validity of all knowledge is known as *svataḥprāmāṇyavāda* and is also followed by Advaita.)[34]

This whole account depends heavily upon the intelligibility of the notion of an authorless revelation and the plausibility of the involved theory of language Mīmāṃsā offers in support of the idea. Moreover, even on the conjectural view of inquiry that *svataḥprāmāṇyavāda* favours, Vedic texts seem to be contradicted by other (heterodox) scriptures. For the Mīmāṃsā, however, this latter point is not seen as a problem since both Jainism and Buddhism hold that their scriptures are the products of (highly developed) authors. Hence on Mīmāṃsā principles they are fallible in a way that the authorless Vedas cannot be. It is interesting to note though that the atheistic Jainas and Buddhists take a view of their scriptures rather similar to the theistic Nyāya account and opposed to the atheistic Mīmāṃsā view of revelation. Thus for Jainism the scriptures are the products of the totally omniscient *tīrthaṅkaras* and their omniscience guarantees the reliability of the scriptures in much the same way as God's omniscience guarantees the reliability of the Vedas for the Hindu theists. This is one motive for the Jaina attribution of the total omniscience usually reserved for divine beings to the human *arhats* and *tīrthaṅkaras*. Similarly, Buddhism attributes the reliability of its scriptures to the reliability of their origin: the Buddha himself.

But the Buddhist position is a bit more complicated than that might suggest. Early Buddhism certainly rejected the authority of the Vedas: it regarded the Vedic texts as the compositions of the early seers, who were in fact bereft of any higher insight.[35] Its own scriptures are the reported words of the Buddha and in those scriptures the Buddha seems to demand a critical attitude towards his own statements.[36] The Buddha's statements are reliable because he knows whereof he speaks, but they are to be tested by his disciples and accepted if found to be true. The Buddha's teaching is claimed to be *ehipassiko*, a "come and see" matter.

In this position there is an implicit tension between a veneration for the Buddha as a model of humanly attainable perfection and a critical attitude towards ancient scriptures which may come to seem incomprehensible or outmoded at a later time. This tension is evident in later Buddhist treatments of the authoritativeness of the scriptures.[37] Thus Vasubandhu (5th century) at the end of the *Abhidharmakośa* addresses this tension and distinguishes between the Buddha as a perfect source of knowledge and the scriptural tradition that gives us imperfect access to the Buddha's truth. The scriptures require interpretation, but adequate interpretation in turn requires

---

[33]Cf. Biderman (1978), pp.140-141.

[34]See, for instance, Dharmarāja's *Vedāntaparibhāṣā*, Ch.7.

[35]Cf. Jayatilleke (1963), Ch.4.

[36]Ibid., Ch.8.

[37]On this theme see Hayes (1984), pp.653-666 to which I am indebted here.

the kind of insight enjoyed by the Buddha and his direct disciples. Since hardly anyone now exists who is competent to provide such interpretation, the scriptures *as they are now understood* are not fully authoritative. Any error, however, is not attributable to the Buddha himself, but only to the imperfections of later interpreters who lack his insight.

Later Buddhist philosophers take over this view and its corollary: viz. that in judging the Buddha's words *as they are recorded in the scriptures* we must be guided by our own experiences and reason. But there remains an unresolved tension in the treatment of the authority of Buddhist scriptures. The writings of the great logician Dharmakīrti, for instance, are revealing in this respect. Thus in the *Pramāṇavārttika* Dharmakīrti accepts the familiar Indian principle that we resort to scriptures for guidance about matters beyond the range of ordinary experience and inference. However, different scriptural traditions present conflicting reports about the nature of the supersensible domain. Clearly we need some way of adjudicating between conflicting claims, some independent criteria by which we can decide upon the merits of a scriptural statement. Dharmakīrti offers two such criteria. First, that action in conformity with the belief expressed in a statement must yield predicted results. (This pragmatic test is proposed as a quite general constraint upon rational belief: any belief which is not proven false by it may be tentatively assumed true.) The trouble with this criterion, however, is that it is only usable when judging actions with immediate consequences. But the scriptures urge upon us actions the results of which lie far in the future, even beyond this present life. Faced with the incompatible demands of different scriptures, the pragmatic test is useless to us in deciding between them.

Dharmakīrti's second criterion rehearses a now familiar pattern of argument. A body of scriptures, he says, is as reliable as the person who is their author. The reliability of the Buddhist scriptures rests upon the reliability of the Buddha. But how do we know that the Buddha was neither mistaken nor deceptive? All Dharmakīrti can do by way of reply is once again to argue in a vicious circle. The Buddha is trustworthy because we know he taught the doctrines all Buddhists believe and practised altruistic exercises and meditations. But our justification for believing this about him is the information about the Buddha's career that we derive from the scriptures, the authority of which Dharmakīrti is supposedly defending.

It is against this historical background that Śāntarakṣita addresses the problem in his *Tattvasaṃgraha.* He claims that the authority of the Buddhist scriptures derives from the omniscience of the Buddha. However, as we have already seen, he argues that only a restricted notion of omniscience is necessary for this purpose: in order to validate the scriptures it is only necessary for the Buddha to be omniscient with respect to all matters relevant to salvation and the means to it. But even this weaker claim to omniscience still has to be defended and Śāntarakṣita agrees that to be in a position to know of the Buddha's omniscience we must have some proof of the truth of his teachings that does not rest upon the assumed truth of the scriptures. This is obvious when we recall that the Jains and some Hindus also claim omniscience for the authors of their scriptures:

> If Buddha is omniscient, then what is the proof for Kapila not being so? If both are omniscient, then how is it that there is difference of opinion between them?[38]

Śāntarakṣita's strategy in dealing with his problem is twofold. First, he tries to

---

[38]*Tattvasaṃgraha*, 3149; Śāntarakṣita (1939), p.1402.

establish the integrity of the Buddha. This is evidenced, he suggests, by the Buddha's invitation to others to examine his teachings closely for errors:

> Those great teachers who are wholly convinced of the obvious rationality of their own teachings and of their own ability to explain them lose all fear .... They dare to say: "Clever people, O monks, should accept what I say after putting it to the test, just as they accept gold after testing it by melting it, scratching it and scraping it on a whetstone. They should not believe what I say out of deference to me."[39]

Secondly, since sincerity is not sufficient for truth, the individual doctrines of the Buddha's teaching must be established one by one. Each doctrine must be compatible with empirical and rational investigation and the whole system must be internally consistent. This is the burden of the huge bulk of the argumentation presented in the *Tattvasaṃgraha*. Satisfied with the results of his investigation Śāntarakṣita can conclude:

> This is a statement for which there is good evidence, namely, that the omniscient lord who has acquired unique talents that distinguish him from the rest of mankind is none other than him whose faultless teaching, in which selflessness is the constantly repeated thesis, is established throughout the present work and is not overturned by any means of knowledge. That being the case, it turns out to be plausible that someone is omniscient, from which it follows that *human* teachings can result in an understanding of truth.[40]

The (restricted) omniscience of the Buddha, then, is the basis for the reliability of the scriptures. But the reason for believing in this omniscience is not just that it is asserted in those scriptures. Rather the doctrines of the Buddha have to be able to stand up to independent empirical and logical investigation. This is why the philosophical activities of Śāntarakṣita in fact form part of an overall religious programme. His dialectical arguments try to establish that the doctrines of rival scriptures do not stand up to philosophical scrutiny as well as those of the Buddhist scriptures.

V

To sum up. We began with some Western attempts to define omniscience, particularly in relation to the notion of an all-knowing God. We saw that a satisfactory account of divine omniscience requires implicit restrictions on the scope of God's knowledge. Such restrictions were defended as not being merely ad hoc. There are good philosophical and theological reasons for them. Moreover there is nothing in the use of the term "all" such that to describe a being as "all-knowing" or "all-powerful" entails that there can be no limits on the powers of such a being. The quantifier might well be being used with an implicit restriction of scope. Indeed we can conceive of a spectrum of degrees of omniscience distinguished according to precisely what the implicit range of the quantifiers is supposed to be.

---

[39] *Tattvasaṃgraha*, 3586-3588; Hayes (1984), p.664.

[40] *Tattvasaṃgraha*, 3641-3645; Hayes (1984), p.665.

Turning to the Indian tradition, we found that Indian uses of the term "omniscience" (*sarvajñatva*) also reflected such implicit restrictions on the scope of the quantifier "all" (*sarva*). Some (like the Jainas) understood omniscience to be *total* omniscience; others (like many of the Buddhists) understood omniscience to be restricted in scope to the class of truths necessary for salvation. The existence of either sort of omniscient being was hotly debated by the various schools. The motivation for these debates was primarily the problem of justifying the authority of the religious scriptures. Most Indian philosophers accepted some scriptures as reliable and in order to justify these they basically opted for one of two positions. Either they claimed the scriptures were self-validating in some sense (Mīmāṃsā, Advaita) or they claimed their validity rested upon the nature of their author. Those that favoured the second option disagreed among themselves as to whether only an unrestrictedly omniscient author could serve to validate the scriptural texts. Both Jainism and Nyāya agreed that only total omniscience will do; where they disagreed is on whether the totally omniscient author could be a human being. Many (but not all) Buddhist philosophers argued that all that is required of the author of the scriptures is that he be omniscient with respect to all the truths necessary for salvation, an attribute they claimed for the Buddha.

The strong claim about the existence of a totally omniscient being is not immediately plausible and it is hard to justify without a viciously circular appeal to the authority of the texts that are in question. The weaker claim about the existence of a restrictedly omniscient being is a little more plausible (if only in virtue of being weaker). But once again it is still difficult to support without lapsing into circularity. The later Buddhist position (as presented by Śāntarakṣita) attempts an interesting compromise. The (restricted) omniscience of the Buddha is still upheld as the source of the truth of the Buddhist scriptures. However *our* knowledge of the truth of the doctrines expressed in the scriptures is based upon independent logical and empirical investigation. Omniscience, then, while it may be possible, is not of much significance for us in deciding what scriptural doctrines we ought to believe (though it may still have religious significance in helping to preserve the ideal of the perfect Buddha as an object of veneration).[41]

REFERENCES

Biderman, Shlomo (1978). "Scriptures, Revelation, and Reason". In Ben-Ami Scharfstein *et al.*, *Philosophy East/Philosophy West: A Critical Comparison of Indian, Chinese, Islamic, and European Philosophy*. Oxford: Basil Blackwell.

Chemparathy, George (1972). *An Indian Rational Theology*. Vienna: De Nobili Research Library.

Craig, William Lane (1979). *The Kalām Cosmological Argument*. London: Macmillan.

Davis, Stephen T. (1983). *Logic and the Nature of God*. London: Macmillan.

Dharmarāja (1942). *Vedāntaparibhāṣā by Dharmarāja Adhvarin*, ed. & trans. S.S. Suryanarayana Sastri. Adyar: Adyar Library and Research Centre.

Geach, Peter (1977). *Providence and Evil*. Cambridge: Cambridge University Press.

Hayes, Richard P. (1984). "The Question of Doctrinalism in the Buddhist Epistemologists" *Journal of the American Academy of Religion* 52: 645-670.

Hintikka, Jaakko (1956). "Identity, Variables, and Impredicative Definitions" *Journal*

---

[41]My thanks to Graham Oddie for his assistance with the material of part II of this paper.

of Symbolic Logic 21: 225-245.
Hintikka, Jaakko (1973). *Logic, Language-Games and Information*. Oxford: Clarendon Press.
Jaini, Padmanabh S. (1974). "On the *Sarvajñatva* (Omniscience) of Mahāvīra and the Buddha". In L. Cousins *et al.* (eds.), *Buddhist Studies in Honour of I.B. Horner*. Dordrecht: D. Reidel.
Jaini, Padmanabh S. (1979). *The Jaina Path of Purification*. Berkeley: University of California Press.
Jayatilleke, K.N. (1963). *Early Buddhist Theory of Knowledge*. London: Allen & Unwin.
Kenny, Anthony (1979). *The God of the Philosophers*. Oxford: Clarendon Press.
Kumārila (1906). *Ślokavārttika*, trans. Ganganatha Jha. Calcutta: Asiatic Society.
Kvanvig, Jonathan L. (1986). *The Possibility of an All-Knowing God*. London: Macmillan.
Murty, K. Satchidananda (1959). *Revelation and Reason in Advaita Vedānta*. Delhi: Motilal Banarsidass, 1974.
Radhakrishnan, Sarvepalli & Moore, Charles A. (1957). Editors. *A Sourcebook in Indian Philosophy*. Princeton: Princeton University Press.
Puccetti, Roland (1963). "Is Omniscience Possible?" *Australasian Journal of Philosophy* 41: 92-93.
Rhys Davids, T.W. (1890). Translator. *The Questions of King Milinda*. Vol.1. Delhi: Motilal Banarsidass, 1969.
Śāntarakṣita (1939). *The Tattvasaṅgraha of Śāntarakṣita with the Commentary of Kamalaśīla*, trans. Ganganatha Jha. Vol.2. Baroda: Oriental Institute.
Singh, Ramjee (1974). *The Jaina Concept of Omniscience*. Ahmedabad: L.D. Institute of Indology.
Solomon, E.A. (1962). "The Problem of Omniscience (*Sarvajñatva*)" *Adyar Library Bulletin* 26: 36-77.
Swinburne, Richard (1977). *The Coherence of Theism*. Oxford: Clarendon Press.

ON THE IDEA OF AUTHORLESS REVELATION (APAURUṢEYA)

Puruṣottama Bilimoria

Deakin University

In the beginning was word
the word was with meaning...

A General Thesis

If the erstwhile theme that has dominated much of traditional (Western) philosophy of religion, namely, the existence of a transcendent being or God, were to be taken as a cue for entering the Indian traditions, there would not be much in the way of an Indian philosophy of religion. For this concern - let it be called, the possibility of *theism* - does not occupy as central a place in the minds of Indian thinkers on religion as it might otherwise appear. Yet, the rejection of theism might provide a more fertile ground for debate, but for a different sort of reason: when this rejection is felt to pose the threat of spiritual and moral nihilism. Is a religion a religion if it is faced, in its fundamentals, with spiritual and moral bankruptcy? And in the absence of a personal God, where would one turn to countenance this threat?

But, as the history of the Indian tradition has well evinced, there was never such a haste to turn to theism, particularly where this would lead to the denial or diminution of the world in favour of the primacy of the Ultimate, conceived of as a transcendent being or God who is endowed with the creation and governance of the world. A delicate tension was poised between belief in a transcendent being or "the Other" qua Being and its antithesis of non-being qua Nothingness (in the widest possible sense) with the implied difficulty of creation. The dialectic would turn upon negating, and, where less decisive, "bracketing" much that is otherwise held to be absolute and sacrosanct in the tradition in its broadest boundaries. And that made for the distinct possibility of non-theistic worldviews.

On the antithesis side, Jainas and Buddhists, it is often said, led the way, with the severest blow coming from Nāgārjunian dialectic: either both the realms are negated, or Nothingness is tipped on the side of "the Other" as well so that, in the same measure, one implies the other. While the Brahmanical schools, it is said, by and large, succumbed to the presence of "the Other", under various guises and in differing degrees. But that has not always been the case, for there has been resistance from within the Brahmanical fold that led to decisive attempts at repudiating theism. Sāṃkhya, for instance, with its structured co-union of the primal principles of *puruṣa* ("spirit") and *prakṛti* ("nature") proposed to solve a number of cosmological/

R. W. Perrett (ed.), Indian Philosophy of Religion, 143–166.

cosmogenic puzzles, albeit non-theistically. Some forms of Vedānta attempted to mend the differentiation of the manifest world of "appearance" and "the Other" by arguing for their substantive unity in a singular frame of reference (Ātman/Brahman) - hence giving God (as Īśvara), at best, a descriptive or "modal" status (*taṭasthalakṣaṇa*). Each of these basically non-theistic responses had its own way of dealing with the problematical threat.

However, in the eyes of the extreme Brahmanical orthodoxy these attempts could not be deemed adequate. What is needed in addition is some kind of epiphany of the sacred, the *Ungrund* of the sacramental or a "transcendental signified" which would stand on its own ground, and therefore sanctify the actions through which this end is to be accomplished. In this way, while repudiating belief in God, one could salvage the spiritual and moral undercurrents of the tradition, and keep alive its soteriological concerns. This is the response of the Mīmāṃsā, and it is a particularly interesting one, if only because it has received such woefully scant and dismissive attention in recent scholarship on Indian philosophy. I contend that the Mīmāṃsā (from the root, *man*, and the desirative suffix, *san*, to know or investigate), known for its moral hermeneutical exegesis, offers a challenge that in a way presents atheism as a possibility, but without, on the one hand, the consequent fears of spiritual and moral nihilism, and, on the other hand, requiring a wholesale commitment to Nothingness. For Nothingness to the orthodoxy is just as threatening as what it perceives of as the nihilism of the Cārvāka-Lokāyata (materialists); indeed, of all heterodox views. And yet the Mīmāṃsā is supposed to be the most *orthodox* of Hindu schools!

Having repudiated belief in God, where would they look for the authoritative source for their moral and spiritual concerns, other than in the resources of man himself? ("Man" is used generically, despite its humanist and sexist connotations; ditto, for the pronomials.) Neither in God, nor in man, is the Mīmāṃsā answer; and yet the Mīmāmsā does not do away altogether with "revelation", broadly understood as a disclosure or unveiling of hidden truth that is otherwise inaccessible to man. A fundamental presupposition for the coherence of such a view rests with the notion of *apauruṣeya*: that is, "authorless revelation"; or, alternatively, the notion of a-personal text.

The view is that the Vedas or, what is the same thing, *śruti* (the formalised "canonical" scriptures of the Hindus) are the authoritative and inviolable source for *dharma/adhikāra* (the spiritual and moral "oughts") and for the invisible good (*adṛṣṭa/apūrva*), but that the Vedas are without any personal agency as their subject or "revealer". The latter claim should stand in its own right as one theory about (scriptural) "revelation", to be scrutinised qua theory, without reference necessarily to the propositional or "magical" contents of the scriptures in question.

Prima facie, this appears to be a rather puzzling claim. How does one make sense of the notion of "authorless revelation"? In order to grasp this notion, I believe, we need to understand at least three things - which correspond to the moves in my protracted enquiry that attempts to show how the Mīmāṃsā goes about this project and to what extent it is successful. Namely: (i) the problem facing orthodoxy, the threat and the closure, as perceived by the Mīmāṃsā; (ii) the peculiar theory of language and the hermeneutic evolved by the Mīmāmsā in its approach to the text of the Vedas; and (iii) the particular motivation undergirding this project.

A question that incidentally arises in this context is whether the term "revelation", such as it is, can be meaningfully applied to the Mīmāṃsā notion of *apauruṣeya*; and conversely, whether the notion of *apauruṣeya* has anything to say on the monolithic notion of revelation (pervasive in the West). One way to appraise this question is to say that, if the argument for revelation is by implication an argument for belief in God, which itself presupposes God's giving of himself in revelation, then stripped of the circularity, belief in God suffers for that. Paradoxically, for the Mīmāṃsā, that would better ensure the authenticity of *śruti*.

For the purposes of the present discussion I will be very brief in my treatment of the issues outlined here. I shall draw on the responses of Kumārila Bhaṭṭa (7th century C.E.[1] and possibly a contemporary of the Buddhist dialectician, Dharmakīrti), Pārthasārathi Miśra (hence the Bhāṭṭa Mīmāṃsā school), and Śabara before them; but textual and other details will be deferred for another occasion.

I

Āstika and *Nāstika*

In traditional India, generally speaking, the question of orthodoxy versus heterodoxy got settled not exactly on grounds of belief or disbelief in the existence of God, but on grounds of the affirmation or the denial of the authority of the Vedas. One who believes in the authority of the Vedas is known as an *āstika* (orthodox), and one who denies the authority of the Vedas in preference for some other authority (or possibly no authority at all) is called a *nāstika* (heterodox). But it is not incumbent upon an *āstika* to, at the same time, believe in God; and conversely, in principle at least, it is not incumbent upon a *nāstika* to disbelieve in God. However, in practice the demarcation was not always so clear-cut, particularly in the eyes of the more theistically orientated believers (e.g. a Vaiṣṇavite), so much so that some scholars have argued that *āstika[tva]* entails belief in God, while *nāstika[tva]* entails the denial of such belief.[2]

Now where does the Mīmāṃsā come in on this debate? Mīmāṃsā identifies itself (staunchly) as *āstika*[3] but is basically atheist (and only just transcendentalist, in a sense to be clarified later) - a stance that has historically not set well with their fellow Hindus. Like the Buddhists of their times (post sixth-century C.E.), the Mīmāṃsakas reject any theodicy that depends for its support on the act or intervention of a deity. But they have the added task of explaining how could they deny the deity and yet believe in the supreme authority of the Vedas. In this task the Mīmāṃsakas find themselves pitted not only against the Buddhists but also against other Hindus. For the latter conflate assent to Vedic authority with affirmation of belief in God since they attribute the origin of the Vedas to some personal source or agency (*pauruseya*), human or divine. In Mīmāṃsā the authority of the Vedas is affirmed, but this authority need not be based on the utterances of a magnificent author.

But the Mīmāṃsā is equally apprehensive of its denial of God being confused with the materialistic and hedonistic preoccupations of the Cārvāka-Lokāyata, the Indian school of materialism.[4] Such tendencies are evident in a concern with the fruits that

---

[1]Dates are in dispute: 590-650 C.E., or 600-700 C.E. See Kaviraj (1983), p vii.

[2]Notably Pashupatinath Shastri (1980) pp.6-9, following Max Muller, has argued for this strict entailment (i.e. *āstika*[Veda] = God-belief; *nāstika*[No Veda] = God-nonbelief). Ganganatha Jha (1964), pp. 135ff; Gopinath Kaviraj (1983), *passim*; and P.V. Kane (1962) p.1217 reject this argument, contending that there is no intrinsic reason why the *nāstika(tva)* should preclude belief in the existence of God or a transcendent being. This is obvious.

[3]Kumārila Bhaṭṭa (1979 edn), *Ślokavārttika* (=*ŚV*), Introductory, #10, p.5, re-asserts Mīmāṃsā as *āstika*.

[4]Kumārila *ŚV* p.5: *prāyeṇaiva hi mīmāṃsā loke lokāyatīkṛtā*. Pārthasārathi Miśra, commenting here, elaborates, as in the text.

might result from Vedic rituals. This wicked fetishism clearly debases the Vedas, and the threat of nihilism becomes ever more pernicious. It would seem that the Mīmāṃsakas, particularly with Kumārila, increasingly construed *nāstika[tva]* as nihilism, which they also associated with the Buddhist doctrine of *śūnyatā* or Emptiness; hence confounding their fears of moral and spiritual degeneration.[5]

Still, the Mīmāṃsakas do not see the need for a theodicy as an alternative to nihilism, for they are able to explain evil in terms of the autonomous operation of the law of cause and effect (karma) and the results of continued actions, both good and bad. Further, in the Mīmāṃsā cosmology, there is no necessity of a deity or deities as the recipient of sacrifices, nor is there need for an apportioner or dispenser of rewards and retributions. (Legend has it that Kumārila entered the fires of immolation in order to expiate his own sins, there being no supreme dispenser.)[6] The regulative function properly belongs to the broader category of *dharma*, the impersonal sempiternal Law, which is conterminous with the world. (I need not rehearse the arguments the Mīmāṃsā advances against the existence of God, which I have discussed elsewhere.)[7]

In this context, however, it may be well to mention that Kumārila denies creation and dissolution of the world (flux of parts is not denied). He rejects cosmological arguments (both Sāṃkhya and Nyāya-Vaiśeṣika)[8], argues for the incoherency of these ideas, and curiously invokes the problem of evil or misery, etc. He bases his denial of a creator God on grounds somewhat similar to his rejection of an omniscient person (*sarvajña*).[9] His basic contention is that no such omniscient person has been known; indeed, such is unknowable. If known, that would make for two such persons (for how can omniscience be incontrovertibly recognised by a mind less than omniscient): but how could we have two omniscient persons both of whom might make conflicting claims about matters in dispute?[10]

This line of reasoning might be weak, but Kumārila has a deeper motive, and that is to foreclose altogether the idea of an omniscient person (*sarvajña*). One reason for this was to counter the threatening assertion of the Buddha's omniscience (*buddhādeḥ sarvajñatvam*).[11] For the Buddhists would then challenge the Vedas and use the Buddha's utterances to falsify, and rival, the authority of the Vedas.[12] Such a situation

---

[5]Ibid., under *nirālambana-vāda* #8, p 157.

[6]The *Bhagavadgītā* presupposes a Mīmāṃsā ontology for its ethics, but then backtracks to introduce grace (*prasāda*) for desireless actions and devotion (in the hereafter), somewhat similar to the Kantian regress.

[7]Bilimoria (1986).

[8]Kumārila *ŚV*, *codanāsūtra*, #47, #68, # 113. Although neither the author of the *Vaiśeṣika-sutras*, Kaṇāda, nor Gautama in his *Nyāya-sūtras*, present any such arguments, let alone entertain theism. It was their respective commentators, Praśastapāda and Uddyotakara, circa 500-600 CE, who began to marshal such arguments, which caught the attention of the Mīmāṃsakas.

[9]Kumārila *ŚV*, *codanāsūtra* #47-59, #114-116, #130, pp. 45-48, 60-61, 63. Pārthasārathi Miśra (1979 edn) in his attached *Nyāyaratnākara* (under *sambandhākṣepaparihāraḥ*) #114, p 477, is precise on the point: *yathā ca buddhādeḥ sarvajñatvam puruṣatvādasmadādivan niṣedhyam, evam prajāpaterapi straṣṭratvam*: "The statement 'The Buddha is Omniscient' cannot be verified, because he is a being like us, hence also the Creativity of Prajāpati (God)".

[10]Kumārila *ŚV*, *codanāsūtra* 117, #130-137, pp.61-64.

[11]See note 9 above.

[12]Kumārila *ŚV*, *codanāsūtra*, #116, #128, #155, #169-172, pp. 60, 63, 68, 71-72.

would be an anathema to Hindu orthodoxy.

Another reason was to reject the attempt to base the authority of the Vedas on the omniscience of a divine author. If omniscience is argued to be an essential and necessary attribute of God (for God must have access to all things, everywhere, after as before creation)[13] then by showing the absurdity entailed in the notion of omniscience Kumārila thought he could score points against the argument the Nyāya-Vaiśeṣika rely upon in their defence of orthodoxy.[14] Namely, one infers the omniscience of God (Īśvara) from the very qualitative character, non-deceiving and benevolent intentionality (*tātparya*) of the Vedas together with their unredoubtable authority (as acknowledged by a multitude of people, or at least by the great minds, *mahājana-parigṛhīta*), for only an omniscient being would be capable of such veracious wisdom. One then deduces the validity of the Vedas on grounds of God's veracity.[15] Clearly a circularity is involved in such an argument; not unlike, we may note, the kind that has often also characterised defence of the Bible in Western theology.[16] Kumārila might further say that, even if we were to grant omniscience (*sarvajñatva*) to the purported author, how would we know that he revealed this and not some other scripture, for such claims can be made for any scripture? Any argument, therefore, that seeks to ground the validity of the scripture in a source external to the texts - more technically on *parataḥprāmāṇya* - is bound to be haunted by uncertainty of one kind or another. The Nyāya move unwittingly weakens the kind of hardline defence needed ultimately for the survival of Hindu orthodoxy, and hence the Mīmāṃsā would have no truck with it.

Kumārila is not so forceful in these arguments, nor is this particularly pressing on him. His primary concern is to defend the Vedas, not to argue against the existence of God (much less for God's *non*-existence), though that should help his cause.[17] It is enough that there is doubt in respect of God's authorship of the Vedas. For now he

---

[13]Although some modern theologians are apt to doubt this one; and it depends on what one means by "omniscience": does it entail knowing everything simultaneously and in all details, past, present and future; or is it sufficient to have at hand general principles and possible permutations of order of things, etc? Is one always omniscient, or can one become so? In the qualified sense, the claim about the Buddha's omniscience need not be as incoherent as the Mīmāṃsakas argue. See *ŚV codanāsūtra*, #130-137, pp.63-64.

[14]Kumārila argues against the derivation of scripture from an omniscient being, *ŚV*, *codanāsūtra*, #118-120, #145-147, pp.61-62, 66-67.

[15]Same comment as in note 8 above applies here. *Vaiśeṣika-sutra* I.3, and repeated in conclusion, seems to have led to this genre of arguments, later championed more vehemently by Udayana in his *Nyāyakusumāñjali*, ch.5: "eight proofs", aimed against the Mīmāṃsā. The *mahājanaparigṛhīta* suggestion is made in Bk.III (#302, 9ff.); for a variant rendering of *mahājana* (*omnis pluribus*) and a candid discussion of the proofs, see Chemparathy (1972), p.97, and p. 53, 69-73. Śaṃkara in his *Brahmasūtrabhāṣya* II.2.38 repeats the charge. And Kumārila *ŚV*, *codanāsūtra*, #97-98 considers and rejects these moves.

[16]See de Broglie (1965), pp.20-31; Hick (1977), p. 2; for a critique see Fichte (1978); Farley (1982).

[17]Pashupatinath Shastri (1980) pp.10, 133ff. says Kumārila nowhere denies God's existence, only that God cannot be the creator if he is also not the dispenser of fruits, and hence calls Kumārila a theist, against all evidence to the contrary. This is like looking for arguments for God's non-existence when all one wants to do is argue against God's existence, which is not at all the same thing.

can simply drop God from the picture.[18] In other words, God or any other omniscient persons are rejected as probable authors of the Vedas.

The Authorless Vedas.

In the absence, then, of God and other omniscient beings, how would the Mīmāṃsā account for the origin and validity of the Vedas? There are really two questions here and they can be treated separately. But for Kumārila, the answers are intertwined. To dispose of the second question first, Kumārila is faithful to the general Mīmāṃsā theory of *svataḥprāmāṇya*, intrinsic validity of knowledge, i.e. truth is self-validating and self-evident.[19] Every cognition, awareness and belief is valid (self-evidentially true) insofar as it is not marred by defects, or shown to be erroneous (i.e. is unfalsified).[20] *Śabda* or words also share this epistemic, "truth-giving", property, provided they are uttered by reliable and trustworthy persons; but this is also an admission to their possible errancy or fallibility. The defect is not in the words as such, or in their capacity to convey meaning (sense), but more usually in the speaker or author, in his intentionality. However, Vedic words are valid for the reason that they convey their own meaning and this meaning is not dependent upon some speaker or author, who might, given personal subjectivity, err, particularly in matters religious.[21] In short, the assertion of the validity of the Vedas is parasitic upon the very denial of the author and the intrusion of personal intentionality (*ŚV* I.i. II,#97). The text is, as it were, "de-personalised" in respect of personal intentionality; but intentionality (*tātparya*) as such is not entirely eroded. There are, of course, a number of questionable assumptions here, but let them pass for now in the interest of the first question.

II

We are tempted to say that this sounds to be a preposterous idea: the Vedas must have had some author, as with any utterance or text. As far as the Mīmāṃsā are concerned the author of the Vedas, whether omniscient or of a lesser state of being, is absent. Could the Mīmāṃsā possibly mean that the author of the Vedas has simply vanished (or withdrawn for other larger purposes, as it appears to be said of the author of the Kabbalistic texts, in the doctrine known as *zimzum*)? But the author or authors could not have vanished, for they are named in the Vedas. The Mīmāṃsā reply is that these names are either fictitious or belong to those who recited the texts, or they refer to evanescent deities that arise instantaneously with sacrifices.[22] So the actual authors

---

[18]One is here curiously reminded of the late 1960's "Death of God" movement in some Anglican-Protestant circles.

[19]Kumārila *ŚV codanāsūtra* #53, #154; p.47, p.68.

[20]The theory is fraught with difficulties; and indeed, not all things valid are "true"; but the main concern here is with sentences (*śabda/vākya*), and of certain sentences, such as speech-acts (illocutionary/perlocutionary) and Goodmanian statements, it is not meaningful to ask whether they are true or false; this wisdom will prevail here, despite the rhetoric of "validity". Kumārila makes a lot of the inerrancy of the Vedic utterances compared with the utterances of the Buddha, etc.

[21]Kumārila *ŚV codanāsūtra* #97, #169, pp.53,71.

[22]Kumārila *ŚV*, *vedanityādhikāra* #4-12, pp. 670-672. On relation between deities and sacrifice see *Śābarabhāṣya* 6.1.2, 6.3.18, 10.4.23, and discussion in Gächter (1983) p.26.

are not known or have been forgotten?

The Mīmāṃsā thesis is that the Vedas are *apauruṣeya*, literally, "without a personal source or agent", or simply: authorless. The doctrine given expression to here is known as *Vedāpauruṣeyatva* : Vedas being without an author, or simply, the authorlessness of the Vedas. Since the Vedas have been merely "heard", but not spoken, they are collectively known as *śruti*: literally, "that which has been heard", or more broadly "what has come through the hearing". The Vedas are, therefore, authorless.[23]

Again, it is not altogether clear what it means to say that *śruti* is without any author. Now the idea of authorlessness suggested can be interpreted in a number of ways as follows. Such person or subject as may have been the author:

(a) is not known, or has vanished;
(b) is a systematised (scriptural) tradition;
(c) is the "community of the wise" (*ṛṣis*);
(d) is wilfully forgotten, so as not to matter;
(e) is the function of a historic-constitutive "tradition";
(f) does not exist, i.e. there was never any;
(g) is constituted in and through language, itself non-originative.

Some overlaps aside, there are doubtless other nuances in currency.[24] I shall very briefly examine a few responses to the suggestions sketched above to illustrate how most interpretations tend to be reductionist and are thus to be rejected. The first possibility has already been dealt with. (Another possibility, namely, the author as a mere intermediary - as with most schools of Vedānta - is implied in (c).)

The Tradition Approach: I

M. Hiriyanna, for one, situates the notion of authorless texts in the context of the history of philosophy. He points out that the Mīmāṃsā were among the first in India to have taken seriously the doctrine of *śabda* ("word", *verbum*) as a *pramāṇa* (means of understanding or knowledge). But *śabda* stood, in earlier times, for *tradition* (and only later the scope was extended to encompass all verbal statements - "verbal testimony" - irrespective of their connection with tradition).[25] The Vedas were part of the vast material of tradition accumulated from earlier times, and as the latter got systematised, the Vedas received preeminence within the *pramāṇa* theory that was also being formalised. The very inclusion of *śabda* qua tradition among the *pramāṇas* or knowledge-sources indicates, Hiriyanna tells us, the appreciation of history in philosophy; but it also indicates the reverence with which the authority of tradition was regarded, which is traceable back to the Brāhmaṇas.[26]

---

[23]*apauruṣeyam vākyaṃ vedah; Arthasaṃgraha* of Laugākṣi Bhāskara (1984 edn) #10 p.7.

[24]One of which (closest to (g)) has become something of a vogue in the postmodern marriage of philosophical and literary thinking: particularly in the works of the Parisian writers Roland Barthes, Michel Foucault and Jacques Derrida.

[25]Hiriyanna (1973), p.178.

[26]Ibid., p.179. The Prābhākara school of Mīmāṃsā, however, equated *śabda* with the Veda (explaining other forms of verbal testimony as mere forms of inference), and this belief continues with the few survivors of this school to this day. For other Mīmāṃsā schools the Veda instantiated, we might say, a more privileged and authentic class of verbal testimony.

Hiriyanna, then, takes *śabda,* and *śruti* as the limiting case, as originally conceived of in Indian philosophy to be nothing more than sytematised "tradition"(b). Tradition, he explains, for some (the heterodox) is reducible to human experiences (*pauruṣeya*), more fundamentally to what can be known through the "higher faculties" of insight, yogic perception and intuition. "For others (the orthodox) it means revelation which, if not exactly, divine or coming from God is ... supernatural (*apauruṣeya*) in some sense or other".[27]

Hiriyanna simply takes *apauruṣeya* to be another way of accounting for the apparently immemorial tradition by those who came to distrust appeal to human experiences (ordinary or paranormal), for such "visions" may be illusory. To avoid this subjectivity and its possible defects, they postulated another *pramāṇa*: viz., *śruti* or "revelation", the inviolable and primary authority (*veritas prima*) that tradition has known, preserved and transmitted.[28] Its source, though, remains a mystery.

Theological analysis aside, however, in his own mind Hiriyanna believes that the truths for which the Vedas stand should eventually be traceable to some human source: "and the fact seems to be implied in the description of those truths having been seen by *ṛṣis* or inspired sages of old".[29] But these truths or insights, as with all "revealed" truths, he argues, must have proved acceptable to the best minds of the community (*mahājanaparigraha*) (c). However here is the rub: the truths must become public and be "ascertained" in the wisdom of the wise ones.[30] He is here invoking the criteria of public certainty and trans-individual commitment. In other words, Hiriyanna seemed to be in favour of reducing *śruti* to an immemorial "tradition", and tradition to a set body of beliefs, informed by the intuition or religious insights of the sages and seers, once they have been adjudged and adopted by the best minds of the community. The propositions of the Vedas are just those intersubjectively corroborated expressions of primal experiences,"the probability of whose truth has already been indicated by reason".[31] In short, *śruti* is a social product - a "race intuition" - that comes to acquire a non-personal authenticity. This is what the "argument from authority" (*śrutiprāmāṇya*), stripped of its mystique, amounts to. Hiriyanna's view combines (b) and (c). But he does not tackle the issue of *apauruṣeya* in any depth, while he self-assuredly defends calling *śruti* "revelation".[32]

Needless to say, Hiriyanna's liberalised reading would not be acceptable to the Mīmāṃsā, as Pārthasārathi Miśra had, as if in anticipation, already repudiated it.[33] It is reductionist and apologetic; in fact, Hiriyanna reads Vedānta (Uttara Mīmāṃsā) backwards into (Pūrva) Mīmāṃsā: not an uncommon tendency in historical

---

[27]Ibid., pp.180, 267. Although Nyāya-Vaiśeṣika also accepted these as legitimate, they did not attribute the real origin of the Vedas to these; these insights were necessary for the primeval seers to "vision" the Vedic corpus even as God (re)issues with each new creation.

[28]Hiriyanna (1952), p.27.

[29]Ibid., p.28.

[30]Ibid.; cf. note 15 above.

[31]Ibid., p.14

[32]Ibid., pp.13-14

[33]Pārthasārathi (1981 edn) deals with other notions of tradition, such as *ṛṣis* waking up with Vedas, and Prājapati's creation of this etc. *Śāstradīpikā (tarkapāda)* at #123.

reconstructions of Indian philosophy.

Revelatio

As to the question of "revelation" and its meaningful use in this context, the debate is far too skewed for me to want to enter into fully here. But basically, if we were break up the doctrine of revelation into, what I prefer to call, the "two dogmas of revelation", we see that the term as it is understood and the pregnant concept it refers to in Western philosophical theology, is controverted in one of its fundamentals by the notion of *apauruṣeya*. The two dogmas are, respectively[34]:

(di) Revelation is something that is not accessible to the normal or supranormal human capacities (i.e. experiences, reason, imagination, deep insight, etc); it is hidden from man.

(dii) This something hidden (i.e. revealed truth) comes to man from beyond him; more specifically, the agent is God: it is God's free self- disclosure.

Now the *Vedāpauruṣeya* doctrine is in one fundamental respect a claim about certain truths not accessible to the normal, or extraordinary, human capacities. These truths pertain to *dharma* and *adharma* ("ought" and "ought not" mandates), *apūrva* ("transcendental" or "the never before" signified potential for the higher good, *niḥśreyasa*), the nature of the self (*ātman*), as also its fate after death, and all such matters that fall under the category of the "invisible" (*adṛṣṭa*). Such truths remain concealed. Hence (di) is satisfied.

However, *Vedāpauruṣeya* falls short of fulfilling the desideratum under (dii), for there is no appeal here to a "higher transcendental reality" or some deeper or "original reality" that "breaks in upon" the human world with these hidden truths[35]. Notwithstanding the Mīmāṃsā appeal to some "transcendental realm or state" - vis-à-vis the notions of *apūrva, svarga* (heaven), and other *lokas* or worlds, as the aftermath in its ritual hermeneutic - we can say that, in respect of (dii), it makes no such appeals. There is no God that reveals; *śruti* does not come about through any intervention in history; rather, if *śruti* is not prior to the world, it is primordially one with the non-created world; it may even "fashion" the cosmos, and provide the constitutive coordinates for a "lifeworld" in a ritual ordering of things. Thus the application of the term "revelation" to the notion of *apauruṣeya* is to be rejected.[36] This is a common argument.

One is then left with no other choice but to predicate the authorless locution within a purely ritual discourse, in terms of an ontologically inconsequential (maybe banal) relation between ritual and text, *yāga* and *mantra*, act and imperative, and so on.[37] But, like all such eliminative comparative judgements, this approach is redolent of

---

[34] I discern this composite sense, in the first instance, from the *Summa Theologiae* of St Thomas Aquinas (1a 1) (1964), pp. 9, 29, and Appendix 7; and for its clearer statement, from Nielsen (1970), pp. 9-10.

[35] Clooney (1985), p.11.

[36] Clooney (1985); this is Clooney's avowed conclusion.

[37] This trend, of course, began with Max Muller and continued through A. B. Keith, S. Radhakrishnan, S.N. Dasgupta, amongst others. For a quick survey of this trend, see D'Sa (1980), pp. 44-45, n.15.

reverse fundamentalism. In the first place, it belies sensitivity to the complexity of the Mīmāṃsā worldview, its philosophy of language and its keen ethical sensibility. And in the second place, it is made despite the inconclusive debate on just what the term "revelation" means and whether the concept it refers to is at all coherent, given its unargued for, and perhaps unarguable[38], logocentric presuppositions, epistemological shifts and ontological assumptions under (dii). (E.g. about the existence of God and his causal activity of revealing.) Moreover there is the circularity involved in its affirmation that revelation is needed for faith, faith presupposes God, and God is necessary for revelation.[39] We are on less precarious grounds with (di) alone, and we might have salvaged something in the idea of revelation; or, perhaps suggested an alternative idea.

Perhaps the shift of focus to (di) might lessen the burden of the (philosophical) difficulty involved in affirming (dii), which, in the Mīmāṃsā view, is largely a consequence of trying to ground the credibility and validity of scriptural utterances on sources external (*parataḥ*) to the text. Perhaps we are being cautioned to look more closely at the scripture itself, its text, its form and language, and all that might be intrinsic to it, before looking elsewhere for its justification. But then, (di) is not sufficient by itself; it calls for a resolution of (dii). The absolute rejection of (dii) without a legitimate substitute would make (di) empty; and whatever is substituted might itself be an incoherent concept, or even self-contradictory, as some believe the notion of authorless revelation to be. And so to that.

Historical Amnesia

One such response has it that this entire authorless idea is a product of what could be termed "retroflexive amnesia". A tradition with a vast body of sacredly regarded doctrines, ideas, liturgical prescriptions and moral teachings, accumulated over a period of time, fails to maintain a well-defined historical perspective of its own past: it collectively forgets its historical roots, and retroflexively identifies its accumulated wisdom with an authority that transcends the mundane processes.

For, as said earlier, with the Mīmāṃsā there is no belief in a supremely transcendental being, and there is no recollection of the progenitors of the vast *śruti* material. Thus the source and authority are identified with an essentially nonpersonal given, namely the word or text itself. So, "the question of its (*śruti's*) being a *pramāṇa* (i.e. means of knowledge) is something which is retroflexive, which is a later projection back on the Vedic material".[40] And we might add, a subconscious, or maybe voluntary, amnesia about the details of the historical past serves to vindicate this peculiar non-originative doctrine. (Hence the (d) interpretation.) It is as though the Mīmāṃsā were interested in Plato's alleged project of *anamnesis*, but without wishing a regressive return to that which makes a tradition, viz. the originary visions. *Śruti* is alive and ready to be appropriated without any need for recollection, *in illo tempore*.

The *apauruṣeya* doctrine then becomes a part of the defence of the claimed ahistoricity of the textual tradition and the Vedas are proclaimed by orthodoxy to be

---

[38]Nielsen (1970), p.9 cites Gordon Kaufman as saying precisely this: that what is amenable to human scrutiny and assessment can be known ipso facto not to be revelation.

[39]Sokolowski (1982), p. 137 comes rather close to saying this; but it is everywhere in classical treatises. For discussion of more complex forms of this assertion see Farley (1982), p. 166.

[40]Ninian Smart made this comment (recorded) in response to papers on "*Śabda* and *Śruti*: Tradition & Authority" at a conference of the Asian & Comparative Philosophy Assocation, Honolulu, 1984.

atemporal, ahistorical and non-originated.[41]

Tradition Approach - II.

Thinking along these lines, Professor J.N. Mohanty argues that "it is too literal an understanding of the thesis of *apauruṣeyatva* of *śruti* to construe it as meaning that the texts are simply not composed by any human author at all, or even that they are not composed at all." And furthermore, "[I]t is totally muddled - and betrays an insensitiveness to the nature of Hindu thought - to say that the *śruti* is *apauruṣeya* in the sense that they contain revealed truths. No less muddled is the cliche that the scriptures express the spiritual experiences of their presumed authors."[42]

So the texts have authors but they are not about the authors' experiences. Then what are they about? Mohanty clarifies that he is not denying the texts in some sense are about the authors' spiritual experiences, but that is not what he claims the texts to be expressing. What the texts express are sedimentations of these founding experiences: that is to say, the experiences "interpreted, transformed into thought, and brought under a conceptual framework".[43] Tradition, it is claimed, has a remarkable way of achieving this by interpreting and incorporating originary experiences into a "thought" and depositing this into language, or texts, thereby giving greater "primacy and autonomy" to the *eminent* texts over the subjective intentionality of the authors. As the text is pushed forward, the intentions of the authors or subjects recede to the background. Thus *śruti* defines, demarcates and constitutes the horizon within which the tradition has understood itself. And it is this constitutive self-understanding that the diaphanous tradition passes on through the exteriority of the text. Perhaps, we might surmise from this argument, the Mīmāṃsā truly lost recollection of the fact that there were subjects of the founding experiences and that the "tradition" at large was the author of the scriptures they are so beholden to.

The argument utilises a basically Husserlian phenomenological perspective tempered by a Gadamarian insight into the historicity of truth-events (*aletheia*), the happening of truth and untruth, in the life of a tradition. But this analysis, challenging as it is, and certainly not without its own merits, is part of a larger project grounded in the quest for an understanding of the Western tradition and its rational/metaphysical movements, from their Greek roots to the present "crisis". It also undergirds a normative concern. Now how this should apply to a distinctive feature of the Indian tradition, without the added assumption of the universality of cultural forms, puzzles me somewhat. I am far from saying that we cannot find, nor look for, parallels, particularly where we are concerned with the interrelations between human subjectivity, intentionality, language and "tradition". My question is: does it really advance our understanding of the Mīmāṃsā doctrine at issue and successfully explain, or explain away, its claims and presuppositions?

Yet it nevertheless has a persuasive force that cannot be overlooked. It is certainly more perspicuous than Hiriyanna's tradition-approach, and is able to liberate texts from, at least, individual intentionality: language is prior to experience. There is much insightful scope here and it provides a useful heuristic. I want merely to caution against a possible universalisation involved here and emphasise the peculiarity of the

---

[41] Mohanty (1982), p. 237; see next note also.

[42] Mohanty (1987), pp.13-14 (more forcefully argued here).

[43] Mohanty (1987), p.14.

Mīmāṃsā theory of language that wants to do away altogether with human intentionality in language. And this is crucial for an understanding the *apauruṣeya* notion. But before that, two other considerations.

Scripture to Text

To give credit to the historicised approach, our attention is drawn by it to the historical fact, of the Vedic corpus having had a long oral tradition before being committed to writing. The immemorial succession of priests and teachers (*gurus*) continued the transmission of the teachings. The several branches of the Vedas were intended to be recited and committed to memory. Given the oral character of the teachings, in what sense did *śruti* constitute what might be called "texts"? The short answer to this is that the structure and organisation of the Vedas conformed very much to the literate or "written" mode, or what might otherwise be called a "text".[44] The Vedas contained, in its oral form, all the devices and techniques of literate speech, such as delimitors, quotations, punctuation and notation markings, accents and appropriate breaks and pauses, so that the compositions could function as texts and be treated as texts or at least as *text-analogue* - indeed, even as "thought". In the course of time writing was developed and the orally recited texts were committed to the written word. But the living tradition of the Vedas remained in the province of oral recitations, not in the written texts (though the latter facilitated their wider access and repeatability). In either case, the expressions continued a career, as if all their own.

It is conceivable, then, as is often with orally handed down traditions, that some or many generations later people tend to forget the subjects or authors of the original expressions as the authors and their intentionality receded into historical oblivion.

The Mīmāṃsakas will have little difficulty with the stress on the facticity of the oral tradition and they may even turn this to their own advantage. For they argue that, as long as it is humanly possible to recollect, there is no knowledge of the authors of the Vedas: all that we know is that they were heard by our fathers, our fathers heard it from their fathers and forefathers, and this line of hearing, reading or whatever, goes all the way back to the ancients, who also heard them.[45] Thus there is a continuous succession of "authorless hearers" (*śrotrīyas*). This is why the Vedas are called *śruti*. It is not self-evident nor is there any real evidence that the Vedas began with some one person or community. This indeed is the mystery. To say that "they should have" or "they can't have", or that it is a confused idea, puts the onus on those who seek to falsify the Mīmāṃsā thesis. Besides, why should the *śruti* diminish in significance merely because its alleged author appears to be absent, or never did exist (f)?

III

Primacy of Language

Should we then take the Mīmāṃsā to be saying that language of the Vedas, and language more generally, was there somehow from time immemorial? Yes, the

---

[44]The Australian Aborigines, one of the oldest surviving language-communities in the world today, developed no written language. But it would be ludicrous to say they had no "texts" or any kind of structured, repeatable, and "objective" language; it is just that this took many other equally complex forms.

[45]Kumārila *ŚV*, (*vedanityādhikāra*) #3, p.670.

Mīmāṃsā would reply, their argument does turn on the primacy of language, the priority of the word, prior to speech. But to say this, it may be objected, is to show a profound ignorance of the origin of language, particularly its social-evolutionary formation. Our capabilities of language have underlying physiological and mental structures, which we have come to possess as human beings as a part of the evolutionary process.[46] The Mīmāṃsā position reminds one of the European Romantic belief in the "givenness" of the language of revelation and supreme poetry, which was disputed by the Enlightenment thinkers.

Now one could refer to anthropological insights into pre-linguistic communities and their peculiar ways of associating signs with their supposed referents or objects. Among so-called "primitive" cultures anthropologists found tendencies to identify primal sounds and symbols with things they correspond to, such that the repetition of these sounds would recall the referents, and the magical invocation of the symbols might causally affect or evoke their corresponding objects, etc. These signs themselves may become signifiers for yet another set of signs, thus establishing a somewhat deferred and autonomous relation between the earlier signs and derivative, albeit more focused signs. There is also a tendency to see synonymity and metonomy between and among signs that ordinarily do not exist. Thus a primitive might associate thunder with the wrath of the gods, and lightning with the damnation of his people, and further associate the two events with his failure to offer sacrifice to the ancestors; next he might develop a system of signs to refer to these phenomena, the acts commensurate with these, and their originary elations.[47]

We see that language here works in an instrumental way once a system of signs is established. The texts into which these signs get codified and recorded become the originative source of the myths, narratives, or legends recounted to later generations.

The Enlightenment Origin of Language Speculations

The anthropologists have echoed, to some extent, eighteenth-nineteenth century speculations on the origin of language, such as those of Condillac (1746), Reid (1764), and Monboddo (1773). Very briefly, the Enlightenment writers had argued that language was an invention, and traced its origins to primitive, natural communicative modes involving self-explanatory visible signs or signals (e.g. gestures, postures, cries), which were replaced in time by arbitrary sounds based on the secondary and unexpected effects of these actions.[48] The signs were gradually improved upon, and more sounds were combined to evolve references to objects, events, etc. not actually present (e.g. warning, heeding, say, a flood ahead). Sounds had greater advantage over all other forms of communication, because they could be easily created, articulated, repeated, and heard at some distance.[49] This led to the deliberate invention of words, conventions for their association, and so on. Thus developed the conventional, articulate oral languages. Questions as to how this language got universalised, diversified, and dispersed among those of lesser skills, remained largely unanswered.

Later there were modifications to this view, but basically it was agreed that language as it exists today consists very largely of sounds whose meanings have been

---

[46]Smart (1985); see also note 50 infra.

[47]This Malinowskian observation is often repeated in social science textbooks.

[48]Wells (1987), pp.10-13

[49]Ibid., p.28

fixed only by convention. Language is thus an invention. Darwin, in his own way, provided a variable twist to the general quest by tracing the possible innumerable steps, "half consciously made", in a biological-evolutionary matrix that led to its accomplishment.[50] Of course this overview is rather crude, but the general drift of the argument is there.

These speculations have all but been discredited and nowadays are regarded largely to be the result of a fruitless endeavour. Not the least, because the belated discovery of Sanskrit in the West threw into disarray such speculations as the antiquity of *Ursprache*, the "original speech", from which the modern languages grew, or perhaps (in Max Müller's Indo-European family-tree typology) degenerated. More damaging were objections of Herder and others, who echoed Rousseau's paradox: "words seem to have been necessary in order to establish the use of words."[51] It was argued that it is impossible to suppose that man invented language, because he could have had no conception of language and its usefulness before it existed. Modern experiments certainly confirm that animals (like chimpanzees) can develop a complicated sign-language from gestures and imitative behaviour, but their "language", thus far, does not converge with the articulated sound-meaning system or speech that human beings possess. Some animals might learn to scribble "sentences" even before they could speak them - which appears to be the converse of what most (human) "origin" theories have supposed. Although, dolphins present another kind of challenge, with their acute sonic capabilities.

It is perhaps, after all, a pseudo-problem; or, one might consider that language is prior to speech, so that, given certain conditions, there is no a priori reason why other sentient beings could not use it, just as the human animal does, or has learnt to.

It is true the Mīmāṃsakas were no anthropologists, nor historians for that matter, although their contributions to linguistic understanding, to Sanskrit, and to Hindu legal jurisprudence, have long been recognised in India. But I believe we have been misled, partly by the Mīmāṃsā rhetoric and partly by earlier Orientalists, in supposing that the Mīmāṃsā were actually commenting on the "origin" of language - anymore than de Saussure or Chomsky could be said to have in their respective quests for the "basic rudiments" of language. What the Mīmāṃsakas want to say is simply that neither they nor others have known a time when language was not. In other words, since no one is able to point to a time when language originated, by default, they assume that language has been with people for as long as human beings have been around, which (given Mīmāṃsā cosmology) must have been an immeasurably long time. It might still betray a faulty inductive reasoning (did they always speak it?); but it would be more correct to say that Mīmāṃsā were interested in getting us away from questions about the progenitors, original speakers, and bearers or subjects of language, and instead to concern ourselves more with what language is, how language operates (even if independently of its speakers and their intentionality), and how it perpetuates itself. The point at issue then is not at all a historical one: it is about the pre-conditions for the possibility of language. This is the stuff of a metaphysic of language, and such questions have indeed also been paramount in the minds of linguists and philosophers alike. It makes one wonder whether the doctrine of *apauruṣeya* was not the result of

---

[50]Ibid. p.5. Although in its revamped neo-Darwinian version this view challenges and rivals all "essentialist" theories of the "basic rudiments" of language kind. See Hattiangadi (1987), pp.5, 25; and in chapter 10, "Mind and the Origin of Language", Hattiangadi presents a variation of the old "imitation" theories, starting with prelinguistic cries.

[51]Wells (1987), pp.11, 103

their reflections on the nature of language itself, and perhaps even derived from their peculiar theory of language?

The Linguistic Turn

I want now to sketch the Mīmāṃsā theory of language in which the notion of *apauruṣeya* finds its support. Now could it be that the Mīmāṃsā entertained the possibility of the preeminence or priority of language over its use in human speech-communities? Could such a possibility be conceivable? What would it mean to conceive of language being there somehow prior to to its bearers or users? Its users would appear, according to such a conception, to be little more than instruments through whose subjectivity and intentionality language operates to manifest the prefigured conventions and (basic) structures that embed meaning. Language "happens" to us.

This view presupposes a kind of essentialism - somewhat akin to that presupposed or argued for in some prominent linguistic theories, such as that of Noam Chomsky, with its basis in an unchanging "Universal Grammar"; but the similarities end here, especially with Chomsky's location of the deep structure in the innate (rational-social) environment of the speaker. Thus, in speaking of the priority of language, we should understand the Mīmāṃsā to be speaking of the *logical* priority of some fundamental feature of the linguistic process, the locus of which is not psychological (i.e. cognitive), nor Platonic for that matter.

One may appeal to common sense: It is certainly the case that in any language community language is there prior to the advent of each new individual born into the community. For as long as we can remember there has been language (although its forms and manifest expressions have tended to vary with time, place, and norms); the young learn it from their elders, and the elders say they learnt it from their elders, forefathers from their ancestors and so on. By this imaginary regress we can demonstrate that language is at least logically prior to individuals who make use of language.

What this really means is that every individual must learn a language the conventions of which are already established or "given", and that goes for the imagined first users of the language. Now if it is the case, as some would argue, that the conventions were created by some prelinguistic individuals, then we fall back to the paradox (canvassed earlier): how could they communicate and explain these conventions to each other and to others unless they already understood the very language made possible by these conventions? Where lies the condition for the possibility of the conventions? To say, using the Wittgensteinian model, that it is determined in the very use of language, as, say, in a game, is unsatisfactory. Imagine again a time when there was no human language, then there was a first time any linguistic device or convention was used, in terms of which, say, a meaning was fixed. But the irony is that at that time there was no usage, and so it would have no meaning; for anything to be used it must have some meaning, and only then it would be adopted.[52]

Now, to get around these conceptual difficulties, the Mīmāṃsā posit a thesis according to which the conventions are thought to be pre-established or *given*, in respect of their pre-condition. We shall call this "the *autpattika* thesis".

---

[52]Hattiangadi (1987), p.30. A convention established by a naming-system, according to which words correspond to the thing that it names, cannot do it either.

The *Autpattika* Thesis.

In what came to be known as the *autpattika sūtra* of Jaimini it is stated: "The relation (*sambandha*) between *śabda* and *artha* is originary (*autpattika*)".[53] Ordinarily *śabda* stands for "sound", "noise", "speech" and may connote "phoneme", "vowel" etc. But in this context *śabda* is best taken to represent the "word", that which denotes; and *artha* is the meaning, that which is denoted. Now Pārthasārathi Miśra observes that in ordinary speech there is a relation between word and meaning, which is of the nature of *pratyāyya* and *pratyāyaka* (that which is denoted and that which denotes). It is by virtue of this denotative character (*pratyāyakatva*) that a word denotes its meaning (in other uses as well) independently of other relations, and of sense-organ contact or inference.[54] The awareness of meaning arises immediately upon the word being presented. This points to a peculiar expressive or signifying capability, i.e. meaning (*abhidhāna*) that the word as a unity of sign signification appears to possess. (It would be best to take "sign" in the Peirceian sense of something that stands for something). The relation then is a significant one: it is one that yields signification. Pārthasārathi characterises this unique relation of *śabda* to *artha* as one of *samjñā-samjñin vācya-vācaka*, which I would like to render as the signifier to signified relation.[55] And this relation is called *autpattika*. What does this mean?

The term "*autpattika*", rooted as it is in *ut-patti* (arising, originating), in Jaimini's use of it at least, would appear to mean "originative", and hence "not given", nor pre-established. In fact, the converse is intended: the relation is "originary", in the sense that the presentment of the word and its meaning is simultaneous, so that there is no moment when they could be separated. In other words, the word and its meaning arise *as if* psychologically co-present.[56] It is as though the word and its meaning are spontaneously united or invariably connected, for the reason that, conventional interferences and habits side, words are never without meanings; and in the process of uttering and hearing, to one familiar with the language, they happen simultaneously. That is to say, the relation is "impeccable", "predelineated" or "prefigured", even "preeminently given". Here I take Jaimini to be utilising a semiotic insight.

The last remark needs explaining; for this we need to turn to Śabara's comments on the relation:

> *Autpatikka* - what we mean by this is *nitya*: it is that (the term) "origin" (*utpatti*) is figuratively spoken of as *bhāva* or presence. The relation between the word and meaning are inseparable by virtue of the presence (of one with the other). The word and meaning do not have their relation constituted after they have been produced.[57]

I have deliberately left the term "*nitya*" untranslated, as its sense is conveyed in

---

[53] *Jaiminisūtra* I.i.5, in *Mīmāṃsādarśana* (1979 edn), p.170: *autpattikastu śabdasyārthena sambandhaḥ.*

[54] Pārthasārathi Miśra (1891 edn), *Śāstradīpikā (tarkapāda)* #89, p.68ff.

[55] Pārthasārathi (1891 edn) #89, p.68.

[56] A description I owe to Professor K.T. Pandurangi of Bangalore, who guided me through these texts.

[57] *Śābarabhāṣya*, in *Mīmāṃsādarśana* (1979) p. 170: *autpattika iti nityaṃ bhrumaḥ. utpattir hi bhāva ucyate lakṣaṇayā. aviyuktaḥ śabdārthayor bhāvaḥ sambandho, notpannayoḥ paścāt sambandhaḥ.*

Śabara's explanation. *Nitya* has the more general connotation of "eternity", "outside time", "beginningless" and so on (a better term is "*śāśvata*"). But here the term "*nitya*", as Biardeau rightly points out, "does not connote eternity nor does it even specifically refer to permanence"; rather it has the sense of an "internal exigency" (*svābhāvika*).[58] And for this there is no dependency on any kind of extrinsic appropriation, such as a qualification of existence in terms of time or its exclusion, or substance by quality, or the sender. It essentially defines a relational structure (hence *saṃbandhena*) that belongs to the very nature of *śabda* and *artha*. The emphatic stress is on the constancy of the relation: "*śabda* is never outside of or apart from the *autpattika* relation".[59] And since *śabda* connotes the unity of the sign with the differential but inseparable relation of the *saṃjñā-saṃjñin* (signifier-signified) it also can be characterised as *nitya* or "non-originative".

The *autpattika* thesis has its parallel in de Sausurre's general semiological insight about the integral union of the signifier [*signifiant*] (a sign-vehicle) and the signified [*signifié*] (meaning) in any system of signs. For Saussure, the linguistic sign is a twofold entity, a Janus-faced thing, both sides or faces of which are absolutely necessary for it to function as a sign.[60] The linguistic sign unites, not a thing and a name, but a concept and a sound-image, as the signified and the signifier respectively. The two elements are intimately united, and each recalls the other. The indissoluble union of the two primordial components is the only essential thing in language, represented thus:

$$\text{Sn} \quad \frac{\text{Sd}}{\text{Sg}} \quad \text{(signification)}$$

signified ⇌ signifier

What is important for us, in the above, is the fundamental unity of the signifier and the signified, and this is what makes it possible for the signifier, by becoming transparent, to allow the meaning (the signified) to present itself; referring to nothing other than its presence. But *aupattika* brings in the added standing-for "power of the sign" (*abhidhānaśakti*) - as with the Peirceian sign - for which a human emitter is not necessary either. For Saussure, however, in language the bond is constituted arbitrarily, and the signs are artifically produced. But Saussure does mean, nevertheless, that there is no "motivation" on the part of the individual to form such a bond or even the power to change it; although Saussure attempts to ground the process in an extended but complex social matrix, dispersed in the history of the particular speech-community, and is suggestive of its indefiniteness.

In principle, at least, we could say that the signifier-signified relation is capable of being relatively permanent, inasmuch as "the signifier, though to all appearances freely chosen with respect to the idea that it represents, is fixed, not free, with respect to the linguistic community that uses it."[61]

---

[58]Cited in Gächter (1983), p.44; see also Staal (1969).

[59]Gächter (1983), p.44.

[60]de Saussure (1959); in Innes (1985), p.36.

[61]de Saussure (1959); in Innes (1985), p.40.

The Mīmāṃsā takes this relation to be paradigmatic of all language, and paramount, in its own estimate, in the language of the Veda. What this means is that the relation between *śabda* and *artha* is not attributable to any individual or human community, but is inseparably or preeminently fixed or "given" in language. In this sense it is non-originative. We should explain, however, that in later Mīmāṃsā thinking, Śabara's use of "*nitya*" in the context of *autpattika* was taken literally to mean "eternal" (i.e. almost in the Platonic sense). Thus Pārthasārathi Miśra, here following Kumārila, takes the relation of *śabda* and *artha* to be inexorably invariant, permanent, even eternal. And he argues that since the relation between word and meaning is eternal, we cannot be in error with Vedic sentences, as we might with ordinary utterances where conventions have so altered the otherwise fixed meanings with their respective words. That is why the ordinary utterance is not an inerrant means of knowledge (*pramāṇa*), unless it comes from a trustworthy person. While in the case of the Veda, the structure that undergirds it is determined according to the fixed relations, and its utterances are interpreted according to fixed rules and schemas, called *tātparyaliṅgas* or "hermeneutical thumb-marks".

Even if we were to disregard the more extreme reading of *autpattika* in later Mīmāṃsā thinkers and return now to Śabara, we see how a move is made from *autpattika* to *apauruṣeya*. Since the relation is non-originative, Śabara denies the "fixing" of this relation to any agency or person: it is *apauruṣeya*.[62] Children learn meanings and the words they are related to from elders, the elders learnt it from their fathers and forefathers, and so on. Through the use of words we learn what particular relation obtains; but use does not create or constitute this relation, although certain usages may impose what appear to be arbitrary relations, by artificially introducing conventions agreed upon by the users and those who adopt them. The originary relation is therefore not reducible to a convention, that, say, establishes a relation between an item *a* and an item *b*, as in the case of technical terms. In this sense also, *śabda* qua the *autpattikatva/nityatva* relation is *apauruṣeya*: a-personal. That is to say, in so far as one cannot trace any constitutive activity in respect of the relation between word and meaning that *śabda* or the word is called *apauruṣeya*. The thesis of *autpattika* for Śabara, then, characterises the fundamental *apauruṣeyatva* of *śabda*. Thus language is freed from conventionality and the necessity of human production.

The implication is that the question of the origin of the relation, and that of its inalienable sign, is indefinitely deferred. If there is any sense to the invariable pairing of word and meaning it must be attributed to an endless succession of their presence, almost as though it were an eternal co-originality. One could object that the fact of the historical repetition and the potential repeatability or "iterability" through the medium of expressions in a communicative environment may give the illusion that no personal agency, at least no individual agency, was responsible for the originary relation: that, therefore, it is non-originative. And further, we can only have access to a finite number of words in any given language at any given moment and from looking at these we cannot pronounce what the Mīmāṃsā want to, other than to spell out the rules that determine and govern conventions. But these are empirical matters that have yet to falsify the *methodological* thrust of the a-personal originary thesis. Another objection that might be brought is that the claim is counterintuitive in that there are words with no meaning, and some words with many meanings, and also many words with the same meaning. It has become a commonplace to suppose that the signifier-

---

[62] *Śābarabhāṣya* on I.i.5: *apauruṣeyah śabdasyārthena sambandhanaḥ... yat śabde vijñāte'rtho vijñāyate.*

signified relation in ordinary language at least is, if not entirely arbitrary, conventionally established or fixed. The debate can go on, as it surely does.

One may grant the virtues of the *autpattika* thesis and its characteristic of *apauruṣeyatva*. But Mīmāṃsā have still to situate intentionality somewhere. And it also has to show how the *autpattika* relation works in respect of sentences. For clearly the Veda is not a mere collection of words, in which case it would be more like a lexicon (and a tighter one at that); like any text or scripture, it is full of sentences, and without sentences no text (barring poetry) can convey as much as the relation between, say, the magnolia flower, its colour, and its likely purpose.

A sentence clearly, as a more complete linguistic expression, is composed of words in a particular relation to each other. If just any word would succeed in achieving what a sentence does, then the random utterance of "Devadatta" now and "home" at another time should be able to convey that Devadatta has gone home. It is also observed that the same words do not behave in the same way in any two constructions. Such considerations lead one to suspect that there is something more to a sentence than a mere concatenation of words, however permanently they may be related to their respective meanings. This something extra appears to be an additional function of the speaker, or his intentions, that follows established conventions of the language-community, shared also by his audience. And this would appear to be true for all sentences. Should this be the case, the thesis of the *apauruṣeyatva* of Vedic sentences, which after all is the real thesis, is undermined.

Mīmāṃsā attempts to respond to these difficulties by suggesting that word-meanings, and not words by themselves, have the capacity to combine to yield sentence-meaning, in terms of certain conditions that ensure their correct combination. But what really determines the connection between individually given word-meanings? Disparate word-meanings are never sufficient, as any new language-learner knows all too well. Again, conventions are indispensible, and these cannot but be due to accepted linguistic practices. Thus the kind of relationship alleged in *autpattika* cannot be said to obtain in the case of sentences. That being the case, we have to postulate the intervention of human agency, i.e. *pauruṣeya,* for this particular *vācya-vācaka* (expressive-expressed) relation to be effective. The *apauruṣeya* analysis cannot go through.

The Mīmāṃsā response to these objections focuses on the form of the sentence and its property of yielding a unified meaning or sense when certain linguistic conditions are satisfied. One might say they are concerned with pointing out the syntactical capabilities of a sentence more than its semantic variations. The simple fact is that sentence-meaning comprehension (*śābdabodha*) arises from hearing a sentence regardless of its source or its organisation. Learning meanings of individual words from elders is not denied, in fact it is necessary; but comprehending a sentence-meaning is another matter. It is to be explained thus.

Words, we said earlier, have a special signifying property, which is called *abhidhāna*. Neither the sentence nor its constituent word-meanings has this capacity. And it is true that words (of a sentence) in isolation from each other also do not yield sentence-meaning. A sentence, however, should not be considered as a concatenation of isolable words that have their own distinct meanings. Rather, the sentence should be seen as a complete utterance in which the word conveys not merely its own meaning, but conveys the meanings of all the words connected with that word, thus creating a "field" of interrelated meanings.[63] The primary or literal meaning gives way to the more relevant connotation in the structure of the sentence. If that does not happen then the words remain expectant (*ākāṅkṣat*): "what with the *cow*...?"; "bring what...". This extended expressive capability, called *lakṣaṇā* by Pārthasārathi Miśra[64], is owed to nothing other than the power (*śakti*) of the word itself, the signifier, which immediately "reveals" its meaning upon one's hearing the utterance. The word forfeits its function the moment its meaning is presented and *lakṣaṇā* takes over. It is as though to say that the word-meaning (or the complex of interrelated word-meanings) is stretched to constitute the sentence-meaning. But the constitutive power of the "field of meaning" is nothing more than an extension of the word-power, according to this analysis.

Secondly, a sentence is centred around a principal element which, for the Mīmāṃsā, is the verb or the action-word, as it provides the *bhāvānas* or incentives to follow through a particular understanding, particularly in regard to certain performatives. The other word-meanings, as it were, gather around this primary unit to convey a unitary meaning with the objective of serving a single purpose. This is how a sentence (*vākya*) is defined by the Mīmāṃsā.

Now as for intentionality, Mīmāṃsā make recourse to a Gricean type analysis, basically by grounding intentionality in the expression itself and shifting the focus to the listener or the "hearer's side" (to use Searle's term).[65] The fundamental contention is that an expression has its own inherent capability of conveying the intended meaning or purport (*tātparya*) to the hearer. This particular competency (*yogyatva*) is called *tātparyavṛtti* and Mīmāṃsā attributes to it a quasi-linguistic status, complemented by other conditions for the efficiency of *śābdabodha* or sentence-understanding, such as *ākāṅkṣā* (verbal expectancy), *āsatti* (contiguity), and *yogyata* (semantic competency). *Tātparya* is one of the generative factors in the comprehension of sentence-sense.

What all this means is that the expression has a way of indicating the relation that obtains between its parts and whether it will "fit" the state of affairs it (re)presents. Thus, for example, the expression "Pot (is) in the house" is fit to indicate the relation of house to pot, but not to cloth or whatever else is in the house. It is not necessary to make reference to the desire (*icchā*) with which the speaker utters this, for the propositional content already specifies this. To this extent, we can speak of the expression as having the "intentionality" (*tātparya*) of indicating the relation of house to pot, as the relation that will satisfy its object or event. Let me elaborate.

If we take utterances to be speech acts (in the broader Austinian sense) then we could say that utterances share with mental states, what Searle calls "Intentional content", meaning they are of or about certain things or state of affairs.[66] There is in the content of the speech act (re)presentation of some object or event a condition and direction of "fit" and the ideal psychological mode (*ākāṅkṣavṛtti*) under which this would obtain. Consider also that the force of certain kinds of speech acts, such as illocutionary acts (asserting, promising, ordering) and perlocutionary acts (act-performing words) rests principally in the very fact or act of their being uttered - in

---

[63] I am glossing over the differences between Prābhākara and Bhāṭṭa on the precise function of words vis-à-vis their meanings ("constructional" versus "contextual" understanding) and presenting a synthesis.

[64] *Śāstradīpikā* (*tarkapāda*), #83. (*Vākyārtha* #6). See also *Mānameyodaya* of Nārāyana Bhaṭṭa (1933), p.96: *vayaṃ tu padārthaṃ lakṣaṇayaiva vakyārthaṃ bodhayantīti*.

[65] Searle (1969), p.37.

[66] See Searle (1983), p.4.

their uttering - rather than in the intentions or otherwise of their presumed utterers. Thus when I say, "I promise ...", or "I name this ship - Queen Elizabeth",[67] I am carrying out a particular activity. The speech is exteriorised and with it remains the intentionality. There are attempts nowadays to situate intentionality in contents outside of the mental states and even to consider that intentionality is a more pervasive feature of reality than just of language qua thought.

Still, one might say that in the foregoing analysis there is a confusion here between how a sentence-meaning is comprehended and how it is, in the first instance, constituted. We do all too often try and understand sentences by the process outlined above (or something close to it), without reference to the intentions of the speaker (or any assumptions about just such a subject). But that in itself does not demonstrate that all sentences are understood in this way. Surely, it is important to know the intention of the speaker if we want to know what particular belief he wants to induce in us through his utterance. But this admission in itself is enough for the Mīmāṃsā (a) to urge that such a wisdom ought also to prevail in the case of the particular sentences whose author or authors are not known or might not exist; and (b) to look for subjective intentions only when an utterance, say, *X*, is made with the intention of inducing a belief by means of the recognition of the intention. But do we need that in order to understand *X* qua *X*? - as Grice would ask.[68] In other words, reference to personal intentions may be necessary for clarificatory purposes and to disambiguate doubtful utterances, for which we often also look to other (circumstantial) factors anyway. The problem for Mīmāṃsā hermeneutics is not how sentences are composed, if at all, but how they are to be understood, and that should not detain us from looking for their a-personal intentionality. The focus, then, shifts to the hearer's side. Greater importance, therefore, is to be attached to the impact of the communication and the action that has to follow.

IV

The Mīmāṃsā believe that something more can be said about the uniqueness of Vedic sentences. There are two classes of Vedic sentences: one class is called *codanā*, which is basically injunctive; the other class is called *arthavāda,* which is descriptive. The differentiation roughly corresponds to Austin's division of speech acts into performatives and constantives. The *codanās* are the performatives or special speech acts of the Vedas (in the sense of illocutionary but also perlocutionary acts), and they involve the use of the optative (*liṅ*). The *arthavādas* are subsidiary texts which merely highlight certain features of the *codanā* and provide other details; they may even have had human authors. It is the *codanā* sentences that are the authoritative source for the mandates. For by exhorting us to certain obligatory actions (*niyoga*) and restraints or prohibitions, they ultimately direct us to the *adṛṣṭa,* the "unseen". The observance of these mandates according to the prescribed rules may result in *apūrva,* the "never before" potency, which is more than a relation between the act and the result: it is the transcendental signified that provides the bridge to the end of the higher good (*niḥśreyasa*) to be accomplished. (The *apūrva* is lodged in the *ātman* or "soul" and is constitutive of the "new" lifeworld; in this sense it is transcendental, but not "transcendence".) The more immediate consequence may be certain expected or unexpected fruits (*phalas*) which follow as a matter of course. Some performatives

---

[67]Of course, I am referring to the famous examples of J.L. Austin. See Austin (1979).

[68]Grice (1957); (1974), p.508. For detailed discussion see Bilimoria (1988), chapter on *tātparya.*

(*niyoga*) are obligatory or categorical (*nityakarma*). Others are prudential imperatives (*kāmyakarma*); thus, *svarga kāmo yajeta*: let him who desires heavenly bliss (*y*) perform sacrifice (*x*), where *y* is the *phala* or fruit, but *z*, implicit in *x*, is the real end.[69]

The Vedas are accordingly said to have two kinds of *bhāvānas*: one in respect of word (*śābdī-bhāvāna*), which leads to the understanding of the performative (what, how and its wherewithal, etc); the other in respect of the object itself (*arthī-bhāvāna*), and the efficiency connected with the fulfilment or the end to be accomplished (*sādhya*). The act would perish, but its efficiency remains in order to bring about the end, which could well be delayed, as it obviously is in the case of *svarga*, a heavenly state or level of being. The invisible can only be reached by the invisible. Human understanding and capacities cannot accomplish these: hence the necessity of the Vedas. The deities that are mentioned in the Vedas only exist with the sacrifices, and they are as momentary as the *mantras* in which their names are recited, and their function is to make efficacious the given.

And all this is done in the name of *dharma* (the very first words of the Mīmāṃsā *jijñāsā* or hermeneutical quest) which, in the end, is the only motivation that drives the Mīmāṃsā to the Veda as the authentic and authoritative source. *Codanālakṣaṇaḥ arthaḥ dharmaḥ: dharma* is to be known as the intended object of the Veda.[70] In the Veda the Mīmāṃsakas have located an autonomous and independent source for their moral necessities. In this sense the source is a priori; freed of the human speculations, relativistic and normative variations, which the orthodoxy of their time had been threatened with. It confers meaning and moral sensibility to the world as it itself changes. That it could be claimed to be *apauruṣeya,* or fundamentally a-personal, as far as the Mīmāṃsā is concerned, guarantees its inerrancy; if it were to be claimed to be *pauruṣeya,* whether of a human or a divine kind, it may not ensure the same degree of validity.

But since the extra-linguistic claims stray into the realm of the transcendental unseen, these claims remain unproven; they remain mere conjectures. Indeed, they are unfalsifiable propositions because they are untestable by the canons of our ordinary investigative methods. Setting up a possible verificationist scenario in the hereafter (or in the near elsewhere), as John Hick tried to for eschatological propositions of Christianity, is fraught with insurmountable difficulties (such as, what would count as a common agreed upon verification language, let alone what would count as evidence). Mīmāṃsā has claimed that *śruti,* as the limiting case of *śabdapramāṇa* or verbal testimony, is self-validating, i.e. truth is intrinsic to their propositions. This is too strong a claim. Besides, they are mostly interested in the speech acts of the Vedas (the Brāhmaṇas); and of performatives, as Austin pointed out, it is more correct to say that they are not non-sensical, yet they are neither true nor false.[71] Thus the Mīmāṃsakas over-extend their claims.

But then that is the prerogative of religious discourse. In the last analysis, the claims regarding the transcendental signified (*apūrva*) and the origin of the scriptures are not that crucial: what is important is that which is to be understood or gathered from the texts, and that too for the sake of *dharma,* a particular form of life, with its own moral discourse, performatives and commitments. Religious language takes on a different meaning to ordinary (and even philosophical) discourse. In this programme,

---

[69] For all this see *Arthasaṃgraha,* #9-13.

[70] *Jaiminisūtra* I.i.2.

[71] Austin (1979), pp. 235ff.

an ethical life is presupposed (as a requisite for undertaking the performatives), and a particular worldview or metaphysics undergirds the discourse. More fundamentally, in its Indian context it offers a response to the fears of spiritual and ethical nihilism in the face of the denial of belief in the deity. It also attempts to elucidate a possible way of conceiving "revealed knowledge" and, incidentally, presents a putative alternative to what in the West is more regimently taken to be revelation. It suggests the feasibility of talk about revelation without a revealer or an author and it does this by trying to show that scriptures, texts, indeed language, need not be a function of an author, speaker or subject. It grounds intentionality, otherwise attributed to the author or subject, in the givenness of language itself. Beyond this, there is no other presence. To me, the notion of *apauruṣeya* suggests the possibility of an Ultimate Absence, with a remainder.

REFERENCES

Aquinas, St Thomas (1964). *Summa Theologiae* (I 1a.1). London: Byre & Spottiswoode.

Austin, J.L. (1979). *Philosophical Papers*. Oxford: Oxford University Press.

Bilimoria, Purusottama (1986). "Hindu Doubts about God: a Critique of Kumārila Bhaṭṭa of the Mīmāṃsā School" (abridged). In *Religious Investigations (The Philosophy of Religion) Reader*. Victoria: Deakin University, pp.133-146.

Bilimoria, Purusottama (1988). *Śabdapramāṇa: Word and Knowledge - a Doctrine in Nyāya-Mīmāṃsā Philosophy*, Dordrecht: D. Reidel.

de Broglie, Guy (1965). *Revelation and Reason*. New York: Hawthorn Books.

Chemparathy, George (1972). *An Indian Rational Theology: Introduction to Udayana's Nyāyakusumāñjali*. Vienna: De Nobili Research Library.

Clooney, Francis X. (1985). "The Co-originality (*Autpattikatva*) of Word and Action in the Mīmāṃsā and its Relevance to the Theory of Revelation". (Presented paper Anaheim: at the American Academy of Religion Meeting)

D'Sa, Francis X. (1980). *Śabdaprāmāṇyam in Śabara and Kumārila*. Vienna: de Nobili Research Library.

Farley, Edward (1982). *Ecclesial Reflection*. Philadelphia: Fortress Press.

Fichte, J.G. (1978) *Attempts at a Critique of All Revelation*. tr. Garret Green. Cambridge: Cambridge University Press.

Gächter, Othmar (1983). *Hermeneutics and Language in Pūrvamīmāṃsā: A study in Śābara Bhāṣya*. Delhi: Motilal Banarsidass.

Grice, H.P. (1957). "Meaning" *Philosophical Review* 66: 377-388.

Hattiangadi, J.N. (1987). *How is Language Possible?* La Salle: Open Court.

Hick, John (1977). *The Myth of God Incarnate*. London: SCM Press.

Innes, Robert E. (1985). Editor. *Semiotics: An Introductory Anthology*. Bloomington: Indiana University Press.

Hiriyanna, M. (1973). *Outlines of Indian Philosophy*. Bombay: George Allen & Unwin.

Hiriyanna, M. (1952). *Popular Essays in Indian Philosophy*. Mysore: Kavyalaya Publisers.

Jaimini (1979 edn). *Jaiminimīmāṃsāsūtras*. In *Mīmāṃsādarśana*.

Jha, Ganganatha (1964). *Pūrva Mīmāṃsā in its Sources*. Benares: Benares Hindu University.

Kane, P.V. (1962). *History of Dharmaśāstra,* Vol V, Part II. Poona: Bhandarkar

Oriental Research Institute.
Kaviraj, Gopinath (1983). Preface to Ganganatha Jha's translation of Kumārila Bhaṭṭa's *Tantravārttika*. Delhi: Śri Satguru Publications.
Kumārila Bhaṭṭa (1979 edn). *Ślokavārttika* (=*ŚV*), with *Nyāyaratnākara* of Pārthasārathi Miśra. Varanasi: Tara Publications.
Laugākṣi Bhāskara (1984 edn). The *Arthasaṃgraha*, ed. A.B. Gajendragadkar & R D Karmarkar. Delhi: Motilal Banarsidass.
Mīmāṃsādarśana (1979 edn). [containing] *Jaiminisūtras, Śābarabhāṣya*, etc., ed. Gajanana Sastri Musalgaonkar. Varanasi: Bharatiya Vidya Prakashan.
Mohanty, J.N. (1982) "Indian Philosophy Between Tradition and Modernity". In S.S. Pappu Rama Rao & R. Puligandla (eds.), *Indian Philosophy Past and Present*. Delhi: Motilal Banarsidass.
Mohanty, J.N. (1987). "A Critique of the Theory of *Śabdapramāṇa* and the Concept of Tradition". (Presented paper, May 23, Oxford: Colloquium on Reason & Scriptural Authority: A Critique of Śabda Pramāṇa).
Nārāyana Bhaṭṭa (1933 edn). *Mānameyodaya*, eds. C. Kunhan Raja & S.S. Suryanayana Sastri. Adyar: Adyar Library and Resarch Centre.
Nielsen, Kai (1970). "On the Logic of 'Revelation'" *Sophia* 9: 8-13.
Pārthasārathi Miśra (1891 edn). *Śāstradīpikā*, ed., Rama Misra Sastri. Banaras; other edition (c.1945), ed., P.P. Subramanya Sastri. Madras: Madras Government. Oriental Series.
Pārthasārathi Miśra (1979 edn). *Nyāyaratnākara* in Kumārila Bhaṭṭa (1979 edn *SV*).
Śabara (1979 edn). *Śābarabhāṣya on Jaiminisūtras*. In *Mīmāṃsādarśana*.
de Saussure, Ferdinand (1959) "The Linguistic Sign", from *Course in General Linguistics*. tr. Wade Baskin; reprinted in Innes (1985), pp.28-46.
Searle, John R. (1969). *Speech Acts: An Essay in the Philosophy of Language*. Cambridge: Cambridge University Press.
Searle, John R. (1983) *Intentionality: An Essay in the Philosophy of Mind*. Cambridge: Cambridge University Press.
Shastri, Pashupatinath (1980). *Introduction to the Pūrva Mīmāṃsā*. Varanasi: Chaukhambha Orientalia (reprint of 1923, Calcutta).
Smart, Ninian (1985). "*Apauruṣeya* of *Śruti*". (Recorded presentation), August, Sydney: International Association for the History of Religions Congress.
Sokolowski, Robert. (1982). *The God of Reason and Faith: Foundations of Christian Theology*. Notre Dame/London: University of Notre Dame Press.
Staal, J.F. (1969). "Sanskrit Philosophy of Language". In Thomas A. Sebeok (ed.), *Current Trends in Linguistics*, Vol 5 . The Hague: Mouton.
Udayana, *Nyāyakusumāñjali*. See Chemparathy.
Wells, G.A. (1987). *The Origin of Language*. La Salle: Open Court.

ŚAṂKARA ON METAPHOR WITH REFERENCE TO GITA 13.12-18[1]

Julius J. Lipner

University of Cambridge

There's a saying in Bengali that when rooting for worms you can come upon a snake.[2] My aim in this essay is a modest one: to analyse aspects of the great 8th century (C.E.) monist or Advaitin[3], Śaṃkara's, understanding of figurative, specifically metaphorical predication, with reference to a pericope of the *Bhagavadgītā*. It may be, however, that the worms of insight I am able to uncover will give a glimpse of something larger. As we shall see, Śaṃkara formulated his views on metaphor in a religious context; it will prove useful, therefore, to consider how these views relate to this theological stance with reference to a passage from scripture.

Let me begin with some preliminary observations. Śaṃkara does not have a full-blown theory of predication, figurative or otherwise. As a Vedāntic philosophical theologian in the classical Hindu mould, he proceeded primarily by way of commenting upon religious texts held to be authoritative in the Vedāntic tradition. The commentatorial method is a limiting one; in making sense of the text at hand, there is little scope for producing full-blown theories. As innovative or systematic as the commentator might be, his or her views on a particular subject tend to be dispersed over a number of works and must be pieced together by the analyst of these views. I do not claim to have made an exhaustive study of what Śaṃkara has to say on metaphor. I do think, however, that this study is representative of Śaṃkara's thought and that it breaks new ground - I have not seen the like elsewhere.

Secondly, the passage chosen comes from the *Bhagavadgītā*. The *Gītā* is strong in imagery about the divine and its relationship with the world, and prima facie uncongenial in its dualist language to Śaṃkara's monistic position. Datable to about the beginning of the Christian era, by Śaṃkara's time it had already been given an important place in the Vedāntic tradition; in interpreting it, the master Advaitin was put on his mettle and forced to give philosophical consideration to graphic language in

---

[1]This essay is dedicated to Raimundo Panikkar on the occasion of his 70th birthday (November 3rd 1988).

[2]*keco khudte khudte sap.*

[3]literally, non-dualist.

R. W. Perrett (ed.), Indian Philosophy of Religion, 167–181.

a religious context. Incidentally, I take it as settled that Śaṃkara is the author of the *Gītā*-commentary usually, though sometimes questioningly, ascribed to him. One or two studies have rendered the genuineness of his authorship as beyond doubt.[4]

Now it is well known that Śaṃkara, as an Advaitin, maintained that in the final analysis there is but one reality, without a second (*ekam evādvitīyam*, see Chānd Up.VI.2.1[5]). The One, called Brahman, underlies the multiplicity of being external to us, and is identical with the Ātman, the underlying principle of our own selves. The world of multifarious being which we experience and of which we, as individuals, are a part, has only a provisional (*vyāvahārika*) reality rooted in the spiritual ignorance (*avidyā*) with which and in which we are born. It is through *avidyā* that we perceive the multiplicity of things, separated dualistically on the one hand into an infinite, personal God (*īśvara*)[6], possessing the familiar attributes of originative causality, omniscience, omnipotence, benevolence etc., and on the other into finite personal and non-personal being. Enlightened or spiritual knowledge (*vidyā*) dispels the dualist conditions which govern our everyday experience and manifests the consuming awareness of sheer non-dual being which undergirds our dualist consciousness. Then there is no distinct experience of "I" and "thou", of finite and divine. There is only the pure, relationless reality of Brahman-Ātman.

Strictly speaking, enlightening knowledge cannot be caused - its "content" lies outside the dualist framework of cause and effect - though we can dispose ourselves to experience it by resorting to various requisite means. These include receiving instruction from a suitable teacher, living the recommended moral and religious life, and the correct understanding of the "testimony of the Word", primarily the Vedic scriptural canon (*śruti*) whose teaching is consummated in the Upaniṣads (also called the Vedānta[7]), but also non-canonical though corroborative texts (*smṛti*) such as the *Bhagavadgītā*.

In his commentary on *Bṛhadāraṇyaka Upaniṣad* (BA Up) IV.4.6, Śaṃkara sums up the essential teaching of the Upaniṣads thus: "We maintain that this is the ascertained meaning of the whole Vedānta: that at all times we are (really) Brahman alone, of homogeneous essence, non-dual, unchanging, unborn, undecaying, undying, immortal, fearless, and of the nature of the Ātman."[8] There is no individual consciousness here, no object of consciousness; at most we can talk of pure awareness. By contrast, it is implied that the provisional, non-Brahmanic, non-spiritual sphere of being - the sphere of *prakṛti* or "matter" - as manifestly multiple in form and number, is subject to origination, change and destruction, is non-conscious and productive of *angst*, and is ultimately sublatable. The human person is a composite of Ātman and non-Ātman, spirit underlying matter. Such a composite experiences through a false, provisional centre of individual awareness, congenitally conflating the attributes of spirit and matter. Thus unenlightened, the individual is

---

[4]The case for Śaṃkara's authorship is made, for example, in Sarma (1932-33) and Mayeda (1965). That Śaṃkara wrote the other commentaries quoted in this article is not disputed.

[5]*Chāndogya Upaniṣad.* In this essay Upaniṣadic references follow Radhakrishnan (1953).

[6]Sometimes referred to in Advaita as the qualified (*saguṇa*) or conditioned Brahman in contrast to the non-dual, unqualified (*nirguṇa*) Brahman.

[7]Vedānta: "end of the Veda" - "end", that is, chronologically and teleologically.

[8]*sarvadā samaikarasam advaitam avikriyam ajam ajaram amaram amṛtam abhayam ātmatattvaṃ brahmaiva sma ity eṣa sarvavedānta-niścito'rtha ity evaṃ pratipadyāmahe.* Ānandāśrama Sanskrit Series, vol.15, p.666.

doomed to endure an indefinite series of physical rebirths, in one living form or other, unless liberated by the saving experience of *advaita*. Without having done justice to the depth and richness of Śaṃkara's analysis of the human predicament and its solution, we have given his metaphysical soteriology in a nutshell; we shall need to keep it in mind to understand aspects of his view on metaphorical predication.

Of relevance too is consideration of the importance, for Śaṃkara, of scripture for salvation. Saving knowledge (*vidyā*) concerning the true nature of Brahman-Ātman and our relationship to It,[9] is necessarily derived from the accredited scriptures. Only the scriptures are a public, authoritative source (*pramāṇa*) of *vidyā*; only the scriptures can inform us about meta-empirical realities. Śaṃkara speaks about scripture's indispensability as follows:

> The source of authoritative knowledge about Brahman is sacred language and not the senses, (inference) etc. Brahman is to be known in accordance with scripture... Even the powers of worldly things like gems, spells, herbs and the like are seen to have diverse opposing effects according as they are subject to the vagaries of time and place. Without instruction, the extent of these powers cannot be known by reason alone: that this thing, for example, has powers which are assisted by these particular factors, or which apply to these particular matters or have these particular uses. Can the nature of the essentially inconceivable Brahman then, be described without recourse to scripture?... Whence knowledge of the true nature of extra-sensory things is founded only on scripture.[10]

But scripture must be correctly interpreted, otherwise it does not yield *vidyā*. To accomplish this, says Śaṃkara, scripture must be understood from within the accredited interpretative tradition (*saṃpradāya*). As an Advaitin he makes this point in deriding the position of the non-Advaitin:

> He who thinks thus (viz. as a non-Advaitin) is the basest of scholars. He thinks that he makes sense of scripture and of this life and liberation, but he commits (spiritual) suicide. Deluded himself, he deludes others, for being outside the right tradition of interpreting scripture, he destroys scriptural teaching and fabricates what is not taught. Thus the person who is ignorant of the interpretative tradition, even if he knows all the

---

[9]The neuter pronoun is meant to indicate that the Advaitic absolute is trans-personal rather than impersonal. Indeed, when he is constrained to describe Brahman-Ātman in positive (analogical) terms, Śaṃkara prefers to use such "person-predicates" as "consciousness" and "bliss".

[10]*brahma śabdapramāṇakaṃ nendriyādipramāṇakaṃ tad yathāśabdam abhyupagantavyam... laukikānām api maṇimantrauṣadiprabhṛtīnāṃ deśakālanimittavaicitryavaśāc chaktayo viruddhānekakāryaviṣayā dṛśyante. tā api tāvan nopadeśam antareṇa kevalena tarkeṇāvagantuṃ śakyante' sya vastuna etāvat ya etatsahāyā etadviṣayā etatprayojanāś ca śaktaya iti. kim utācintyasvabhāvasya brahmaṇo rūpaṃ vinā śabdena na nirūpyate... tasmāc chabdamūla evātīndriyārthayāthātmyādhigamaḥ.* From Śaṃkara's commentary on *Brahma Sūtra* 2.1.27; Dhupakar & Bakre (1904), p.400.

> scriptures, is to be despised as a fool.[11]

Śaṃkara, of course, claimed to belong to the right tradition of scriptural interpretation, i.e. Advaita; it was from this vantage point that he sought to make sense of scriptural utterances (especially about the supreme being), figurative or otherwise.

As an exegete, Śaṃkara distinguished between two main kinds of linguistic usage in scripture: literal (*mukhya*) and figurative (*gauṇa, aupacārika*). It was an important rule of Śaṃkara's exegetical tradition that figurative meanings could be resorted to only if it was clear (or clearly shown) that the literal meaning did not apply. In other words, there was an exegetical onus to understand scripture figuratively only as a last resort. The plain sense of scriptural utterances could not lightly be tampered with. This prompted Śaṃkara to make some extremely interesting exegeses, philosophically and theologically, in defence of Advaita, not least where he thought analogical (rather than figurative) speech about Brahman obtained. But we cannot go into this now. Here we are interested in Śaṃkara's views on figurative, specifically metaphorical, utterance in a religious context, with special reference to a text of the *Bhagavadgītā*.

At this point it should be noted that Śaṃkara does not take pains to distinguish effectively between different kinds of figurative expression, such as metaphor, simile, metonymy, synecdoche, catachresis etc. In a western context, a (largely) successful attempt to distinguish between these tropes has been made recently in Soskice (1985); see especially ch.4. However, as we shall see, Śaṃkara did articulate his views on figurative predication in terms of what western philosophers of language call "metaphor". It is thus that we claim to be analysing Śaṃkara's views on metaphorical usage in this essay. The general principle underlying the non-literal understanding of scripture is given by Śaṃkara in this revealing statement:

> Scripture's (*śruti*) cognitive authority applies not to matters of perception etc., but to matters not known from such other authoritative sources of knowledge as perception and so on - for example, with respect to the practice and fruits of the *agnihotṛ* sacrifice etc. Even if a hundred scriptural utterances were to say that fire is cold or that it does not glow, they would have no cognitive authority. If scripture were to say that fire is cold or that it does not glow, we would have to assume that it intended some other meaning, otherwise it would cease to have cognitive authority. For such utterances cannot be understood as opposed either to the other authoritative sources of knowledge or to themselves.[12]

There is no licence here for indiscriminate recourse to non-literal interpretations of

---

[11] *evaṃ manvāno yaḥ sa paṇḍitāpasadaḥ saṃsāramokṣayoḥ śāstrasya cārthavattvaṃ karomīti, ātmahā ca; svayaṃ mūḍho' nyāṃś ca vyāmohayati śāstrārthasampradāyarahitatvāt, śrutahānim aśrutakalpanāṃ ca kurvan. tasmād asampradāyavit sarvaśāstravid api mūrkhavad evopekṣaṇīyaḥ.* From Śaṃkara's commentary on *Gītā* 13.2; Sadhale (1935-38), vol.3, p.16. In Sadhale this passage appears under 13.3, since he gives as 13.1 a verse not admitted by most classical commentators (including Śaṃkara). For ch.13, though we shall quote from Sadhale for Śaṃkara's comments on the *Gītā*, we shall follow the standard numeration of the text.

[12] *pratyakṣādipramāṇānupalabdhe hi viṣaye' gnihotrādisādhyasādhana-sambandhe śruteḥ prāmāṇyam, na pratyakṣādiviṣaye, adṛṣṭadarśanārthatvāt prāmāṇyasya...na hi śrutiśatam api "śīto' gnir aprakāśo vā" iti bruvat prāmāṇyam upaiti. yadi brūyāt "śīto' gnir aprakāśo vā" iti, tathāpy arthāntaraṃ śruter vivakṣitam kalpyaṃ, prāmāṇyānyathānupapatteḥ, na tu pramāṇāntaraviruddhaṃ svavacanaviruddhaṃ vā kalpyam.* Śaṃkara on *Gītā* 18.66; Sadhale (1938), p.409.

scripture. On the contrary, scripture must be interpreted as internally coherent and as in external conformity with the other sources of knowledge such as the senses, inference and so on. But it does have its own proper (extra-empirical) domain, and where necessity dictates is to be understood non-literally. We can now turn to Śaṃkara's understanding of metaphor; it will be useful to begin with a distinction he makes between two kinds of oblique predication (*lakṣaṇā*).

I do not say "between two kinds of *figurative* predication" because at least one of these forms of *lakṣaṇā*, it seems to me, is regarded by Śaṃkara as applying in another context (that of *Taittirīya Upaniṣad* II.1.1) to what we would call the analogical use of words ("linguistic analogy" for Soskice (1985), p.64). And analogical discourse, while not straightforward, is also not figurative; a literal core is retained in this kind of usage. As Soskice remarks: "Linguistic analogy concerns stretched usages, not figurative ones."[13] In any case, we must leave the topic of Śaṃkara on analogical discourse about Brahman for another occasion. Let us now examine his distinction regarding *lakṣaṇā* or oblique predication.

In his commentary on *Brahma Sūtra* 3.3.9, Śaṃkara discusses four different ways in which we may make a prima facie identity statement. He begins with "superimposition" (*adhyāsa*). For example, a Hindu devotee may say of a duly consecrated icon of Viṣṇu that the icon *is* Viṣṇu. What happens here, says Śaṃkara, is oblique predication (*lakṣaṇāvṛtti*) in respect of the words associated with the cognition (*buddhi*) of Viṣṇu superimposed on the icon.[14] In other words, we cannot say straightforwardly that the icon is Viṣṇu.[15] We shall return to Śaṃkara's notion of superimposition later. A second kind of identity statement considered by Śaṃkara is that by "sublation" (*apavāda*). We start by positing an identity, in whole or part, e.g. we say that the biological organism is the true self (Ātman). But when enlightened as to the real distinction between the things identified, viz. that the Ātman is not the body, we deny or sublate the identity. A third way is by affirming an actual identity by the use of synonyms, as when we say (in accordance with custom) that the Brahmin is the noblest of the twice-born castes. Finally, we may say that *A* is *B* by way of "qualifiers" (*viśeṣaṇa*). Here we refer to the whole by means of the part (or vice versa) as when we say, "She's a willing hand" or (of an important or representative person of a group or institution), "Here comes (that group/institution)".[16] The subject is identified with its qualifiers (and can be identified through its qualifiers). It seems that at least some instances of this fourth way are synechdocal.[17]

In this context, we are interested in Śaṃkara's comments on *adhyāsa*, by which he means using words indirectly when superimposing a cognition directly associated with one thing onto some other thing directly associated with another cognition. Taking a duly consecrated icon of Viṣṇu for Viṣṇu is a case in point. When it is said that the icon is Viṣṇu some cognition relating to Viṣṇu is being superimposed on what is known to be only an icon. It is in this connection that Śaṃkara distinguishes between

---

[13] Soskice (1985), p.66.

[14] *tatrādhyāse tāvad yā buddhir itaratrādhyasyate tacchabdasya lakṣaṇāvṛttitvaṃ prasajyeta...*; Dhupakar & Bakre (1904), p.687.

[15] So much for any simplistic notions of "idolatry" in this context.

[16] The examples of the first three ways are (approvingly) assigned by Śaṃkara to the interlocutor; the examples of the last way are our own.

[17] See Soskice (1985), p.57.

two kinds of *lakṣaṇā*:

> As to oblique predication there is closeness or remoteness (of the primary sense of the relevant word/s in relation to the assumed meaning of the word/s). In the case of superimposition, where the cognition of one thing is superimposed on something else, the *lakṣaṇā* is remote. But in the case of qualifiers, where by a word expressing a whole we understand the part, we have proximate *lakṣaṇā*. Words referring to wholes are commonly applied to the parts, as in the instances of "cloth" and "village" (viz. we say that the cloth is burnt when only a part of it is, and that the village is on fire when only some of its huts are).[18]

That metaphorical utterance, as we understand it, qualifies as an instance of remote *lakṣaṇā* for Śaṃkara becomes clear from his commentary under *Brahma Sūtra* 4.1.6. Śaṃkara explicitly exemplifies remote indirect/oblique predication by metaphor. In the general context of superimposition again, he considers the meditation enjoined by the obviously metaphorical (though somewhat obscure) statement: "This (earth) is the hymn (*ṛk*), fire is the chant (*sāman*); that chant is raised on this hymn."[19] The text requires that the hymn be meditated upon as the sacrificial earth (altar) and the chant as the sacrificial fire. Śaṃkara comments: "The words 'hymn' and 'chant' are used indirectly of earth and fire respectively. Now oblique predication obtains according as (the assumed meaning) is proximately or remotely related to the primary sense."[20] Clearly this is a case of "remote" *lakṣaṇā* for Śaṃkara, for during the meditation the aspirant is to superimpose the cognition of one thing (i.e. the hymn, the chant) on to what is known to be something quite different (viz. the altar, the fire), and where superimposition of this kind occurs, says the Advaitin, the *lakṣaṇā* expressing it is remote (see note 17). In other words, for Śaṃkara metaphor implies the use of words where the assumed meaning is remote from the primary or literal sense of the relevant word/s. Several points emerge from this.

In the first place, behind Śaṃkara's reference to the "primary sense" or "sense proper" (*svārtha*) of a word in his description of *lakṣaṇā*, lies his acceptance of the traditional Vedāntic view that the Vedic (Sanskritic) "naming word" (*nāmaśabda*) or substantive[21] has an inherent relation with a sort of metaphysical "form" (*ākṛti*) of the empirical object it denotes. (This inherent relation between a word and its form is known technically as *śabdārthasaṃbandha*.) Thus the terms "*gaur*" (ox) and "*siṃha*" (lion), for example, have a pre-established relation to their respective *ākṛtis*. It is by virtue of this relationship that they denote individual oxen and lions. The primary (lexical) sense of a Vedic naming word then is supposed to be a well-defined one. In this context, the contrast between "primary" and "assumed" meanings is starker than it would have been otherwise. But the main point I am making is that Śaṃkara discusses

---

[18] *lakṣaṇāyām api tu saṃnikaraṣaviprakarṣau bhavata eva. adhyāsapakṣe hy arthāntarabuddhir arthāntare nikṣipyata iti viprakṛṣṭā lakṣaṇā viśeṣaṇapakṣe tv avayavivacanena śabdenāvayavaḥ samarpyata iti saṃnikṛṣṭā. samudāyeṣu hi pravṛttāḥ śabdā avayaveṣv api vartamānā dṛṣṭāḥ paṭagrāmādiṣu.* Śaṃkara on *Brahma Sūtra* 3.3.9; Dhupakar & Bakre (1904), p.688.

[19] *iyam eva ṛg, agniḥ sāma, tad etad etasyām ṛcy adhyūḍhaṃ sāma...* Chānd Up. I.6.1.

[20] *lākṣaṇika eva pṛthivyagnyor ṛksāmaśabdaprayogaḥ. lakṣaṇā ca yathāsaṃbhavaṃ saṃnikṛṣṭena viprakṛṣṭena vā svārthasaṃbandhena pravartate.* Dhupakar & Bakre (1904), p.840.

[21] This view seems not to apply to proper names.

metaphor chiefly in its *scriptural* context. Here the metaphorical paradigm is in Sanskrit and makes use of the substantive rather than other parts of speech. No doubt this explains in large measure why Śaṃkara's own examples of metaphor follow this paradigm. However, it is important to note that notwithstanding the implications and restraints of this scriptural context, Śaṃkara's analysis of metaphor does seem intended to apply, *mutatis mutandis*, to metaphorical usage in general, not least to language that is not Sanskrit and to non-substantives, though it is not always clear how these correlations are to be made.[22]

Secondly, "assumed meaning" in Śaṃkara's description of *lakṣaṇā* must not, I think, be taken to mean that in addition to their primary senses metaphorical words have separate hidden or secondary senses lying in wait to come into play at the metaphorical moment! - a view at least in part inveighed against by Donald Davidson in his article, "What Metaphors Mean".[23] As we shall see, for Śaṃkara the assumed meaning of a metaphor is dependent on the whole context in which that metaphor works, and as such is not on a par with the primary senses of words.

Finally, to say that for Śaṃkara metaphor implies the use of words where the assumed meaning is *remote* from the primary or literal sense of the relevant word/s is to say that he regards it as crucial that a significant semantic hiatus characterises the metaphorical use of words. Śaṃkara does not expatiate on the nature of this hiatus here. To understand more clearly what he has in mind, we must now consider his important distinction between metaphor and error.

The distinction is made in Śaṃkara's commentary on *Brahma Sūtra* 1.1.4. Here our account of his view on the nature of the human person must be kept in mind. The interlocutor claims that the identification (*abhimāna*) we make between our true self (Ātman) and the psycho-physical organism which the Ātman animates and pervades, resulting in such (composite) judgements as "I am Devadatta", "I am a man", "I am fair", is not a *false* judgement but a *figurative* one.[24] This is not so, says Śaṃkara:

> For figurative and literal predication obtain when the distinction between things is clearly recognised. (To explain). Where the distinction between things is clearly recognised - for example, when something having a distinctive configuration which includes a mane etc. is known to be the primary referent of the word "lion" and its corresponding idea, by the process of agreement and disagreement[25], and *something else*, a man, is known to be endowed with the qualities of a lion, that is, much fierceness, might, and so on - there we have figurative (viz. metaphorical) predication, the word "lion" and its corresponding idea being applied to the man (as in the statement: Devadatta was a lion on

---

[22]This harks back to our earlier observation that Śaṃkara does not have a full-fledged theory of metaphor. Metaphor, of course, is not expressed only through nouns.

[23]Davidson (1984), essay 17, pp.245-264.

[24]*dehādivyatiriktasyātmana ātmīye dehādāv abhimāno gauṇo na mithyeti*. Dhupakar & Bakre (1904), p.96.

[25]*anvayavyatirekābhyām*: experience teaches that a certain "naming" word in its primary sense and the concept associated with it, are invariably connected with a particular object (e.g. "*gaur*" and its concept with the ox) - this is the agreement - and that this word and its concept are not directly associated with some other thing; this is the disagreement. These are the grounds for the basic confidence we have in the use of language.

> the battle-field). This is not the case when the distinction between things is not recognised. Here the word and its corresponding idea belonging to one thing are applied to something else *as a result of error*, and not figuratively, as for example when, to something not clearly apprehended in poor light - a stump in fact - we apply the word "man" and its corresponding idea: "there's a man here" we say) of the stump-object; or when, stumbling upon mother-of-pearl we say and think confidently that it's silver. Similarly, when one says of one's bodily complement that it's really oneself, the relevant words and ideas not being used on the basis of discrimination between the Ātman and the non-Ātman, how can we say that here the words and ideas involved are figurative?[26]

Here I wish to single out two features of metaphor which this passage brings to light. First, note that for Śaṃkara, metaphor has to do with intention which itself has to do with *context*. For a metaphor to work, it must be intended as metaphor and understood as such by the hearer. This is the implication of Śaṃkara's emphasis on "the distinction between things" being "clearly recognised" (*prasiddho vastubhedaḥ*). This is why a metaphorical utterance is not an erroneous one. Error has to do with mistaken identity (we mistake nacre for silver), but not metaphor (we do not mistake the warrior Devadatta for a lion), even though superficially both error and metaphor assume that same syntactical identity-form: "This (nacre) is silver", "Devadatta is a lion". Because metaphor is contextual - a transaction between utterer and hearer - we cannot speak of metaphor containing ready-made hidden senses which pop out independent of the context. Metaphorical meanings are the yield of the metaphorical transaction itself and are not entirely predictable; they are not on a par with the primary (lexical) senses of words. The distinction between error and falsehood (in the sense of lying) vis-à-vis metaphor will further clarify the matter. Though lying also has to do with intention and context, in lying utterer and hearer are at cross purposes, whereas in metaphor they work in harmony. One of the features of metaphor Śaṃkara is addressing in the passage above is this transactional harmony.

But a second, and perhaps more important, feature of metaphor for Śaṃkara is that metaphor is based on the perception of difference. Metaphor occurs when there's a realisation that the subject of the metaphor (e.g. Devadatta) is different from the referent/s to which the metaphorical words would apply straightforwardly (e.g. lion). Because we know full well that Devadatta the man is not really a lion, is far removed from being the natural referent of the sense proper (*svārtha*) of "lion", we can refer metaphorically to Devadatta in appropriate context as a lion. Śaṃkara's reference to the presence of a semantic hiatus in remote oblique (metaphorical) predication, noted earlier, now becomes more clear. The remoteness of the assumed metaphorical meaning from the primary sense of the relevant word/s is based on the radical difference perceived to exist between the subject of the metaphor and the referent/s to which the metaphorical words would apply straightforwardly. Śaṃkara admits, of

---

[26] *prasiddhavastubhedasya gauṇatvamukhyatvaprasiddheḥ. yasya hi prasiddho vastubhedaḥ, yathā kesarādimān ākṛtiviśeṣo' nvayavyatirekābhyāṃ siṃhaśabdapratyayabhāṇ mukhyo' nyaḥ prasiddhah, tataś cānyaḥ puruṣah prāyikaiḥ krauryaśauryādibhiḥ siṃhaguṇaiḥ saṃpannaḥ siddhaḥ, tasya puruṣe siṃhaśabdapratyayau gauṇau bhavato nāprasiddhavastubhedasya. tasya tv anyatrānyaśabdapratyayau bhrāntinimittāv eva bhavato na gauṇau. yathā mandāndhakāre sthāṇur ayam ity agṛhyamāṇaviśeṣe puruṣaśabdapratyayau sthāṇuviṣayau, yathā vā śuktikāyām akasmād rajatam iti niścitau śabdapratyayau, tadvad dehādisaṃghāte' ham iti nirupacāreṇa śabdapratyayāv ātmānātmāvivekenotpadyamānau kathaṃ gauṇau śakyau vaditum.* Dhupakar & Bakre (1904), p.96.

course, that metaphor is also based on similarity. He points out that Devadatta may be called a lion because his prowess may be compared with distinctive qualities attributed to lions. But the overriding insight here is that the comparison is rooted in contrast. The perceived difference between Devadatta and lions enables the metaphorical comparison to be made. For Śaṃkara, at the root of metaphor lies difference, not similarity.

Śaṃkara's position is elaborated somewhat, with further examples, in the following statement taken from his commentary on *Gītā* 18.66. The relevant examples make it clear that by "figurative" (*gauṇa*) Śaṃkara means what we understand by "metaphorical". Once more the interlocutor suggests that the identification we make between the Ātman and its bodily complement is figurative, not false. He says: "The notion one has that one's bodily complement is the self is figurative, like (the awareness expressed) when one says of one's son, 'My son, you are my very self', or when people say, 'This ox is my very life'."[27]

Śaṃkara denies the analogy. One's everyday self-idea is mistaken, not figurative, as in the case of the stump misapprehended for a man. If everyday self-awareness were figurative, he argues, its consequences would be of the same order, without literal effect. But this is not the case.

> There is no real substance to the consequence of a figurative (i.e. metaphorical) awareness whose aim is to praise the referent by means of a statement containing a suppressed comparison. Thus we say, "Devadatta is a lion" or "The lad's fire" only to praise the referent, viz. Devadatta or the youth, because they are similar in fierceness and lustre (to a lion and fire respectively). No consequence pertaining to a (real) lion or fire is accomplished by the figurative awareness or expression at all. However a false awareness can have positively harmful consequences. One is alert to what is involved in a figurative awareness, for example, that Devadatta is not really a lion or that the lad is not really fire. In the same way, an action done when the Ātman is only figuratively identified with one's bodily complement would be (regarded quite rightly as) an action not really done by the Ātman which is the subject of one's self-consciousness. Indeed, no action done by a figurative lion or fire could be an action done by a real lion or fire!... Moreoever, those being praised (in the examples) know that they are not really a lion or a fire and that the actions of lion or fire are not their own. Similarly, (if we identified the Ātman with the bodily complement only figuratively) it would be more appropriate to say, "The action of my bodily complement is not really the Ātman's" (and we would not suffer the undesirable consequences of mistaken identity between Ātman and body etc., which in fact we do).[28]

---

[27] *ātmīye dehādisaṃghāte' hampratyayo gauṇaḥ, yathātmīye putre "ātmā vai putra nāmāsi" iti. loke cāpi "mama prāṇa evāyaṃ gauḥ" iti tadvat.* Sadhale (1938), p.407.

[28] *na gauṇapratyayasya mukhyakāryārthatvaṃ, adhikaranastutyarthatvāl luptopamāśabdena. yathā "siṃho devadatto' gnir māṇavakah" iti siṃha ivāgnir iva krauryapaiṅgalyādisāmānyavattvād devadattamāṇavakādhikaraṇastutyartham eva, na tu siṃhakāryam agnikāryaṃ vā gauṇaśabdapratyayanimittaṃ kiñcit sādhyate; mithyāpratyayakāryaṃ tv anartham anubhavati. gauṇapratyayaviṣayaṃ ca jānāti "naiṣa siṃho devadattaḥ syāt", "nāyam agnir māṇavakaḥ" iti. tathā gauṇena dehādisaṃghātenātmanā kṛtaṃ karma na mukhyenāhampratyayaviṣayenātmanā kṛtaṃ syāt. na hi gauṇasiṃhāgnibhyāṃ kṛtaṃ karma mukhyasiṃhāgnibhyāṃ kṛtaṃ syāt... stūyamānau ca jānītaḥ*

It is Śaṃkara's intention here to show how metaphorical awareness - the statements exemplifying the kind of awareness Śaṃkara has in mind are indubitably metaphorical - differs from that conflation between Ātman and non-Ātman we invariably and ordinarily tend to make. The relationless, actionless, ineffable Ātman, the true subject of our self-awareness, does not literally (*mukhyena*) perform the (bodily) actions we attribute to It. But we do not attribute figuratively; we attribute mistakenly. Hence the undesirable consequence we experience of repeated birth in the stream of existence (*saṃsāra*).

In making the distinction between the two kinds of awareness, Śaṃkara emphasises the two features of metaphor noted earlier. Metaphor is contextual: both utterer and hearer (viz. Devadatta, the lad) are alert to what's going on - that language is being used figuratively, not literally. And metaphor is differential: both utterer and hearer know perfectly well that Devadatta and the lad are not a lion and fire respectively. That is why the metaphors work.

We can now consider two further features of metaphor intimated by Śaṃkara. The first is metaphor's *cognitive* nature. This is intimated by the expression that metaphor contains an (elliptical) comparison (*luptopamā*). A successful metaphor entails the making of comparisons based on perceived contrast - (comparatively) superimposing the cognition of one thing on what is known to be something else (to quote Śaṃkara in an earlier context) - in other words, "accessing" particular relationships between different things. Metaphor is not just an ornamental or emotive form of speech; it enlarges our horizons of knowledge. Sometimes familiarity makes the cognitive content of metaphor rather trite, as when we regularly compare valiant fighters to lions. But sometimes metaphoric insights can be more stimulating, as when a particular hymn is identified metaphorically with the sacrificial altar, and a particular chant with the sacrificial fire. In both cases, the actualisation of the greater or lesser imaginative possibilities in metaphor transforms the world for us; we know and experience our environment in a different way. Śaṃkara would approve of the Greek etymology of "metaphor", viz. a carrying across of meaning from one side to the other (*meta-pherein*); metaphor is a form of semantic bridgebuilding, the networking of separate things. No less would Śaṃkara approve the following statement, summing up the western cognitivist view of metaphor (e.g. of M. Black, I.A. Richards, J.M. Soskice):

> A good metaphor may not simply be an oblique reference to a predetermined subject but a new vision, the birth of a new understanding, a new referential access. A strong metaphor compels new possibilities of vision.[29]

But what does Śaṃkara mean by saying that metaphor contains an *elliptical* comparison? That metaphor is equivalent semantically to simile? That simile is a syntactical expansion of metaphor? In the west much has been written about the relationship between metaphor and simile, often to the detriment of simile. Simile tends to be treated as the poor relation of metaphor. To my mind, however, Soskice has rehabilitated simile, and put simile, at least in one of its modes, on a par with

---

"nāhaṃ siṃhaḥ", "nāhaṃ agniḥ" iti. "na hi siṃhasya karma mamāgneś ca" iti tathā "na saṃghātasya karma mama mukhyasyātmanaḥ" iti pratyayo yuktataraḥ syāt. Sadhale (1938), p.407.

[29] Soskice (1985), pp.57-58.

metaphor.[30] Śaṃkara himself does not expatiate on his reference, and I doubt if it would be profitable to speculate on his silence further.

The second feature we are considering here follows hard on the first: metaphor's *open-endedness*. Not only does metaphor enlarge our knowledge, it carries a "surplus of meaning" which is neither fully predictable nor defined. When we identify two (or more) things metaphorically we contemplate a virtually indefinite range of comparative possibilities. Some of these possibilities spring to mind: that Devadatta has lion-like fierceness and might, for example. Other possibilities depend on more particular circumstances: the mane-like hair of Devadatta, perhaps, or his fearless carriage, or his battle-cry, or the way he pounces on his hapless enemies. The possibilities could be extended circumstantially. Perhaps this open-endedness of metaphor is intimated by the many scriptural injunctions in Hinduism to *meditate* upon certain metaphorical utterances, for instance, that the hymn is the altar and the chant the sacrificial fire. Śaṃkara could have had this feature in mind when he says, in the context of the Devadatta-lion example, that the similarity is based on fierceness, might *and so on* ("*ādi*" in the Sanskrit). As commentators confirm, "*ādi*" in philosophical Sanskrit often has a technical function, as well it might have here, meaning "and other qualities, depending on what's intended". The characteristic embracing these two features, viz. metaphor's cognitive and open-ended nature, is that metaphor is "reality-referential": in its own way it describes, gives information about the world we live in. In other words, there is such a thing as metaphorical no less than literal truth.[31]

No doubt, Śaṃkara's view of metaphor as analysed hitherto, leaves a number of things unclear or problematic. One or two of these grey areas have been adverted to; others include his tendency (for which a reason has been suggested) to instantiate metaphor in the "*A* is a *B*" form (a tendency which has rightly been criticised as severely limiting the scope of metaphor[32]), and a predilection, perhaps, for the "two-referents" theory of metaphorical predication.[33] But I suspect that his insights concerning metaphor's reality-referential, contextual, and especially differential features are more than just vermicular ones; with respect to the nature of figurative language, cognition and indeed reality itself, when teased out they may well bring something more potent into sight. Finally, let us examine how Śaṃkara's view of metaphor seems to come into its own in his exegesis of *Bhagavadgītā* 13.12-18 which I now translate in full:

(Kṛṣṇa, God descended in human form, is speaking to his friend, Arjuna).

13.12 The To-be-known I will declare, knowing which one attains the Immortal - the beginningless, highest Brahman.[34] It is said to be neither existent nor non-existent.

13.13 With hands and feet everywhere, eyes, heads and mouths everywhere,
With hearing everywhere, It stands in the world enveloping all.

13.14 Reflecting the qualities of all the senses, yet devoid of all the senses,

---

[30]See Soskice (1985), pp.58f.

[31]Metaphorical truth obtains even in fictional contexts, of course. Successful metaphors in novels, for example, fulfil their truth-bearing function.

[32]Śaṃkara's examples follow this form because scriptural paradigms do so (see earlier). Soskice (1985) criticises its limitations; pp.18f.

[33]See Soskice (1985), pp.20, 38f.

[34]Following Śaṃkara's interpretation of "*anādimat-paraṃ brahma*".

Detached yet supporting all, free from (Nature's) elements yet experiencing them,
13.15 Outside yet within all beings, unmoving yet moving about,
Ungraspable because of its subtlety, far away yet close at hand!
13.16 Undivided in all beings, yet fixed in them, divided as it were,
That To-be-known is knowledge itself, as knowledge's goal It is established in the heart of all.
13.18 Thus knowledge, its object and the To-be-known have been declared in brief;
Knowing this my devotee is able to become one with Me.[35]

In the context of Śaṃkara's thought, this striking passage is peculiarly suited to our purposes. It contains a tension between apophatic and cataphatic references to the supreme being, described as the beginningless Brahman, the "To-be-known" (*Jñeya*). Thus, after warning Arjuna that the *Jñeya* is said to be neither existent nor non-existent, in other words, ineffable (13.12b), Kṛṣṇa goes on to describe the *Jñeya* in clearly metaphorical (13.13,13.16b) and paradoxical (13.14,13.15 etc.) language. Śaṃkara's interpretative problem pivots around the tension adverted to. In the light of our analysis of his view on metaphor, we shall be especially concerned with his interpretation of 13.13.

With Śaṃkara, it is important that we attend to the pericope's linguistic bias in its reference to Brahman. Rather than positing ontological relationships between Brahman and the world, the text as a whole is concerned with how we may acceptably speak about, refer verbally to, the ultimate reality. Hence the bounding, "I will declare" (*pravakṣyāmi*) and "Thus... have been declared" (*iti... uktam*) of 13.12 and 13.18 respectively, and the "it is said" (*ucyate*) of 13.12b and 13.17 in between. This puts 13.13 in context. As part of the whole passage, 13.13, when taken, as it must be, in conjunction with the apophatic reference of 13.12, clearly intimates how we may speak *figuratively* of Brahman. Śaṃkara acknowledges this, but the first major point he makes is that the pericope begins by indicating how one may *most appropriately* refer to the transcendent Brahman, viz, as "neither existent nor non-existent", or apophatically. He stresses the point: "In all the Upaniṣads, Brahman, the *Jñeya* , is referred to by a denial of distinguishing characteristics, as e.g. in (BĀ Up III.9.26) '(Brahman) is not this, not that' and (BĀ Up III.8.8) '(Brahman) is not gross, not fine' etc. Because Brahman is beyond our ken, statements like 'It's so and so' do not apply."[36]

The purpose of *Gītā* 13.12 too, says the Advaitin, is to insist on Brahman's ineffability. We know that an everyday object, e.g. an earthen pot, "is" or "is not" on the basis of sense-experience. Brahman, the *Jñeya*, however, transcends the senses

---

[35] *jñeyaṃ yat tat pravakṣyāmi yaj jñātvāmṛtam aśnute anādimat paraṃ brahma na sat tan nāsad ucyate* (13.12). *sarvataḥ pāṇipādaṃ tat sarvato'kṣiśiromukham sarvataś śrutimal loke sarvam āvṛtya tiṣṭhati* (13.13). *sarvendriyaguṇābhāsaṃ sarvendriyavivarjitam asaktaṃ sarvabhṛc caiva nirguṇaṃ guṇabhoktṛ ca* (13.14). *bahir antaś ca bhūtānām acaraṃ caram eva ca sūkṣmatvāt tad avijñeyaṃ dūrasthaṃ cāntike ca tat* (13.15). *avibhaktaṃ ca bhūteṣu vibhaktam iva ca sthitam bhūtabhartṛ ca taj jñeyaṃ grasiṣṇu prabhaviṣṇu ca* (13.16). *jyotiṣām api taj jyotis tamasaḥ param ucyate jñānaṃ jñeyaṃ jñānagamyaṃ hṛdi sarvasya viṣṭhitam* (13.17). *iti kṣetram tathā jñānaṃ jñeyaṃ coktaṃ samāsataḥ madbhakta etad vijñāya madbhāvāyopapadyate* (13.18).

[36] *sarvāsu hy upaniṣatsu jñeyaṃ brahma "neti neti", "asthūlam aṇu" ityādiviśeṣapratiṣedhenaiva nirdiśyate nedaṃ tat iti vāco'gocaratvāt*. Sadhale (1938), p.47.

(*atīndriya*) and is knowable only by scripture.[37] As such, unlike pots and so on, It is not the object of empirical awareness. In other words, we cannot predicate "existence" and "non-existence" of Brahman and pots etc. univocally; we cannot say that Brahman and empirical objects exist in the same sense of "exist". Implicit here is a position on analogical predication which we cannot go into now.

Śaṃkara elaborates:

> It stands to reason that Brahman cannot be signified plainly (*ucyate*) by such words as "existent" and "non-existent", for every word is used (ordinarily) to reveal an object, and when heard by its hearers, makes its object known conventionally by referring to genus, action, attribute or relation. We do not ordinarily use words otherwise. Thus "ox" and "horse" refer generically; "he cooks/studies" refers action-wise; "white" and "black" refer by way of attribute, while "wealthy" and "ox-owner" are relational. But Brahman belongs to no genus, whence It cannot be directly signified by such words as "existent". Nor does It possess attributes which make It denotable by attribute-words, for It is without attributes (*nirguṇa*). Nor is It denotable by action-words, for It is actionless. For scripture says that Brahman is "without parts, without action, serene" (Śvetāśvatara Up.VI.19). Further, since It is not relational, and since It is non-dual and not the object but only the subject (Ātman) (of experience), it is proper to say that Brahman cannot be denoted by any word. And so attest such scriptural passages as (Taittirīya Up.II.9.1, when referring to Brahman, viz.) "From which words turn back...".[38]

Thus Śaṃkara contends that the most appropriate way to refer to the transcendent Absolute is apophatically or negatively, viz. by saying what Brahman is not. In this, as a theologian, whether in east or west, he is not alone. For example, the traditional official theologian of the Catholic Church, Thomas Aquinas, was similarly minded. "Speaking of God by saying what he is not, is the most appropriate," he affirms, "because (the divine essence) is unknown (to us) not on account of its obscurity but on account of its overwhelming clarity."[39] So too could Śaṃkara speak of Brahman, "the very light of lights" (*Gītā* 13.17).

Well then, if we cannot plainly refer to Brahman as existent or non-existent, can

---

[37] *idaṃ tu jñeyam atīndriyatvena śabdaikapramāṇagamyatvān na ghaṭādivad ubhayabuddhyanugata-pratyayaviṣayam, ity ato "na sat tan nāsat" ity ucyate.* Sadhale (1938), p.48. Also see notes 9 & 11.

[38] *upapatteś ca sadasadādiśabdair brahma nocyata iti. sarvo hi śabdo'rthaprakāśanāya prayuktaḥ śrūyamāṇaś ca śrotṛbhir jātikriyāguṇasambandhadvāreṇa saṅketagrahaṇaṃ savyapekṣārthaṃ pratyāyayati, nānyathādṛṣṭatvāt. tad yathā "gaur aśvaḥ" iti vā jātitaḥ, "pacati paṭhati" iti vā kriyātaḥ, "śuklaḥ kṛṣṇaḥ" iti vā guṇataḥ, "dhanī gomān" iti vā sambandhataḥ, na tu brahma jātimat,ato na sadādiśabdavācyam. nāpi guṇavat yena guṇaśabdenocyate, nirguṇatvāt nāpi kriyāśabdavācyaṃ, niṣkriyatvāt "niṣkalaṃ niṣkriyaṃ śāntam" iti śruteḥ. na ca sambandhikatvād advayatvād avisayatvād ātmatvāc ca na kenacic chabdenocyata iti yuktaṃ "yato vāco nivartante" ityādiśrutibhyaś ca.* Sadhale (1938), p.48.

[39] *nominatio Dei quae est per remotionem, est maxime propria... (quia essentia divina) non est ignota propter obscuritatem, sed propter abundantiam claritatis.* Mandonnet (ed.), *Super De Divinis Nominibus Expositio* vol.2, p.259.

we say anything about It at all? One kind of answer, rejoins Śaṃkara, is provided by *Gītā* 13.13: the transcendent, ineffable Brahman is said to possess hands, feet, eyes, heads, mouths and ears on every side, thereby enveloping everything. The purpose of this verse is (i) to affirm the existence of Brahman, and (ii) to do so in a particular way. The verse affirms the existence of Brahman as the "*kṣetrajña*" (that is, as "the knower-pervader of the domain of empirical existence"[40]) by figuratively ascribing to Brahman the sense-organs and limbs of living beings.[41] 13.12 (and 13.14) makes it clear that Brahman does not really possess such features and it would be false (*mithyā*) to say that It literally does.[42] In other words, Śaṃkara is making the point that for 13.13 to work, its proper context as metaphor must be understood.

The organs attributed to Brahman are only "*upādhis*", superimpositions, taken from the manifold field (*kṣetra*) of everyday experience.[43] Metaphor's reality-referring nature is being brought to the fore. 13.13 not only affirms but also depicts the reality of Brahman. This affirmation-depiction takes place by the ascription of various organs to Brahman. Our sense-organs are our instruments of communication with, pervasion of, each other and the world in which we live. They are the means by which we participate in and control our environment. By this graphic imagery, then, we get an inkling of the way in which the transcendent Brahman communicates with, pervades, participates in and controls the domain of empirical existence. The organs mentioned in the text do not, in their figurative application, exhaust the pervading power of Brahman. The metaphor is open-ended: "the field of experience is differentiated *in many ways* through (the organs of) hands, feet *and so on*."[44] But a genuine cognitive basis has been provided for an inkling of how Brahman is related to the world. Why this metaphor - this kind of depiction - rather than some other? Because scripture in its wisdom chooses so to provide. The scriptural context of this metaphor gives it a privileged place in the development of our spiritual enlightenment. Here scripture, more loving towards us than a thousand parents as the Vedāntins are wont to say, is fulfilling its role of securely guiding us towards the realisation of those liberating insights which will encompass our salvation.

But the knowledge we thus metaphorically acquire is only an inkling. We are *pointed* in the right direction; we have no real cognitive *purchase* on Brahman's ineffable being. The rationale underlying the metaphorical ascription of 13.13 is intimated by Śaṃkara thus: "Since in all instances, hands, feet etc., in so far as they are the parts of all bodies, are known to be the effects (of the *Jñeya*), resulting from the power of the *Jñeya* existing within them, they are pointers to the existence of the *Jñeya* and as such are predicated figuratively of It."[45] Since we are constitutionally constrained by our feeble minds to think and talk about Brahman positively, scripture indulges us by providing guidelines. Some idea of our goal is thereby given us, it is true - but at all times this inkling must be set in the context of the non-dual Brahman's awesome ineffability. Here Śaṃkara's insight that metaphor is based on the perception

---

[40] the "knower": virtually in the biblical sense of "know".

[41] *sarvaprāṇikaraṇopādhibhiḥ kṣetrajñāstitvaṃ vibhāvyate.* Sadhale (1938), p.52.

[42] *kṣetropādhibhedakṛtaṃ ca viśeṣajātaṃ mithyaiva kṣetrajñasya...* Sadhale (1938), p.52.

[43] *kṣetrajñaś ca kṣetropādhita ucyate.* Sadhale (1938), p.52.

[44] *kṣetraṃ ca pāṇipādādibhir anekadhā bhinnam.* Sadhale (1938), p.52.

[45] *sarvatra sarvadehāvayavatvena gamyamānāḥ pāṇipādādayo jñeyaśaktisadbhāvanimittasvakāryā iti jñeyasadbhāvaliṅgāni "jñeyasya" ity upacārata ucyante.* Sadhale (1938), p.52.

of difference (and how much more mutually different can Brahman and sense-organs be!) and his conviction that the Advaitic tradition out of which he theologises is the right one converge in the following comment he makes: "Whence we have this dictum of those who know the interpretative tradition: 'The Unmanifest is described by means of attribution and negation.'[46] We attribute to Brahman (e.g. sense-organs), and in attributing, deny. It is not the case that two chronologically separate steps - first attribution and then denial - are involved here. Informed (metaphorical) predication of Brahman attributes and denies what is thus plainly attributed, in one and the same act. Attribution and negation are two phases, logically separate moments, of the same event. But the denial is not a denial of everything: a residual, a metaphorical awareness remains. We deny the literalness of the attribution by an act that is on the whole what Śaṃkara calls an imaginative ascription (*"jñeyadharmavat parikalpya"*). It is only in this way that the predication can be cognitively fruitful rather than cognitively misleading.

There is much in Śaṃkara's view of metaphor, especially in its theological context, for further study. I do not think, however, that the distinctive theological context diminishes the value of his general insights regarding the nature of metaphor: that it is contextual, cognitive, open-ended, differential. As I have already indicated, these will repay further analysis. Here we have done no more than give some promise of harvest, perhaps, by breaking a little ground.

REFERENCES

Davidson, Donald (1984). *Inquiries into Truth and Interpretation.* Oxford: Clarendon Press.

Dhupakar, Ramchandra Shastri & Bakre, Mahadeva Shastri (1904). Editors. *Brahmasūtraśāṃkarabhāṣyam śrīgovindānanda-vācaspati-ānandagiripraṇīta-ratnaprabhā-bhāmatī-ānandagirīya-(nyāyanirṇaya)-vyākhyātrayopetam.* Bombay: Tukaram Javaji.

Mayeda, Sengaku (1965). "The Authenticity of the *Bhagavadgītābhāṣya* Ascribed to Śaṃkara" *Wiener Zeitschrift für die Kunde Süd- und Ostasiens und Archiv für indische Philosophie* 9: 155-197.

Radhakrishnan, Sarvepalli (1953). *The Principal Upaniṣads.* London: Allen & Unwin.

Sadhale, Shastri G.S. (1935-38). *The Bhagavad-Gītā with Eleven Commentaries.* 3 vols. Bombay: Gujerati Printing Press.

Sarma, B.N. (1932-33). "Śaṃkara's Authorship of the *Gītābhāṣya*" *Annals of the Bhandarkar Oriental Research Institute* 14: 39-60.

Soskice, J.M. (1985). *Metaphor and Religious Language.* Oxford: Clarendon Press.

---

[46]*tathā hi sampradāyavidāṃ vacanam - "adhyāropāpavādābhyāṃ niṣprapañcaṃ prapañcayate" iti.* Sadhale (1938), p.52.

SALVATION AND THE PURSUIT OF SOCIAL JUSTICE

Shivesh C. Thakur

University of Northern Iowa

I

To what extent, if any, is it our duty, as humans, to strive towards social justice? This is an important enough contemporary question in its own right. What makes it specially so in the context of "religions of salvation" is the plausible supposition that they cannot pay more than lip service, if even that, to the pursuit of social justice on earth, here and now. And since Indian religions are, almost without exception, religions of salvation (*mokṣa*, *nirvāṇa*, *kaivalya*, etc.), it would seem to be desirable to explore whether they can be said to require, encourage, tolerate or forbid individual effort directed towards procuring social justice for all. That is the question I wish to explore here. The crux of the problem, to put it very briefly at first, is this. If human destiny ultimately lies in transcending the world and worldly processes, and if this is a goal which, by and large, each one of us must achieve for ourselves individually, then social action, or even any action whatsoever, which is not instrumental to salvation, should either be shunned altogether, or, at best, considered optional. So there are at least two important, but separate, aspects to this problem: (1) why act at all; and (2) why act altruistically?

It will be recognized instantly that the issues involved here have been debated in Indian philosophy of religion for a very long time. But it should not be thought that they are, by any means, exclusive to the Indian tradition. There are, in fact, grounds for thinking that at least "European" Christianity has been very ambivalent between "other-worldly" salvation, and the effort to mitigate human misery in this world. This is clearly the reading of historical Christianity put forward by Liberation Theology.[1]

---

[1]"Liberation Theology" is the name usually given to the thoughts of certain Latin American theologians - all influenced by Marxism, to varying extents - who claim, among other things, that Christianity, before it came under the influence of European culture, was a religion primarily seeking the political and economic emancipation of the poor and the oppressed, rather than the salvation of the soul; and that, therefore, "European" Christianity, insofar as it emphasizes the latter, is a distortion of the true spirit of original Christianity. Some of the better-known Liberation Theologians are: Hugo Assman, Leonardo Boff, Paulo Freire, Gustavo Gutierrez and Juan Luis Segundo.

R. W. Perrett (ed.), Indian Philosophy of Religion, 183–193.

Nonetheless it can be plausibly argued that in the context of Indian religions, the idea of salvation, especially in conjunction with the attendant doctrines of *dharma*, *karma*, *saṃsāra*, and the like, raises intractable barriers to the pursuit of social justice.

Anyone familiar with the vast literature on the subject available in Indian philosophy of religion will readily concede that it is impossible to deal with the actual or possible answers of *all* Indian religions in the space of one paper. I will, therefore, confine my investigations to Hinduism, especially since it is, in so many important ways, the source of the other Indian religions. At the very least, it is safe to say that the concepts of *dharma*, *karma*, *saṃsāra*, etc. are as central to them as they are to Hinduism, although the details of the doctrines surrounding these concepts are frequently different. By way of a further narrowing of the focus, I should say at the outset, that even among Hindu sources, I will be relying mainly on the *Gītā*. My choice is determined not just by the fact that the *Gītā* doctrine of *karma-yoga* is likely to be most relevant to the subject under discussion, but also by the additional fact of its importance in Hindu religious literature, and of the many similarities between some of its contents and Buddhist teachings.

I should point out, too, that I intend here to discuss not social action in general nor even social justice in general, but rather the narrower segment of social justice, commonly known as "distributive justice". As I see it, distributive justice refers primarily to "economic goods", and certain attendant political conditions, which can be distributed across society by, say, a government through legislation, or by a body of enlightened persons through persuasion. What the principles and procedures of such distribution should be is a hotly debated issue among philosophers of various persuasions, such as libertarians, liberals and socialists. Fortunately, the issues involved in this larger debate can be left aside here. Let us assume that everyone will agree that no society can be said to be just unless all its members enjoy the right to have their basic needs fulfilled: such as adequate food and nutrients, housing and sanitation and access to medical care. It is this minimal sense of "social justice" that I will be concerned with here. The two specific questions that I will be exploring are the following: (1) is the pursuit of social justice compatible with the Hindu goal of salvation; and (2) can the pursuit of social justice be said to be obligatory for the Hindu seeker of salvation? It should be obvious that if the answer to the first question is negative, then the same must be true of the second: in fact, the latter then becomes redundant. But an affirmative answer to the first does not, by itself, entail an affirmative answer to the second: the latter would be a strong claim, the former a comparatively weak one. I intend to discuss first, the weak claim, and then, the strong one, in separate sections. But, before anything else, I will try to outline some arguments why salvation may be said to be incompatible with social action, or, indeed, any action.

II

The main reason why the pursuit of social justice, or any other socially-oriented action, may seem to be incompatible with the goal of salvation is that the latter is normally deemed to be a transcendental state, so that what happens in, and to, this world, may be said to be scarcely relevant to a person's ultimate destiny. If the soul (*ātman*) is merely trapped into the worldly process, then wisdom, not to mention common sense, would seem to dictate that it ought not to waste a moment longer than necessary in that process. Whether by knowledge, devotion or "action" (of the strictly instrumental kind), it ought to escape this process as expeditiously as possible. Such antinomian readings of salvation as the ultimate goal, are not uncommon in other religions; but, especially in the case of Hinduism, may be said to have a long, and not-too-undistinguished ancestry. As Arjuna says to Kṛṣṇa in the *Gītā*: if understanding the real nature of things is what leads to liberation, then why do you advise the path of action, especially fighting a savage war?[2]

A pretty similar set of conclusions would seem to emerge if one took the cognate doctrines of *saṃsāra* and *māyā* into account. Even if one desisted from interpreting *māyā* as complete illusion, there is no doubt left that this world, that is, the physical world and the tedious cycle of generation, decay and death, *saṃsāra*, is not the soul's final abode. Anyone who even vaguely "senses" the less-than-real character of the world, could have only one sensible wish: i.e., to "wake up", and to do all, and only, those things that are likely to destroy the factors causing the slumber. It is interesting to note that, by most accounts, the very desire for liberation, *mumukṣutva*, presupposes at least this vague sense or feeling that this world is not what counts. Once this awareness, *jñāna*, has dawned, all actions, other than those that are directly instrumental to salvation, are bound to appear as unnecessary, if not also as detrimental.

The doctrine of *karma*, so very much part of the larger metaphysics of Hinduism, can be easily rendered to lend emphatic support to the line of argument pursued above. All actions produce not only immediate consequences, but, more importantly, subtle potencies, which cannot be destroyed - not ordinarily, anyway. Immoral, or evil, actions certainly "bind" us to the wheel of *saṃsāra*. But even good actions, in general, have the same tendency i.e., ensuring that the soul is reborn, although under more enjoyable circumstances. And if the cessation of rebirth is the essential mark of liberation, then prudence, and perhaps wisdom, too, might dictate refraining from action as the only sensible path to take. In any case, there would seem to be room only for those actions that are directly, or indirectly, conducive to the ultimate goal of salvation.

Since the attainment of liberation may not be possible in this life, it would, naturally, be right to avoid "sinful" actions, so as not to be trapped, in the "cycle" for longer than absolutely necessary by the especially powerful potencies, *karmas*, generated by them. By a corollary, since "sin" often accrues merely from the avoidance of ceremonial, ritual or caste-duties, it would seem to be prudent to ensure that such "negative" accumulation of "sin" does not take place. And insofar as avoidance of such "sin", *pāpa*, or the acquisition of merit, *puṇya*, through the performance of conventional duties, entails what might amount to social action, one would be unwise not to undertake such social duties. But, otherwise, it would seem to be wiser to perform only those actions that are conducive to one's own liberation. Being trapped into *saṃsāra* is something that has happened to *my* soul; and it is my responsibility, not someone else's, to get me out of this mess. Likewise for every other soul. So acting altruistically may, in general, be no more than self-indulgence, for reasons of pride, honour or pleasure - all pre-eminent expressions of egoism, *ahaṃkāra*. In the pursuit of salvation, pleasurable actions may be no less an obstacle than painful ones; altruistic effort no less a barrier than ill-considered selfish endeavour.

It should be clear that, as long as the general position taken is that salvation is not compatible with social action, it is not to be expected that the choice of paths - knowledge, *jñāna*, devotion, *bhakti*, or action, *karma* - would make a difference.

---

[2]*Bhagvadgītā*, Chapter III, verse 1. All references to the *Gītā* are to the edition of Radhakrishnan (1960).

Nonetheless, it may be easier to make a case for the incompatibility in respect of the first two paths. If the path chosen is knowledge, for example, then obviously the seeker of salvation has to devote all his energies to studying, thinking about and meditating on, the higher truths: namely, that the soul is not of this world and that this world is a mere veil which has to be lifted in order to realize the true identity and destiny of the soul. What the seeker should be after is *viveka-jñāna,* the kind of wisdom that separates the real from the unreal. And since this world is part of the unreal, his appropriate attitude would be one of withdrawal from the world of the senses, as a tortoise draws in its limbs inward when sensing danger.

The path of devotion seems to fare no better, although for somewhat different reasons. The devotee's ultimate goal is to realize communion with the object of his love, namely God. He must ceaselessly think of God, recite His many names and recognize his own utter dependence on God. This recognition of dependence also entails the realization that he is not a true agent of action, that his love of worldly pleasures or of his family, friends, etc., is a product of ignorance and egoism. He must, therefore, aim at overcoming his attachment to these "false" objects of love and surrender himself entirely to his true love. This generally negative message regarding social action may be reinforced by some implications of the doctrine of grace, *prasāda* or *anugraha.* Salvation for the devotee, it may be argued, is not so much a function of the intensity or quality of his devotion, but rather a result of God's grace: God may select anyone He pleases for this purpose. According to the "radical" model of the operation of grace, God may pick even the vilest of "sinners", who may have done nothing to deserve this privilege, in the way that the cat picks its helpless kitten by the scruff of its neck (*mārjāra nyāya*). On this model, personal effort of any sort, including social action, e.g., alms-giving, etc., may be redundant. There is a bit more room for personal effort in the alternative model (*markaṭa nyāya*), according to which, although God bestows His grace out of His own free choice, the devotee may help, to some extent, by his own behavior and character - rather like the monkey which, of course, carries its baby, but the latter helps the mother by clutching her body. It should be unnecessary to add that the first model is perfectly compatible with complete passivity, which the second only allows for actions comparable to clutching, i.e., prayer, worship, recitation of holy names etc., in the context of devotion.

The path of action is obviously more likely to accommodate social action. But, if interpreted narrowly, these actions need not go beyond the various kinds of conventional ritual and caste-duties. That is how *dharma* is often understood. And if the perspective is one of caste and ritual duties, then there may be no room for action undertaken to bring about social justice in the relevant sense. For it is not assumed to be accidental that a particular person has a specific position in the social order and enjoys or suffers privileges or privations of certain sorts. Distributive justice may well require social action to change the lot of the oppressed or deprived; but changing their lot will inevitably involve changing the social order, and that cannot be a dictate of traditional *dharma.*

Undoubtedly, a lot more arguments can be constructed to demonstrate the apparent incompatibility we are here trying to make a case for. But I doubt that their spirit can be much different from that of the ones outlined above. I will, therefore, conclude this section by drawing attention to one additional source of incompatibility. Whatever might be the case regarding the incompatibility between salvation and social action, in general, there is a special conflict between economic justice and the goal of salvation. For the former has everything to do with material well-being, while the latter is a spiritual goal; and for those who maintain that the material and the spiritual realms do not mix, it is perfectly natural that the quest for salvation will either belittle, or altogether ignore, prevailing economic injustices. It may not be necessary even to appeal to the possible fatalistic implications of the doctrine of *karma* - namely, that the circumstances in which an individual is born, including poverty, for example, are largely determined by one's actions in a previous life; and that, therefore, it may be neither desirable nor possible to alter them. Once these implications are brought into play, however, the case for incompatibility may seem to be well-nigh complete.

III

Despite arguments to the contrary in the preceding pages, I think there is a good case for what I earlier called the weak claim, namely, that salvation and social action are compatible, after all. This should not be thought to imply that the arguments developed in the previous section were merely "straw men", waiting to be "slain" at one's convenience. But is is true that they represent only one set of implications to be drawn from the relevant concepts and doctrines. In what follows, I will, clearly, be looking at things from a different end of the spectrum; and I hope that the analysis presented here will be at least as plausible as the one in the previous section.

What needs to be laid to rest at the earliest opportunity is Arjuna's provocative, but "deluded", suggestion that, if wisdom, *jñāna*, is superior, then action may be unnecessary. Not surprisingly, Kṛṣṇa attacks the suggestion instantly by arguing that the apparent choice between action and inaction is an illusion. "Nature" will compel everyone to act: *prakṛti*, ceaselessly impelling through its *guṇas* (*prakṛtijairguṇaih*)[3], will drive the individual to action - in one way or another, at one level or another. We may, indeed, choose to restrain our organs of action - at least for short durations. But this is taking a very superficial view of action. For it takes account of physical action only, and not of its mental or psychological source (*manasā smaran*).[4] As long as these "springs of action" - desires and impulses - have not been brought fully under control, nothing is gained by merely disengaging the motor organs. While we are embodied, survival alone will compel action. Hence, Kṛṣṇa is emphatic in his advice that action is better than (apparent) inaction.[5] The choice really is not between action and inaction but between kinds of action. Even the decision not to do anything, for a while, or in a given situation, is action - although of a different kind, namely, the exercise of the will to withhold physical action. This may, to some, appear to erode the distinction between decision and action. But every language has idioms which imply that deciding may be acting, although perhaps only in contrast to indecision, hesitancy or inertia. Besides, even if the motor organs were inactive, the sense organs would not have ceased acting, anyway. If one were to include involuntary "actions", such as breathing etc., then, of course, the *Gītā* would be absolutely right in asserting, as it does, that no one can remain inactive even for a moment. It may be possible to interpose here that only if continued survival were one's aim would incessant action be necessary. What if one chooses not to survive? But the choice of death will only alter the course of actions, not stop action itself. The *yogin* may seem to be an exception, since tradition regards him as capable of suspending action of any sort, including breathing, etc., for indefinite periods. But a true *yogin* will be unlikely to refrain from

---

[3]Ibid., III, 5.

[4]Ibid., III, 6.

[5]Ibid., III, 8.

action, and, indeed, must ceaselessly remain active for the benefit of others. This is explained elsewhere in the *Gītā*, and we will discuss that later.

As for the argument that this world is illusory, *māyā*; and that, therefore, action is pointless, it should be easily seen that the force of the earlier argument about the impossibility of inaction, could serve as adequate rebuttal: illusion or not, as long as we are in the world, we have to act, even if the action is merely a charade. Moreover, it is only Advaita Vedānta which may be said to interpret *māyā* as illusion, *adhyāsa*. For practically every other school of Hindu thought, *māyā* is understood as the mysterious power of God to create the world, *yogamāyā*[6]; and the fact that we may not fully understand why things are the way they are, is not sufficient ground for inaction: on the contrary, it may provide reasonable grounds for letting those who might know better, e.g., Kṛṣṇa, dictate how we ought to act. It is true that, even if we do not regard the world as illusory, we may have reason to see it as the sphere of birth, decay, death and rebirth again, and thus to be convinced of its futility. But futile or not, as long as we are in it, *saṃsāra*, we cannot ignore it or its dictates, i.e., the laws governing it. The fact that there is a transcendent level of reality may cause schizophrenia or ambivalence; but is not entirely a justifiable excuse from conventional, including moral, duties: our duties to God do not always absolve us from our duties to "Caesar"!

What can one say regarding the argument that, according to the Law of Karma, all actions, and not just bad ones, produce potencies which bind the soul to *saṃsāra*; and, consequently, if one must act at all, one ought to confine oneself to those that bring "merit" and thus lead to salvation? There seems to be nothing seriously wrong with this conclusion, as far as it goes. But when further plausible deductions are added, it is no longer incompatible with social action, nor even with the narrower subclass of social action, identified as the pursuit of social justice in the first section of this paper. For we do not know precisely how *karma* operates; and it may entirely be the case that the pursuit of social justice might be part of "meritorious" action, and, thus, possibly part of the "enabling conditions" of salvation. Discussions of *dharma*, or duty, in the scriptures frequently indicate that altruistic action paves the way to salvation, no less than the performance of ritual and conventional caste-duties etc. But even if we did not know this to be the case with certainty, prudence might demand that we allow for this possibility: a sort of "Pascal's wager" might be advisable! Finally, in this matter, the *Gītā* makes it sufficiently clear that what "binds" us to *saṃsāra* is not action itself, but the passions driving us to action: what may be appropriate, then, is the cultivation of "detachment" from desires, *naiṣkarmya*[7], rather than abstinence from altruistic social action.

This general conclusion - namely, that one needs to cultivate the spirit of non-attachment to desires and the expected or imagined consequences of action, rather than abstinence from social action - seems to hold, irrespective of what path of salvation has been chosen. It is true that the path of knowledge demands the acquisition of wisdom; but, as the *Gītā* points out emphatically, *niṣkāma karma*, is itself part of "wisdom". Wisdom entails freedom from attachment, fear, anger, etc., (*vītarāgabhayakrodha*)[8], precisely the condition of non-attached action. Similarly, the path of devotion does, indeed, primarily demand love and worship of God; but this is entirely compatible with other actions, if the latter are performed in the spirit of dedication to God and obedience to His commands.[9] And if the devotee's choice includes the active pursuit

---

[6]Ibid., VII, 25.

[7]Ibid., III, 4.

[8]Ibid., IV, 10.

of social justice for all, then he may, indeed, justifiably devote his energies to that task, undertaken as a homage of service to God. The path of action, naturally, enjoins action, and, in the first place, perhaps only the ritual and conventional duties. But it is not difficult to see that, even on the conventional view of duties, some social action is inevitably entailed. A *brāhmin* must, among other things, teach; a *kṣatriya* defend society against enemies; the *vaiśya* produce food; and the *śūdra* till the soil, etc. - all involving the discharge of socially required functions.

As for the irrelevance of material well-being to the spiritual goal of salvation, there is a counter-argument, based, initially, in common sense. The fact that salvation may be our ultimate goal does not automatically entail that the realm of the body, of nature, *prakṛti*, either can, or ought to, be ignored while we are still in it. Besides, Hindu tradition, while clearly advocating *mokṣa* as the ultimate goal, does prescribe *dharma*, the performance or moral, ritual and caste duties; *artha*, the acquisition of material wealth; and *kāma*, the satisfaction of bodily needs and desires, as legitimate proximate goals. These are three of the prescribed ends or goals, *puruṣārthas*, *mokṣa*, being the fourth one. Further, as the *Gītā* strongly implies, this is God's world;[9] and, as His agents, we do as He does. And we know that He incarnates Himself from time to time in order to establish or restore justice.[10] One only needs to be reminded that the war between the Pāṇḍavas and the Kauravas takes place simply because the latter have usurped the power and wealth of the former, who are fighting to restore justice. One may view this war as waged primarily to restore political legitimacy and the rule of righteousness; but material wealth is not altogether out of the reckoning. Distributive justice, as understood at the time and in the specific context, seems also to be involved. And we know whose side Kṛṣṇa is on - namely: on the side of those who had been dispossessed, the Pāṇḍavas.

IV

I am aware that in the last section, I may have been "batting on a relatively easy wicket". For the *Gītā* itself has already made the case for the compatibility of social action with salvation. Indeed, the distinctive message of the *Gītā* has frequently been taken to be just that. Where I wish to depart from this familiar perception is in claiming that some of the ideas found in the *Gītā* convey a much stronger message than the mere compatibility of social action with salvation. I think that there may be very good reasons to conclude that the *Gītā* stands for what I earlier called the strong claim, namely, that it is our duty, as human beings, to fight for social justice: that when we do not, we are guilty of dereliction of duty, just in the way individual members of the Pāṇḍava and Kaurava clans were, in letting things drift (through their inaction on appropriate occasions) to a point where justice could only be restored through war. I concede that this strong claim can only be made entirely defensible by a certain amount of reinterpretation of some of the relevant concepts and doctrines, and by filling in "gaps" that the tradition itself might have left unfilled. But I doubt that the reconstruction (or "deconstruction") involved is altogether too radical. It does indeed require exploiting existing ambiguities and switching levels of discourse; but only, I believe, within permissible limits, and along lines that have already been suggested in the long tradition of Hindu thought.

I want to start with a general question in philosophical psychology. We noticed in

---

[9] Ibid., III, 30.

[10] Ibid., IV, 8.

the earlier section that the *Gītā* doctrine of *karma-yoga* entails the cultivation of "desirelessness"[11] in the performance of actions. But desires and passions have quite correctly, at one level, been deemed as "springs of action". If so, then it would seem that "desirelessness" would destroy the very incentive, the "spur", to the striving for social justice. It may, then, appear that the doctrine of *niṣkāma karma*, while ostensibly preaching activism, in fact, discourages it. If we do not desire to bring about social justice for all, then the latter will not come about; and all talk regarding the pursuit of social justice will be empty talk. What needs to be said in answer, in the context of the *Gītā* doctrine, is that, in a very important sense, the crucial difference between self-regarding and other-regarding actions may lie just in the fact that the former may be initiated by desire, while the latter by one's sense of duty, or the rational conviction that they need to be done; and that, as rational, moral agents, we have an obligation to see that they are done. This is not to restate any sort of Kantian formalism, but a recognition of the psychological fact that altruistic action may not be said to originate in desire, but in one's sense of duty. The beginnings of the state of desirelessness, then, may also be the first steps towards altruism: the latter is made possible by the dictates of an "enlightened" conscience.

Understood this way, *mumukṣutva*, the necessary condition of liberation, frequently translated as "the desire for liberation", may, in fact, be seen as implying not desire, but the emergence of the sense of obligation to extend, or alter, the scope and focus of one's actions. They need no longer be rooted in the desire for personal gratification, but transformed into felt duty to secure the well-being of all. What might have, at first, arisen as a desire for mere personal salvation, may, with the dawn of "enlightenment", *jñāna*, appear to be the duty to seek the economic and political emancipation of all: *mokṣa*, after all, simply means "that which releases..."! This rendering, I suggest, is not in the least fanciful when taken in the context of such phrases occurring in the *Gītā* as *lokasaṃgraha*[12], "the good of the people", and *sarvabhūtahita*[13], "the well-being of all creatures". It might be of interest to note also that Praśastapāda, one of the recognized "law givers" of Hinduism, adds *bhūtahitatva*, seeking the good of all creatures, to Manu's and Yājñavalkya's lists of generic or universal duties, *sādhāraṇa dharma*.[14]

The well-being of creatures, etc., may, then, be an indispensable quest of the individual, as a seeker of salvation. But the complete rationale for this quest does not rest entirely in this contingent link between salvation and seeking the good of all. At least for those willing to follow the reasoning of the *Gītā*, there is a very important additional reason. And that is that the true devotee must follow the example of the Lord: whatever is judged to be the wish of the Lord, by precept or example, becomes the duty of the devotee. That is the "logic" of devotion. It is evident from the words of Kṛṣṇa, the Lord, that He incarnates Himself for the establishment or restoration of "justice" (*dharma saṃsthāpanārthāya*), whenever there is a rise in injustice (*ahhyutthānam adharmasya*)[15]; to save the good, and punish the wicked, or the oppressor (*paritrāṇāya sādhūnām, vināsāyaca duṣkritām*)[16]. To this, if necessary,

---

[11] Ibid., II, 70-71.

[12] Ibid., III, 20.

[13] Ibid., V, 25.

[14] Maitra (1925) p.10.

[15] *Gītā*, IV, 7-8.

[16] Ibid., IV, 8.

could be added the general theistic thinking, but especially Rāmānuja's, that God is *akhilaheyapratyanika*, i.e., one who actively cancels or removes all evils, imperfections and obstacles from the path of creatures, just as light cancels darkness; and that, therefore, we, as devotees, must always do as God might have done in the situation facing us. This entails, for example, giving knowledge to the ignorant (*jñānaṃ ajñānaṃ*), power to the powerless (*śakti aśaktānāṃ*) etc.[17] This is, it seems to me, no more than an explicit rendering of the message contained in the *Gītā*.

There is an important question regarding *dharma* that needs to be settled here. Granted that Kṛṣṇa incarnates Himself for the establishment or restoration of *dharma*. But if *dharma* simply refers to duties accruing to someone from his place in the system of castes and stages, *varṇāśrama dharma*, then it is unlikely that the *Gītā's* message could have any bearing on the pursuit of social justice in the particular sense of the phrase I am concerned with here. There is little doubt that the *Gītā* is sometimes talking about caste-duties etc: hence the exhortation to do one's own *dharma*, for trying to do someone else's may be perilous, etc.[18] But it is important to note that the overall language of the *Gītā* in this respect is, at the very least, ambiguous: the sense of *dharma* as justice, morality, righteousness and the law etc., is never entirely missing. Indeed, I think that the latter may even be its primary sense. Otherwise, it becomes difficult to give a coherent account of the emphasis placed on such terms as *loksaṃgraha, sarvabhūta hitatva*, etc., as also of the more inclusive tone of the phrases used in the elucidation of the purposes of divine incarnation: i.e., to save the good, to destroy the evil and to establish justice etc. Arjuna is being exhorted to fight his cousins - who naturally, also belong to the same *kṣatriya* caste - because they have violated principles of justice: usurped, by unjust means, what did not belong to them. As I have argued elsewhere[19], "justice" is an evolving term, which has acquired new dimensions of meaning over the centuries and millennia. That it is the right of all humans to be fed and housed properly, is undoubtedly a modern extension of the scope of the term, whether in the West or the East. But it is an extension which, in my opinion, is in harmony with the overall tone, context and language of the *Gītā*. It should be recalled that the Pāṇḍavas decide to fight the war only after Duryodhana, the leader of the Kauravas, has flatly declared to Kṛṣṇa, the mediator, that he will give nothing to his cousins, not even anything measuring the point of a needle, without war. The war, therefore is about giving or returning (distributive justice); and the point of a needle, as a measure, can only refer to material or economic goods, such as land. The *Gītā* can, in other words, serve quite adequately as a suitable text for anyone today wishing to do battle for universal social justice, including, I believe, the battle against inequities created by caste itself; for *dharma*, as justice, may, rightly, override *dharma*, as caste-duties.

It has already been pointed out that the theistic schools of Hinduism regard *māyā* primarily as the mysterious creative power of God, which mere mortals cannot comprehend. Even the privileged, such as Arjuna, can at best get a glimpse into the mystery. The *Gītā* certainly does not encourage the view that the world is any sort of illusion. It is true that it refers to the worldly processes, in typical Indian fashion, as the "wheel", *cakram*. But, far from conveying any sense of futility, and, therefore,

---

[17]Maitra (1925), p. 22.

[18]*Gītā*, III, 35.

[19]Thakur (1986).

possibly encouraging any "inactivism", it emphatically declares that anyone who does not help to turn the wheel, once it is set in motion, is "evil in his nature, sensual in his delight, and ... lives in vain".[20] Its view of *karma* seems to be that it is not action that binds the soul to the wheel, but the selfish desires and passions underlying it. Unattached, or desireless action, undertaken simply as duty, leads to release from the fetters of *karma* (*mucyantete' pi karmabhiḥ*)[21]. The secret of such release is the art, *kauśala*[22], of performing one's duties without attachment to the fruits of one's actions.

This brings us to a very emphatic statement made in the *Gītā*, possibly the most pertinent in the context of the strong claim that I am defending, i.e., its affirmation that *yoga* is the outlook of equality of all creatures, *samatvam yoga ucyate*[23]. Although there are several other verses in the *Gītā* which convey this message of equality (e.g., V, 18), the one just partially quoted turns *samatva* into the very definition of *yoga*, or union with God; and thereby gives the message much greater force, amounting, in my opinion, to moral obligation. The true *yogin* perceives himself in all things, and all things in himself; because he has realized his union with God.[24] He no longer has personal interests or limitations, no selfish desires or passions; because he has literally enlarged himself and so identifies himself with the interests of all living beings: he regards them as himself. This is not mere "universalizability", as the principle of morality, but actual universalization, or identification, with all creatures, *samatva*. The cultivation of the art of performing one's duties without attachment, culminates in the attainment of release: at once union with God, *yoga*, and felt equality with all beings, *samatva*. And if release is, by definition, this outlook of equality, then there is no longer any additional reason needed for the pursuit of social justice.

I conclude that the *Gītā* offers no excuses to any seeker of salvation tempted to construe his goal selfishly or narrowly: not even the one that the seeker may have chosen to adopt the path, not of action, *karma*, but of knowledge, *jñāna*, or of devotion, *bhakti*. For it turns out, on closer examination, that, according to the *Gītā*, the three distinct paths merge: knowledge, devotion and action complement each other. The true seeker knows that there is no escape from action, and so allows his "wisdom" to propel him towards the only alternative open, namely, a non-attached performance of his duties; and, all the while, he consecrates his actions to the Lord, knowing that He is the real doer, the agent of actions. As his devotion matures, he attains union with God; and realizes not only that all beings are God's creatures, just like himself, but also that, as souls, they are just as much part of the "greater soul", *paramātman*, as himself. The feeling of equality with all, consequently, is, on the one hand, the effect of release from personal limitations; and, on the other, the cause of commitment to action for the benefit of all creatures, *sarvabhūta hite ratāḥ*. This *samatva* that the *Gītā* speaks of will not, it seems, serve as a license for hedonism; but nor will it absolve the seeker from the duty to pursue the political and economic well-being of all. Indeed, it is possible to render Rāmānuja's phrases, "*jñānam ajñānaṃ*" and "*śakti aśaktānāṃ*", as the equivalents of the Marxist revolutionary slogans, "raising the consciousness of the (ignorant) masses", and "power to the (oppressed) people"!

---

[20] *Gītā*, III, 16.

[21] Ibid., III, 31.

[22] Ibid., II, 50.

[23] Ibid., II, 48.

[24] Ibid., VI, 29.

REFERENCES

Maitra, S.K. (1925). *The Ethics of the Hindus*. Calcutta: University of Calcutta.
Radhakrishnan, Sarvepalli (1960). *The Bhagavadgītā*. London: George Allen & Unwin.
Thakur, Shivesh C. (1986). "Social Justice: An Informal Analysis" *International Philosophical Quarterly* 26: 213-222.

CASTE, KARMA AND THE GĪTĀ

Bimal Krishna Matilal

University of Oxford

I

In Chapter IV, verse 13 of the *Bhagavadgītā* Lord Kṛṣṇa says:

> The assembly of four *varṇas* (castes) has been created by me in accordance with the division of "qualities" and actions. But although I am its creator, know me as a non-creator and imperishable (undiminished).

The context is rather odd for talking about the origin of the four *varṇas* or the caste-system of Hinduism. And yet the first line of this verse has often been quoted by modern apologists to show that the hierarchy prevalent from time immemorial in the Indian Vedic (Hindu) society, known as the caste-system, was actually based upon merits and capabilities rather than on heredity. But, paradoxically, heredity seems to have been the general practice throughout. For caste is usually determined by birth, and birth is something over which the person does not have any control. If hierarchies are determined by birth, then there is something about which a human being (a rational being, that is) has a right to feel uneasy. For it is somewhat unfair. Hence there is an apocryphal (but also very ancient) line attributed to the well-known *Mahābhārata* character, Karṇa, which says

> *daivāyattam kule jamma madāyattam tu pauruṣam.*

I translate,

> My birth in a family is under the control of the "book of Fate"[1]

[1]It is difficult to translate "*daiva*" in English. In the Indian tradition it is usually opposed to *puruṣa-kāra*, which means what humans can achieve by their own effort. A parallel, though not quite the same, distinction in the West is between freedom of will and determinism. I believe "the Book of Fate" captures essentially the core sense of the word in the context.

R. W. Perrett (ed.), Indian Philosophy of Religion, 195–201.

> but I myself control my qualities as a human being.[2]

The significance of this line is obvious in the context. A person may be born in a lowly family, but through effort, determination and cultivation of virtues she or he may rise in life and be *somebody*. Karṇa became a great hero, and a king; in fact in the *Mahābhārata* he was the only match for the invincible Arjuna, although he was supposed to be the son of an ordinary charioteer. It can match a modern story where a cabbie's son becomes a prince or a general.

That the heredity-determined hierarchy in a society is somewhat unfair and even irrational was felt much earlier in the tradition. Karṇa's assertion quoted above (apocryphal though it may be) expresses the protest of the dissident groups in the society. A human being's worth must be judged by her actions, virtues and merits, by what she makes of herself, not by her birth. Support of this point comes from another source, which is by no means apocryphal in any sense. Poet Bhavabhūti writing in 8th century A.D., said in his *Uttararāmacarita*:

> *Gunāh pujāsthānam guṇiṣu no liṅgam na ca vayaḥ* (Act IV, verse 11)

This has been said about Sītā, the abandoned wife of Rāma. The argument of the verse was that Sītā excelled all others by her virtue and merit, hence the abandonment was entirely unjust. I translate the above line:

> Qualities of the qualified persons are worthy of our adoration,
> not their sex, nor age.

This was a remarkable assertion in the predominantly sexist society of the so-called traditional India. It is no doubt charged with sexist reflexes, as are, alas, many statements heard in modern society today. I believe our language is *given* to us and as such it always suffers from the defects of the Orwellian Newspeak. Anything you say in it does not really sound right in the light of the newly gained consciousness of injustice, domination and tacit discrimination. Hence it seems to me that the concept of *muting*, developed by the sociologist E. Ardener, is a very suitable one in this context. The subdued group is often the *muted* group.[3]

But let us go back to the *Gītā*. I had read the *Bhagavadgītā* many times in my youth. And I must admit that I did not understand many things because I did not know much Sanskrit at that time. At that time its appeal was more in the form of an inspired "song" sung by Lord Kṛṣṇa to persuade reluctant Arjuna to do his duty. So the crude message was: We must do our duty no matter what. We have been taught to treat the book with reverence. It is regarded (mostly by European scholars) as one of the "Hindu Scriptures". In the orthodox Indian tradition, the *Gītā* is regarded as part of our *smṛti*, not *śruti* (in fact, "scriptures" is a poor translation of the Sanskrit *śruti*, if not totally wrong). In our Vedānta parlance, the *Gītā* is one of three *prasthānas*, the other two being the Upaniṣads (*śruti*) and the *Brahmasūtra*. Hence anybody interested in the Vedānta (both Advaita and non-Advaita) cannot afford to ignore the *Gītā*.

---

[2] "*pauruṣa*" is derived from "*puruṣa*" = "man"; hence, heroism, prowess, achievements etc., could be indicated by the same form.

[3] Ardener (1975).

Western scholars generally identify the *Gītā* as a "Vaiṣṇava text".[4] But it is not exclusively for the Vaiṣṇavas, although Kṛṣṇa/Viṣṇu is the main speaker here. In fact, this is a text which is accepted as authoritative even outside the Vedāntic circle. Apart from the Advaitin Śaṃkara, Abhinavagupta, the well-known Śaivite author, wrote a commentary on this text. This falsifies the idea that it is exclusively for the Vaiṣṇava. Besides, I believe this sort of "exclusivism" which tries to discover a clear-cut and sharp line of demarcation between Vaiṣṇavism and Śaivism and other "-isms" in the Indian context is a product of Western *reading* of Indian culture. It is, mildly speaking, a discourse constructed by the perceptions of the Western Indologists.

If the message of the *Gītā* is to be taken seriously (as we must from the Hindu point of view at least), then certain paradoxical questions do arise regarding the concept of ethics and morality. These issues have been debated over the ages and many ad hoc but not very satisfactory solutions have been given. We sometimes do not wish to see the paradoxes but go on acting according to some dictum or other and believe that these are *given* to us. Must we always indulge in rational thinking before acting? We do not like to share Arjuna's doubts and reluctance. For if everything has been decided for us by the supreme intelligence of Kṛṣṇa, who are we to think about the propriety or justification of the moral codes that the *Gītā* presents?

There are philosophers and other people who believe that there cannot arise any moral or ethical dilemmas because there is always some *right* answer to all apparently paradoxical questions. It is our duty to know the right answers. We may not be able to discover these right answers, but persons with superior intellects can conduct the rigorous "critical level" thinking (as R.M. Hare insists)[5] and discover the right answers for us, and our duty would be to follow them. There are, however, others who believe just the opposite. Dilemmas are realities. They do arise and a totally satisfactory resolution of them through rational means may be simply unavailable to us.

I wish to concentrate upon one particular issue: the paradoxicality of caste and karma. This paradoxicality has often gone unnoticed. To uncover the paradoxicality as well as complementarity of the two notions of caste and karma, we have to go back to Max Weber. The caste-hierarchy was anti-rational for it was underwritten by the ritual sanction of pollution, as well as by heredity rather than merit. Predominance of hierarchy is found in all civilized societies, including the egalitarian ones, and its usefulness is not in question here. The question is whether it should be heredity-based or merit-based. Rationality supports the second alternative, whereas practice makes the first alternative more acceptable. The doctrine of karma, on the other hand, is, or at least seems to be, an example of ethical rationalism. For Weber this doctrine represents a coherent theodicy. He saw in the caste-*dharma* and its tie-in with karma, a completely unique concept; the combination of the two produced for Max Weber "the most consistent theodicy ever formulated".[6] It produced a persistent social order. From the point of view of an internalist - an orthodox Hindu, for example - the karma

---

[4]A curious anecdote: Once a colleague of mine in Oxford used the expression "a Vaiṣṇava text" to describe the manuscript of the *Gītā* which was on display at Bodleian Library Manuscript Display Room. It was an exhibition of the Sanskrit manuscripts in the Bodleian. But an Indian who came to Oxford to see the exhibition was upset because he was an Advaitin (not a Vaiṣṇava) and still regarded the *Gītā* as one of his scriptures. He complained. But of course, my colleague did not want to change the description just to please him. For Western Indologists have for a long time identified the *Gītā* as a Vaiṣṇava text; it makes categorization easier.

[5]Hare (1981).

[6]Weber (1958).

doctrine must also be complementary to the caste-hierarchy, for it may resolve the tension created by the unaccounted for inequalities nurtured in a hierarchical society.

The mixture of caste and karma, however, was, as J. Heesterman has recently put it, "volatile"[7] The two notions are also mutually opposed to each other. Karma or ethical rationalism emphasizes the "merit-based" nature of the social order, while the caste-hierarchy emphasizes its "heredity-based" nature. The first allows freedom and self-responsibility, the second closes the door to freedom and accentuates the givenness of social duties and responsibilities. But at the same time their combination became feasible. If the heredity-based caste-hierarchy made the social system anti-rational and unfair, the karma theodicy was introduced for the rationalization of the existing practice. The social order that resulted therefrom was not a rational, but a rationalized order. However the inner conflict did not disappear completely. For the heredity-based hierarchy presumably received a rational support as well as a ritual sanction, and the merit-based hierarchy was not given the prominence it deserved.

The merit-based nature of a hierarchy, however, seems to be rational. This awareness became more and more a shared feeling among the members belonging to this social order. The feeling found expression in various forms. Those who denounced orthodoxy rejected the hereditary nature of caste-hierarchy. Those who became renouncers went the same way. But within the tradition itself, many asserted that the merit-based nature of the hierarchy is a more acceptable alternative. Thus *brāhman*-hood is not dependent upon birth or family, but it is constituted by a set of several moral virtues, several duties and responsibilities. Similarly *kṣatriya*-hood or *vaiśya*-hood. It is the echo of this view - the critical view rather than the view of the conformist - that I believe we find in the line of the *Gītā* that I quoted in the opening sentence.

II

The caste duties are talked about in the *Gītā* in at least four different places: Chapter 2, 31-37; Chapter 3, 35; Chapter 4, 13; and Chapter 18, 41-48. The context of Chapter 4 is rather odd, as I have already mentioned. Lord Kṛṣṇa is dwelling on the point that although in this world (*iha*) people perform sacrifice desiring success and do obtain such success (verse 12), God (who created the world, divided people into four *varṇas* according to their merit, etc.) should not be regarded as an agent. For agency belongs to the humans (who work with desire in their mind), not to the Changeless One, God. The idea is probably that God works without any desire and the fruits do not cling to him (as is made explicit in verse 14). Hence, although there is no emphasis on how the *varṇa*-division came to be, it nevertheless is pointed out that the caste-classification is not really created by the divine will, but by the distribution of merit according to the law of karma. The commentators (e.g. Śrīdhara) note that since the inequalities were not created by God but by the law of karma which God only administered, the so-called problem of evil is somehow averted.

Chapter 2, 31-37: Here Lord Krsna tells Arjuna that it is his duty as a *kṣatriya* to fight this battle to recover his kingdom. This is the action prescribed by the *kṣatriya* code of duty. In fact, it is morally binding by the principle of group-morality. If Arjuna as a *kṣatriya* fails to act in the prescribed manner, he would be disgraced and condemned by all other warriors. The *kṣatriya* code is also the "death before dishonour" code. The situation is this: As a human being, as a loving member of the royal family, he feels that the killing of a grandfather and other relatives is bad; but as

---

[7]Heesterman (1985), p.195.

a *kṣatriya* he is told that it is his sacred duty to fight and kill - a classic case of moral conflict, which tends to inspire moral scepticism.

Chapter 3, 35: It emphasizes again that one must follow one's own *dharma*, duties prescribed by the code, even when performance of such duties could be faulty or devoid of any merit. The expression "*svadharma*" (the key expression in all such contexts) is intriguing, for it is also interchangeable with *svabhāva*, "own nature" or simply "nature".[8] Thus it may be read as the advice to follow one's own nature, natural inclination, in choosing the course of action. One should try always to be one's own self, not somebody else. Arjuna was by nature a warrior, not a forgiving, self-sacrificing recluse. Hence, Kṛṣṇa seemed to be saying, Arjuna's sudden decision to turn back and run away from the battlefield to be a recluse (cf. *bhaikṣyam apīha loke*, Arjuna's pious wish: I would rather be a mendicant) would be acting against his nature. That is, against the grid of a natural warrior, a *kṣatriya*, who always fights for his honour. Thus Arjuna's own *dharma* at this stage is just to fight as best as he can. It would be doing what he can do best and to do otherwise would be dangerous and fatal (cf. *bhayāvaha*).

Chapter 18, 41-8: Lord Kṛṣṇa says that the four *varṇas (brāhman, kṣatriya, vaiśya* and *śūdra*) have their duties assigned to them according to the "qualities" arising from their "own-natures". Śaṃkara, in his commentary on verse 41, introduces, as he does on many other occasions, the three Sāṃkhya *guṇas*: *sattva*, *rajas* and *tamas*. The first is connected with anything that is good and pious. The second is connected with activity: the dynamic qualities, drive, passion, etc., which are not always good, but not bad either. They are, however, much needed for a life of action. The third is connected with ignorance, darkness, confusion, the non-intelligent, mechanical labour etc. Śaṃkara connects the origin of the *brāhmans* with *sattva*; the *kṣatriyas* with *rajas* mixed with *sattva*; the *vaiśyas* (peasants, tradesmen, artisans etc.) with *rajas* mixed with *tamas*; and the *śūdras* with *tamas* mixed with a bit of *rajas*. This is a neat classification which acknowledges the different natures (*svabhāva*) we witness in various human beings.[9] But it does not explain the origin of this variety. Both Rāmānuja and Śaṃkara add another crucial comment here. According to them, one's caste or birth is predetermined by one's former lives, i.e. former karma. This seems to be an acceptable rationalization of the prevalent caste-hierarchy. Your previous karma (in former lives) is responsible for what you are today (what status in the hierarchy you have).

This type of rationalization was enough to fire the imagination of Max Weber, who even quoted from the *Communist Manifesto* to show how much more acceptable the caste-karma system would become:

---

8 *sva-dharma*: On this Heesterman writes, "it is better to perform the duties of one's own caste, one's *svadharma*, indifferently than those of others with outstanding distinction" (p.196). This clearly identifies *svadharma* with one's caste-duty. Though this is the general understanding of the term, I believe it misses at least one subtlety: "*sva*" refers to the person himself or herself. Besides, if the division of castes is according to natures of human beings, then what is proper for one's own caste is also proper for one's own self or nature. I believe *sva-dharma* can be interpreted in the second way on several occasions, without emphasizing the caste-bound duties. Manu also refers to "*svasya ca priyam*" (verse II/2) as well as to "*ātmanas tuṣṭir eva ca*" (verse II/6), as one of the authorities on *dharma*, over and above the Vedas etc.

9 Indian society was pluralistic and hence we find ready acceptance of multiple interpretations of the textual tradition. That the *Gītā* has a multivalent character is today well recognized by even the most devout Hindu. See also Sharma (1986), pp.248-252.

> "... they (the proletariat) have nothing to lose but their chains, they have a world to win", the same holds for the pious Hindu of low caste, he too can gain Heaven and become a god - only not in this life, but in the life of the future after rebirth into the same world pattern (p.122).

Verses 42-44 give four lists of virtues and assign them to the four *varṇas* respectively. Thus calmness, self-restraint, ascetic practice, purity, tolerance, uprightness, wisdom, knowledge and faith - all constitute *brāhman*-hood. High courage, ardour, endurance, skill, not turning back on the battlefield, charity, majesty - all these constitute *kṣatriya*-hood. Cultivation, cattle-rearing, trade - these are the constitutive properties of *vaiśya*-hood. Finally, service to others is what makes a *śūdra* a *śūdra*.

III

To list the constitutive properties of *brāhman*-hood etc., was in fact a significant development. For if we depend upon the constitutive properties to assign hierarchical status, lower or higher, then birth or family (i.e., heredity) becomes immaterial for such status distinction. I shall conclude after relating a relevant story from another part of the *Mahābhārata*.

In the *Vanaparva*, Yudhiṣṭhira, the *dharmarāja*, had an encounter with a huge python, who was in fact king Nahuṣa, one of the forefathers of Yudhiṣṭhira. Nahuṣa, through his good deeds and piety, obtained as his reward the throne of Heaven, but then his downfall started. For he became too proud and forgot the distinction between *dharma* and *a-dharma*. He kicked at the head of sage Agastya and was cursed, which turned him into a python for thousands of years. He had been waiting, in the form of the python, for a long time to be saved by pious Yudhiṣṭhira through a discourse on *dharma*. So he one day got hold of Bhīma and was about to crush him when Yudhiṣṭhira appeared in search of his brother. The fabulous power of Bhīma, who used to kill almost endless numbers of demons, elephants, pythons, etc., was of no avail. Nahuṣa was more powerful for he had a noble mission - a discourse on *dharma*. Nahuṣa said to Yudhiṣṭhira, "I will let your brother go, if you answer my questions on *dharma*." So the discourse started. The first question was: What makes a *brāhman* a *brāhman*? Yudhiṣṭhira listed a number of virtues: truthfulness, generosity, forgiveness, goodness, kindness, self-control and compassion - all these qualities together constitute a *brāhmin*. The list is not very different from the one found in the *Gītā*, chapter 18, verse 42. The python asked, "But this goes against the principle of four *varṇas*. For even a *śūdra* may have all these virtues. Virtues cannot be the monopoly of any caste." Yudhiṣṭhira replied in unambiguous language, "Indeed, if a *śūdra* is characterized by all these virtues, he is to be 'defined' (cf. *lakṣya*) as a *brāhman*. And if a *brāhman* lacks them then he is to be regarded as a *śūdra*." The python asked again, "But if *brāhman*-hood is constituted by a number of virtues, then birth (in a *brāhman* family) would be in vain, where such virtues are conspicuous by their absence." Yudhiṣṭhira replies, "Indeed. Since through sexual urge (*rāga*) people copulate and produce children (and copulation is not always between husband and wife of the same caste), birth is always a dubious criterion in such matters. Therefore, the old sages depend upon good conduct (*śīla*) as the indicator of a better person. Even one who is a *brāhman* by birth would be a *śūdra* through poor and despicable conduct". Yudhiṣṭhira even referred to the "self-originating" Manu as his authority.[10]

I believe this reflects the presence of what I call the "internal criticism" within the tradition about the prevalence of the heredity-based caste hierarchy. Hence, if one portion of a whole text is to be treated as a commentary on another portion, then this discourse on caste may be regarded as a commentary on the remarks on caste in the *Gītā* Chapter 4, verse 13, or Chapter 18, verses 41-48. In the light of the above remarks a comment such as "*guṇa-karma-vibhāgaśaḥ*" is to be regarded more as a criticism of the existing heredity-bound caste system, than an assertion of an already existing practice. But Weber's commendation of the caste-karma order was a bit premature. The undercurrent of rationality in the tradition no doubt interpreted the karma doctrine in such a way as to make it adjustable to the heredity-bound caste-hegemony. But then we are back with the same old quandary. If one's responsibility extends not only to what one does in this life but also to what one is supposed to have done in one's many (hypothetically construed) former lives, then the thin thread of rationality that presumably tied karma to the heredity-bound caste hierarchy becomes too elusive to allow freedom and autonomy. And, paradoxically, karma becomes almost synonymous with Fate or Destiny.

It may be argued that my interpretation of these passages of the *Gītā* is only an intepretation, a novel or modern one. But that is all we can do with a text like the *Gītā*. The multivalent character of this text (or scriptural texts in general) is well-known and well-documented.[11] I believe the history of the ever changing social and religious ethos of Indian society is to be gleaned from the enormous body of the textual material we have at our disposal. Very broadly speaking, hierarchical society was heredity-bound from time immemorial, which was found unsatisfactory because of its "irrational" nature. The karma doctrine was reinterpreted to rationalize it. My point is also very general. There existed (and I believe, still exists) an internal critique of this within the tradition itself. And this was based upon what I must call a form of rationality not very different from what we call rationality today. This form of rationality came into conflict with the form of relativism which the caste-relative set of *dharma*-prescriptions encourages.

REFERENCES

Ardener, Shirley (1975). Editor. *Perceiving Women*. London: Malaby Press.

Hare, R.M. (1981). *Moral Thinking*. Oxford: Clarendon Press.

Heesterman, J.C. (1985). *The Inner Conflict of Tradition*. Chicago: University of Chicago.

Sharma, Arvind (1986). *The Hindu Gītā: Ancient and Classical Interpretations of the Bhagavadgītā*. La Salle: Open Court.

Weber, Max (1958). *The Religion of India*. New York: Free Press.

---

[10]It may be that what Yudhiṣṭhira was made to say here was against the prevalent and dominant views of the society. It is undoubtedly a form of social criticism to ridicule the hereditary nature of the social hierarchy. Hence it seems to me that an authority, like that of a Svayambhu Manu, was needed to combat the authority of other *dharmaśāstrakāras*.

[11]Sharma (1986), p.252.

CONTRIBUTORS' ADDRESSES

Shlomo Biderman: Philosophy Department, Tel Aviv University, Ramat Aviv, Tel Aviv 69978, Israel.

Puruṣottama Bilimoria: School of Humanities, Deakin University, Geelong, Victoria 3217, Australia.

Arindam Chakrabarti: Philosophy Department, University College London, Gower Street, London WCIE 6BT, United Kingdom.

Peter Forrest: Philosophy Department, University of New England, Armidale, NSW 2351, Australia.

Arthur L. Herman: Philosophy Department, University of Wisconsin-Stevens Point, Stevens Point, Wisconsin 54481, U.S.A.

David J. Kalupahana: Philosophy Department, University of Hawaii at Manoa, Honolulu, Hawaii 96822, U.S.A.

Julius J. Lipner: The Divinity School, University of Cambridge, St John's Street, Cambridge CB2 ITW, United Kingdom.

Bimal Krishna Matilal: All Souls College, University of Oxford, Oxford OX1 4AL, United Kingdom.

Roy W. Perrett: Philosophy Department, Massey University, Palmerston North, New Zealand.

Ninian Smart: Religious Studies Department, University of California at Santa Barbara, Santa Barbara, California 93106, U.S.A.

Shivesh C. Thakur: Philosophy and Religion Department, University of Northern Iowa, Cedar Falls, Iowa 50614, U.S.A.

Keith E. Yandell: Philosophy Department, University of Wisconsin-Madison, Madison, Wisconsin 53706, U.S.A.

INDEX

STUDIES IN PHILOSOPHY AND RELIGION

1. FREUND, E.-R. *Franz Rosenzweig's Philosophy of Existence: An Analysis of* The Star of Redemption. 1979. ISBN 90 247 2091 5.
2. OLSON, A. M. *Transcendence and Hermeneutics: An Interpretation of the Philosophy of Karl Jaspers.* 1979. ISBN 90 247 2092 3.
3. VERDU, A. *The Philosophy of Buddhism.* 1981. ISBN 90 247 2224 1.
4. OLIVER, H. H. *A Relational Metaphysic.* 1981. ISBN 90 247 2457 0.
5. ARAPURA, J. G. *Gnosis and the Question of Thought in Vedānta.* 1986. ISBN 90 247 3061 9.
6. HOROSZ, W. and CLEMENTS, T. (eds.) *Religion and Human Purpose.* 1987. ISBN 90 247 3000 7.
7. SIA, S. *God in Process Thought.* 1985. ISBN 90 247 3103 8.
8. KOBLER, J. F. *Vatican II and Phenomenology.* 1985. ISBN 90 247 3193 3.
9. GODFREY, J. J. *A Philosophy of Human Hope.* 1987. ISBN 90 247 3353 7.
10. PERRETT, R. W. *Death and Immortality.* 1987. ISBN 90 247 3440 1.
11. GALL, R. S. *Beyond Theism and Atheism: Heidegger's Significance for Religious Thinking.* 1987. ISBN 247 3623 4.
12. SIA, S. (ed.) *Charles Hartshorne's Concept of God.* 1989. ISBN 0 7923 0290 7.
13. PERRETT, R. W. (ed.) *Indian Philosophy of Religion.* 1989. ISBN 0 7923 0437 3.